CAMBRIDGE

active GRAMMAR

LEVEL 1

Without answers

Fiona Davis and Wayne Rimmer
Series editor: Penny Ur

Shaftesbury Road, Cambridge CB2 8EA, United Kingdom

One Liberty Plaza, 20th Floor, New York, NY 10006, USA

477 Williamstown Road, Port Melbourne, VIC 3207, Australia

314–321, 3rd Floor, Plot 3, Splendor Forum, Jasola District Centre, New Delhi – 110025, India

103 Penang Road, #05–06/07, Visioncrest Commercial, Singapore 238467

Cambridge University Press & Assessment is a department of the University of Cambridge.

We share the University's mission to contribute to society through the pursuit of education, learning and research at the highest international levels of excellence.

www.cambridge.org
Information on this title: www.cambridge.org/9780521173681

First published 2011

40 39 38 37 36 35 34 33 32 31 30 29 28 27 26 25 24 23

Printed in Great Britain by Ashford Colour Press Ltd.

A catalogue record for this publication is available from the British Library

ISBN 978-0-521-73251-2 Paperback with answers and CD-ROM
ISBN 978-0-521-17368-1 Paperback without answers and CD-ROM

Introduction

What is Active Grammar?

Active Grammar is a grammar reference and practice series for secondary students and university students. It is divided into three levels, corresponding to the levels of *The Common European Framework of Reference for Languages* (CEF). Level 1 corresponds to A1–A2, Level 2 to B1–B2, and Level 3 to C1–C2. The books give comprehensive coverage of grammar at each level, while also covering reading, composition and discussion. The books are suitable for students who are preparing for Cambridge ESOL exams.

How are the books organised?

Each unit includes

- a short **presentation** text which shows the grammar in context and provides authentic content in areas such as geography, history, social studies and science.
- easy-to-understand **grammar explanations** with plenty of examples.
- **Tip** boxes which highlight common errors or other interesting facts about the grammar.
- graded grammar **practice exercises**, many of which are in the style of Cambridge ESOL exams, aimed at building students' confidence.
- a **My Turn** activity, where students can actively apply the grammar to their own experiences, opinions and personal preferences.
- a **My Test** section which allows students to check their understanding of key points.

Also included in the book

- regular **Review** units which provide contrastive practice of previous units.
- the **Appendices**, which include a **Glossary** with definitions for all highlighted words in the units.

The CD-ROM includes:

- extra activities for all the grammar covered in the book.
- printable progress tests.

How do I use the book?

You can work through the book unit by unit from Unit 1. Alternatively, you can use any unit or group of units separately if you want to focus on a particular area of grammar.

The book can be used for self-study, or in the classroom. For teachers, a comprehensive online teacher's guide gives practical tips on how to use the material in class.

www.cambridge.org/elt/activegrammar

Contents

Introduction 3

1 Word class and word order 6
In the world today

Present

2 *Be* 8
Are you my son?

3 Present simple 1: statements 10
Maybe you know her.

4 Present simple 2: negatives and questions 12
Do you like zoos?

5 Present continuous 14
She's wearing a bright yellow dress.

6 Present continuous and present simple 16
I'm walking – I don't have a car.

7 Imperatives 18
Stay calm!

R1 Review: present simple and present continuous 20

Past

8 Past simple 1: *was, were* 22
He was a popular hero.

9 Past simple 2: regular past forms 24
She lived in a tree.

10 Past simple 3: irregular past forms 26
They spoke Celtic languages.

11 Past continuous 28
Everyone was talking about the alligators.

R2 Review: past simple and past continuous 30

12 Present perfect 1 32
They've already invented it!

13 Present perfect 2 34
Have you ever tried mustard ice cream?

14 Present perfect 3 36
They have lived there for centuries.

15 Present perfect or past simple? 38
The company has invented the Mac and the iPod.

16 *Used to* 40
Sick people often used to sleep in temples.

R3 Review: present perfect and *used to* 42

The future

17 *Will, shall, won't* 44
I hope you'll enjoy yoga.

18 Present continuous with future meaning 46
She's flying to Glasgow tomorrow.

19 Be going to 48
I'm going to use magic.

R4 Review: The future 50

Modal verbs

20 Modal verbs: *can, could, be able to* 52
How can dogs help us?

21 Modals for requests: *can, could, may* 54
Could we go on a safari?

22 *Must, have to* and *can't* 56
I have to stay here.

23 *Should, ought to* 58
You should take off your shoes.

24 Modals of possibility: *may, might* 60
We may never know ...

R5 Review: modals 62

Questions and answers

25 Yes / no questions and short answers 64
Are beetles important? Yes, they are!

26 Question words: *Where? When? Why? How? Whose?* 66
How did he die?

27 Object and subject questions 68
Who studied at Hogwarts?

28 *Be like* and *look like* 70
What does Wolverine look like?

29 *What?* and *Which?* 72
Which of them is the queen bee?

30 *How ...?* questions 74
How cold is the Channel?

31 *So* and *neither* 76
Neither do I.

32 Question tags 78
Chocolate is bad for you, isn't it?

R6 Review: questions and answers 80

Verbs

33 *Have* and *have got* 82
Have you got a favourite crocodile?

34 *Make, do* and *get* 84
Do you get angry?

35 Prepositional verbs 86
Think about it!

36 Phrasal verbs 88
A friend to tidy up your room.

37 Verbs with two objects 90
Tell your friends the truth.

38 Verb + *-ing* or verb + *to*-infinitive; *like* and *would like* 92
Learn to speak any language in two weeks!

39 State verbs 94
Imagine a story.

R7 Review: verb structures 96

Articles, nouns, pronouns, etc.

40 Countable and uncountable nouns 98
Where does sand come from?

41 Plural nouns 100
He ate 47 sandwiches in ten minutes.

42 Articles 1 102
Do you know the answer?

43 Articles 2 104
Play music and watch the birds.

R8 Review: nouns and articles 106

44 *This, that, these, those* 108
This is me.

45 *Some, any, no, none* 110
There are no trains or buses.

46 *Something, everywhere, nobody, anyone* 112
Say nothing.

47 *Much, many, a lot of, a little, a few* 114
A lot of fun!

48 Subject and object pronouns 116
I don't know them and they don't know me.

49 Possessive *'s* 118
My great-grandfather's letters

50 *Whose?, my, mine* 120
Whose bag is this?

51 *There* and *it* 122
It's a very unusual book.

R9 Review: pronouns, possessives and quantifiers 124

Adjectives and adverbs

52 Adjectives 126
It's a wonderful place.

53 Order of adjectives 128
... wonderful golden shoes ...

54 Comparatives 130
It's nearer than you think.

55 Superlatives 132
The lowest point on Earth

56 Adverbs of manner 134
Eat healthily.

57 Comparative and superlative adverbs 136
Which will fall faster?

58 *-ed* and *-ing* adjectives 138
Is it exciting?

59 *Too* and *enough* 140
This chair is too soft.

60 Adverbs of frequency 142
We always have dreams.

R10 Review: adjectives and adverbs 144

Prepositions

61 Prepositions of place 146
I've left my keys at home.

62 Prepositions of time: *at, in, on* 148
It happened at night.

63 Prepositions of movement 150
Get off the boat and swim to the island.

R11 Review: prepositions 152

The passive

64 Passive: present and past simple 154
A lot of rubbish is produced.

Conditionals

65 Zero and first conditionals 156
If you study chemistry, you'll never stop learning.

66 Second conditional 158
I'd throw a cake at him if he didn't stop.

R12 Review: passive and conditionals 160

Reported speech

67 Reported speech 162
She said she would never have a party again.

68 *Say* and *tell* 164
She told me to meet her.

Relative clauses

69 Defining relative clauses 166
A ball game that is played in many countries

R13 Review: reported speech, say / tell and relative clauses 168

Linking words and sentences

70 Linking words: *and, but, or, so, because* 170
What is 6,700 km long and made of stone?

71 Time and sequence adverbs: *first, then, afterwards* 172
After lunch we visit the Peguche Waterfall.

72 *Both, either, neither* 174
They both live in a fantasy world.

73 Word order 176
Outside the port today

R14 Review: linking words and word order 178

Appendices

Verb tenses 180
Irregular verbs 181
Spelling: verbs 182
Spelling: adjective, adverbs and nouns 183
Glossary 184
Grammar index 186

1 Word class and word order
In the world today

In the world today, people speak around **2,700** different languages.

More than **750** million people use the English language.
But only about **350** million people speak it as a first language.

About **885** million people speak Chinese as their first language.

About **80%** of the information on the world's computers is in English.

There are **26** letters in the English alphabet. The sentence
The quick brown fox jumps over the lazy dog uses all 26 letters.

? Underline the correct option: English is the first language of around *350 / 750 / 885* million people in the world.

Answer: 350

Word class and word order

1 **A noun can be singular (e.g. *world*) or plural (e.g. *computers, people*).**
Examples of nouns are:
man, girl (people)
fox (animals)
computer, letter, language (things)
world (places)
success (qualities)

2 **A pronoun can replace a noun.**
Examples of pronouns are:
I, me, you, she, him, it, we, them

3 **An adjective describes a noun.**
Examples of adjectives are:
quick, brown, first, different, good

4 **Adjectives usually come before the noun.**
a first language NOT ~~*a language first*~~

Adjectives have no plural form.
different languages NOT ~~*differents languages*~~

5 **A verb can refer to the past, present or future.**
Examples of verbs are:
speak, jump (actions)
be, like, stay (states)

6 **An adverb can describe a verb, an adjective or a whole sentence. Examples of adverbs are:**
carefully, slowly (adverbs that describe a verb)
very, extremely (adverbs that describe adjectives)
however, sometimes, luckily (adverbs that describe sentences)

7 **A sentence usually contains a subject (S) and a verb (V).**
He (S) *won* (V).
Williams (S) *was* (V) *the winner.*
Our team (S) *is playing* (V) *in the big stadium.*

8 **Many sentences contain an object (O). In these sentences the word order is SVO.**
She (S) *won* (V) *the race* (O).

9 **Adverbs which describe a verb usually come at the end of a sentence.**
*My brother speaks English **quickly**.*

Practice

A Find examples of nouns, pronouns, verbs, adjectives and adverbs in the following sentences and write them below.

1 The alphabet has 26 letters.
2 750,000,000 people use the language.
3 It has five vowels: a, e, i, o and u.
4 The quick brown fox jumps over the lazy dog.
5 He studied the new words very carefully.

Nouns: *alphabet, letters,* ....
Pronouns: ....
Adjectives: ....
Verbs: *has,* ....
Adverbs: ....

B What is the subject in each of the sentences in Exercise A?

1 *the alphabet* 2 ....
3 .... 4 ....
5 ....

C Complete the sentences with an appropriate word. Use the part of speech in brackets.

1 He's a *happy* child – he's always smiling. (adjective)
2 .... loves her. (pronoun)
3 She .... to the pool every Saturday. (verb)
4 Can you speak more ....? I can't understand you. (adverb)
5 They're both very .... and thin. (adjective)
6 Luckily, the weather is .... good. It has been sunny all week. (adverb)
7 I study at school. I'm a ....(noun)
8 My teacher .... really good stories. (verb)
9 They work at the ....They're nurses. (noun)
10 My cousins live in Brazil. .... speak Portuguese. (pronoun)

D Make sentences by putting the words in the correct order.

1 walks / he / quickly *He walks quickly.*
2 we / speak / Russian ....
3 a / woman / strange / is / she ....
4 very badly / drives / my aunt ....
5 they / live / in this street ....
6 he / two brothers / has ....
7 the dog / my sandwich / ate ....
8 we / film / the / new / saw ....

MY TURN!

Use the words in the box to complete the table below.

adjectives adverbs ~~nouns~~ pronouns verbs

1	*nouns*	bee country game giraffe leaves man moon Morocco pizza spider station tennis match woman
2	....	I they we
3	....	beautiful crazy purple small stripy tall ugly wonderful young
4	....	be dance eat go have watch win
5	....	angrily happily quickly quietly sadly slowly

Now use the words from the table to make ten or more sentences and write them in your notebook. Use the verb in any appropriate tense. Your sentences must be correct but they can be crazy!

Example: *The tall man ate his pizza slowly.*

MY TEST!

Circle the correct option.

1 My sister and I love computer games. .... all the time. a We play them b Them play we c Play we them
2 My uncle speaks four .... a different languages b languages differents c differents languages
3 My mother is Spanish and my father is Japanese, but .... both speak English with me. a we b them c they
4 I like the book and my friend likes .... too. a book b him c it
5 *Cat, rabbit, dog* and *snake* are .... a adverbs b nouns c pronouns

My Test! answers: 1a 2a 3c 4c 5b

2 Be

Are you my son?

The Prince and the Pauper (1881) is a book by Mark Twain. The book **is** about two boys, Tom and Edward. They **are** 15 years old but their lives **are** very different. Tom **is** a poor boy but Edward **is** a prince. They change places by mistake so Edward **is** a poor boy and Tom **is** a prince. The old King, Henry VIII, **is not** well but he **is** Edward's father and he wants to know the truth ...

The King visits the prince (or is he the poor boy?).

King: I don't understand! **Are you** my son?
Tom: No, **I'm not** a prince, **I'm** poor.
King: **Are you** sure? Your clothes **are not** very old!
Tom: **They're not** my clothes. **They're** Edward's clothes. **He's** poor now.
King: Oh no! This **is** terrible! **Is it** true?
Tom: Yes, it **is**. **I'm** really sorry, King Henry. **You aren't** my father, **you're** my King.

Underline the correct option: Edward is Henry's *father / brother / son.*

Answer: son

Be

1 **Use *be* to give and ask for information.**
I'm Tom.
*The story **isn't** true.*
***Is** he in England?*

2 **Use *be* with ages.**
*Two boys **are** 15 years old.*

3 **Use *be* and *a / an* with jobs.**
She's a teacher.

4 **Use *be* to describe the weather.**
It's cold.

5 **Use *be* to talk about time and place.**
It's six o'clock.
*Edward **is** in London.*

6 **There is a full form and a short form.**
***I am** → **I'm**.*

In conversation, the short form is more common.
*'**They're** not my clothes.'*

In writing, the short form is used mainly with pronouns, not nouns.
*The old King **is not** well, he's sick.*

▶ **See Units 25 and 32 for more information on *be* in questions.**

statement ✓	negative ✗
I **am** ('m)	I **am not** ('m not)
You / We / They **are** ('re)	You / We / They **are not** (aren't / 're not)
He / She / It **is** ('s)	He / She / It **is not** (isn't / 's not)

question ?	short answer ✓✗
Am I ...?	Yes, I **am**. No, I **am not** ('m not).
Are you / we / they ...?	Yes, (they) **are**. No, (they) **are not** (aren't / 're not).
Is he / she / it ...?	Yes, (he) **is**. No, (he) **is not** (isn't / 's not).

TIP **English sentences normally need a subject.**
***It is** cold.* NOT ~~*Is cold.*~~
***I am** sure.* NOT ~~*Am sure.*~~

Practice

A Underline the correct option.

1 I *be / am / is* twelve years old.
2 They *be / am / are* in the garden.
3 It *am / is / are* six o'clock.
4 You *be / is / are* a dentist.
5 I *am / is / are* in the station.
6 It *am / is / are* very hot.
7 My sister *am / is / are* at work.
8 I *be / am / are* hungry.
9 We *am / is / are* students.
10 The book *be / is / are* about tigers.

B Complete the sentences from stories with the present simple of *be*. Some are negatives or questions.

1 The poor boy has no coat. He ...'s... cold.
2 We are the three bears. We .... in the woods.
3 Cinderella is running home. It .... 12 o'clock.
4 Tweedledum and Tweedledee have the same parents. They .... brothers.
5 The monster has a very ugly face. He .... handsome.
6 The wicked queen is asking her mirror: .... I beautiful?
7 Achilles and Hector fight. They .... friends.
8 Robinson Crusoe has no friends on the island. .... he unhappy?

C Complete this book review of *The Prince and the Pauper* with the present simple of *be*.

The Prince and the Pauper [1] ...is... a very good book. I [2] .... 11 years old and I [3](not) .... very interested in history but I really like this book. Mark Twain [4] .... a great writer. It [5](not) .... a true story but the characters [6] .... very realistic. The story [7](not) .... difficult. It [8] .... easy to understand and enjoy the book. Tom [9] .... a simple English boy. His family are poor and they [10] .... always hungry. Edward [11](not) .... poor because he [12] .... a prince. The boys [13] .... very different but at the end of the book they [14] .... friends. There are many films of the book too but they [15](not) .... very good – the book is the best!

D Make Tom's questions, using the words given and *be*. Then make Edward's replies with short answers using *be*.

1 you / prince?
Tom: ...Are you a prince?...
Edward: ...Yes, I am....
2 King Henry / your father?
Tom: ....?
Edward: ....
3 your mother / the Queen?
Tom: ....?
Edward: ....
4 we / brothers?
Tom: ....?
Edward: .... I don't have a brother.
5 your sisters / here?
Tom: ....?
Edward: .... They're in France.
6 you / very rich?
Tom: ....?
Edward: ....
7 it / cold / in your house?
Tom: ....?
Edward: .... It's always warm.
8 I / your friend?
Tom: ....?
Edward: .... I like you.

MY TURN!

Use the verb *be* to make these sentences true for you.

1 My mobile phone ...isn't... new.
2 Today .... Monday.
3 Coffee .... my favourite drink.
4 I .... a good cook.
5 My eyes .... blue.
6 It .... warm today.
7 My shoes .... clean.
8 I .... at home.
9 History books .... interesting.
10 My bed .... next to the door.

MY TEST!

Circle the correct option.

1 Tom and Edward ....
a have 15 years b is 15 years old c are 15 years old
2 Paul .... doctor.
a isn't a b aren't c isn't
3 A: What's the time? B: .... 11 o'clock.
a Is b It c It's
4 A: Are you my son? B: No, ...
a I'm not b I amn't c I am
5 A: .... today? B: No, it isn't. It's warm.
a Is cold b Is it cold c It cold

My Test! answers: 1c 2a 3c 4a 5b

3 Present simple 1: statements

Maybe you know her.

There's a new girl at school.

Maybe you **know** her.

She **has** beautiful black hair down to her waist.

Her big, brown eyes are pools of chocolate.

The new girl's name is Layla. My sister and I **see** her every day. We **think** she's 15. She **lives** in the apartments on the corner of our street. She **goes** to the library after school. I **hope** she is happy.

Layla **has** a young brother. They **walk** to school together. Her mum **works** as a cleaner at our school. She **comes** from Egypt. I **don't know** much about Egypt. My dad **says** that it never **rains** in Cairo.

? True or False? Layla lives in Egypt.

Answer: False

Present simple 1: statements

1 **Use the present simple for:**

– things that are always or usually true
*It never **rains** in Cairo.*

– regular or repeated events
*They **walk** to school together.*

– states, with verbs such as *feel, hate, know, like, look, love, prefer, think, understand, want.*
*We **think** she's 15. Maybe you **know** her.*

2 **Use the infinitive without *to* with *I, you, we* and *they*. Add *-s* with *he, she* and *it*.**

statement ✓	
I / You / We / They	think
He / She / It	thinks

TIP

In the present simple, the verb only changes with *he, she* or *it*. So remember ...

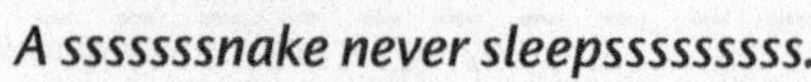

A sssssssnake never sleepssssssss.

3 **Spelling of the final *-s*:**

With most verbs, just add *-s* after the verb.
think → he thinks

After verbs which end *-o, -ch, -sh, -ss, -x*, add *-es*.
go → she goes
catch → he catches
push → she pushes
miss → it misses
fix → she fixes

When the verb ends in consonant + *-y*, drop the *-y* and add *-ies*.
fly → the bird flies

But add *-s* when the verb ends in vowel + *-y*.
play → he plays
enjoy → she enjoys

Irregular forms:
have → he has

► **See page 182 for more spelling rules.**

Practice

A Change the infinitive without *to* of these verbs into the correct present simple form with *it*.

1 play *it plays* 2 do .... 3 enjoy ....
4 fix .... 5 miss .... 6 say ....
7 teach .... 8 think .... 9 try ....
10 wash ....

B Complete these facts about Egypt. Use the correct present simple forms of the verbs in the box.

buy	come	~~have~~	have	live	show	study	visit

1 Egypt *has* a population of around 80 million.
2 17 million people .... in Cairo.
3 The name 'Egypt' .... from the Greek word *Egyptos*.
4 Around 6,000,000 tourists .... Egypt every year.
5 Every tourist .... presents from a night market.
6 Egypt .... about 100 pyramids.
7 Tourist guides .... people the pyramids of Giza.
8 An egyptologist is a person who .... Egyptian history from a long time ago.

C Complete Layla's letter using the correct present simple forms of the verbs in brackets.

Every morning I [1] *make* (make) breakfast for my brother and me. I [2] .... (walk) to school with my brother. We [3] .... (see) the same two girls. They always [4] .... (say) 'hello'. I [5] .... (feel) lonely sometimes, but I really like my new school. The school [6] .... (have) a very good library. My brother [7] .... (go) to primary school. He always [8] .... (wear) his old red coat. My mother [9] .... (go) to work early in the morning. She [10] .... (work) very hard. Thank you for the card. You [11] .... (write) very good letters. Write again soon!
Love, Layla

MY TURN!

In your notebook, write present simple statements about your school morning.

1 Every morning I *have breakfast with my family.*
2 I always ....
3 You never ....
4 My teacher ....
5 The school ....
6 My friends sometimes ....
7 We ....

MY TEST!

Circle the correct option.

1 .... to the shops. a They walks b She walk c He walks
2 Layla's mum .... by bus. a go b gos c goes
3 .... in Cairo. a It never rains b It never rain c It's never rain
4 .... big brown eyes. a Layla have b Layla haves c Layla has
5 Her mum .... English. a study b studys c studies

My Test! answers: 1c 2c 3a 4c 5c

4 Present simple 2: negatives and questions

Do you like zoos?

Do you like zoos?
Do you think zoos are a good idea?

Welcome to Animal World Park in California, USA. The park is different from other zoos. We help animals in danger. When it is possible, we return young animals to their homes.

We have more than 30 gorillas in the park. A mother gorilla doesn't have many babies. A baby gorilla stays with its mother for three years.

You often find colobus monkeys in zoos. They are in danger because they have beautiful fur. Young colobus monkeys don't have black and white fur – their fur is white.

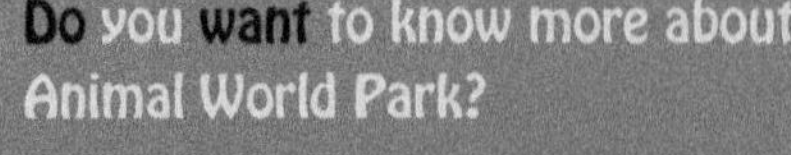

Do you want to know more about Animal World Park?

Click here for more information.

Yes, I do!
Please tell me more.
My email address is

PARK FACT
Does the park cost a lot of money?
Yes, it does. Over $7 million every year!

Find the names of the animals in the photos.

Answer: a gorilla and a colobus monkey

Present simple 2: negatives and questions

1 **To make negative forms in the present simple, use *don't* and *doesn't* + the infinitive form without *to* of the verb.**
*They **don't have** black and white fur.*
*A mother gorilla **doesn't have** many babies.*

negative ✗	
I / You / We / They	**do not** (**don't**) believe
He / She / It	**does not** (**doesn't**) believe

There is no -s on the main verb after *does* or *doesn't*.
She doesn't think ... NOT ~~*She doesn't thinks ...*~~
Does she know? NOT ~~*Does she knows?*~~

2 **To make a question, use *do* or *does* in front of the subject.**
***Do** you **like** zoos?*
***Does** the park **cost** a lot of money?*

3 **Use *do* or *does* in the affirmative short answer and *don't* or *doesn't* in the negative short answer.**
*Yes, I **do**.*
*No, he **doesn't**.*

question ?			short answer ✓✗
Do	I / you / we / they	**like** ...?	Yes, (I) **do**. No, (I) **don't**.
Does	he / she / it	**like** ...?	Yes, (he) **does**. No, (he) **doesn't**.

Practice

A Underline the correct option.

1 I *don't know* / *doesn't know* the answer.
2 Most trees *don't grow* / *doesn't grow* very quickly.
3 *Do* / *Does* Sara understand this?
4 *Do* / *Does* you want to talk about it?
5 The price *don't include* / *doesn't include* service.
6 I *don't think* / *doesn't think* he's very nice.
7 We *don't see* / *doesn't see* our grandparents very often.
8 They *don't live* / *doesn't live* very near.

B Complete the text about black rhinos using the correct present simple forms of the verbs in brackets.

We [1] have (have) a large number of rhinos living here. Black rhinos [2] .... (not live) in groups. They [3] .... (prefer) to live alone. Black rhinos are in danger because of their horns. People [4] .... (use) the horns as medicine. A mother black rhino [5] .... (not have) many babies. A baby [6] .... (stay) with its mother for three to four years. The mother rhino [7] .... (not stay) with the father. Rhinos [8] .... (not fight) with other animals in the park. In fact, they are friendly animals.

C Make present simple questions from the words, then answer the questions in your notebook using short answers.

1 a mechanic / fix cars
Does a mechanic fix cars?
2 you / work at the weekend
Do you work at the weekend?
3 a vet / look after animals
....
4 zoo keepers / work in shops
....
5 a young colobus monkey / have white fur
....
6 we / go to school on Sundays
....
7 nurses / work in a hospital
....
8 you / do sport in the evening
....

D Read part of an interview with a gorilla keeper. Complete her answers, using the verbs in the box.

not eat	not fight	~~get up~~	not go home	have	have	not look after	love

1 Yes, I get up at 6.30 every morning.
2 Yes, but they .... bananas all the time. They like a lot of other fruit, too.
3 The gorillas in the park are all friends. They ....
4 Yes, it does. The park .... more than 50 gorillas.
5 Yes, they do. We .... a baby gorilla in the park at the moment.
6 Yes, but sometimes a mother .... her baby. Then we help the baby.
7 Yes, I give the baby milk every four hours, day and night. I .... in the evening. I sleep at the park.
8 I .... my job! No day is the same!

MY TURN!

What did the interviewer ask? Make present simple questions using the words in brackets and write them in your notebook.

1 Do you get up early? (early)
2 .... ? (bananas)
3 .... ? (fight)
4 .... ? (a lot of gorillas)
5 .... ? (have babies)
6 .... ? (stay with its mother)
7 .... ? (drink milk)
8 .... ? (like)

Now think of at least three more present simple questions for the gorilla keeper and write them in your notebook.

MY TEST!

Circle the correct option.

1 A: .... to go to the zoo? B: No, I don't.
a You wants b Want you c Do you want
2 We .... zoos very often.
a aren't visit b don't visit c doesn't visit
3 My sister .... zoos.
a doesn't like b doesn't likes c don't like
4 She says the animals .... a very happy life.
a not have b doesn't have c don't have
5 A: Do the rhinos fight with other animals?
B: No, ...
a doesn't they b it doesn't c they don't

My Test! answers: 1c 2b 3a 4c 5c

5 Present continuous

She's wearing a bright yellow dress.

Mark: Hi, Monica. Are you looking for Nicole?

Monica: Mark, hi. Yes, we're waiting for her at the party. She isn't answering her mobile. Is she getting ready?

Mark: No, she isn't. She's lying on the sofa.

Monica: Are you serious? Everyone's arriving now.

Mark: She isn't feeling well.

Monica: That's a shame. We're having a great time. Diego's playing his new guitar and some people are dancing. That strange girl Bianca is here too. She's wearing a bright yellow dress and a green hat. She's ... Are you listening?

Mark: Wait a minute ... Nicole is coming now ...! See you there, Monica.

? Who is ill? **a** Mark **b** Monica **c** Nicole

Answer: c

Present continuous

1 The present continuous describes a temporary activity in progress at or around now.

*She **is lying** on the sofa now.*

past — present — future

*I'**m reading** this book at the moment.*
*Mark **is speaking** on the phone.*
***Are** you **listening**?*

2 Make present continuous statements with *am* / *is* / *are* + *-ing* form of the verb.

*I **am watching** TV.*
*Monica **is washing** her hair.*
*We **are drinking** coffee.*

3 Make negatives, questions and short forms like this:

*I **am not watching** TV.*
***Is** Monica **washing** her hair?*
*A: **Are** they **drinking** coffee?*
*B: Yes, they **are**.*

statement ✓	negative ✗
I **am** ('m) **working**	I **am not** ('m not) **working**
You / We / They **are** ('re) **working**	You / We / They **are not** (aren't / 're not) **working**
He / She / It **is** ('s) **working**	He / She / It **is not** (isn't / 's not) **working**

question ?	short answer ✓✗
Am I **working**?	Yes, I **am**. No, I **am not** ('m not).
Are you / we / they **working**?	Yes, (you) **are**. No, (you) **are not** (aren't / 're not).
Is he / she / it **working**?	Yes, (he) **is**. No, (he) **is not** (isn't / 's not).

If a verb ends in *-e*, drop the *-e*.

dance → *People **are dancing**.* NOT ~~*danceing*~~

If a verb ends in one vowel and one consonant, double the consonant.

stop → *The train is **stopping**.* NOT ~~*stoping*~~

▶ See page 182 for more spelling rules.
▶ See Units 6 and 18 for more information on the present continuous.

Practice

A Underline the correct option.

1 She is walking / are walking down the street.
2 People *is singing / are singing* too loudly.
3 We *isn't waiting / aren't waiting* in the right place.
4 I *am running / is running* because I'm late.
5 Hello? *Are I speaking / Am I speaking* to Lucy?
6 The guests *is not enjoying / are not enjoying* the party much.
7 At the moment I *am living / are living* with my friend.
8 *Is that boy smiling / Are that boy smiling* at me?

B Complete the sentences using the present continuous of the verbs in brackets.

1 ......It's raining...... (rain)
2 The baby ......is not crying...... now. (not cry)
3 We .... our holiday. (plan)
4 I .... to school. (walk)
5 They .... very fast. (not run)
6 The cat .... some milk. (drink)
7 I .... a good time. (not have)
8 He .... a computer upstairs. (carry)
9 She .... hard today. (not work)

C Complete the telephone conversation using the present continuous of the verbs in brackets. Some are negatives or questions.

'Hello, Dad. Yes, I'm still at the party. What's happening? Well, everyone [1] ...'s dancing... (dance) but I [2] .... (sit) on the sofa. Geoff [3] .... (tell) some friends about his holiday and he [4] .... (show) them the pictures. Diego and Bianca [5] .... (look) at the pictures because they think they are boring. What? Oh, that's Helen. She [6] .... (shout), she just speaks very loudly. I'm glad she [7] .... (sing) – she is a terrible singer! Wait ... Nicole [8] .... (come) in the door. She looks OK now. Everyone [9] .... (smile). Anyway, what about you, Dad? [10] .... (do) anything interesting? I see. Great, they [11] .... (bring) the food. I'm hungry! I'll phone later. Bye.'

D Complete the sentences using the present continuous of the verbs in the box. Some are negatives or questions.

carry	feel	play	stay	study
talk	try	~~watch~~	wear	write

1 ......Are you watching...... this film?
2 I .... very well.
3 A: Be quiet! We .... to listen to the radio!
B: Sorry.
4 A: My team are losing again!
B: They .... very well this season.
5 Sarah, ... my red dress?
6 A: Where's Robert?
B: He .... a letter.
7 A: .... you .... anything dangerous with you, Sir?
B: No, there's nothing dangerous in my suitcase.
8 Everyone .... about her purple hair.
9 .... Alice .... Economics at university?
10 A: Can I phone you at the hotel?
B: No, I .... there.

MY TURN!

Answer the questions in your notebook using short answers.

1 Is it raining?
...Yes, it is....
2 Are you watching TV?
...No, I'm not....
3 Are you wearing jeans?
4 Are any of your friends sitting near you?
5 Are you feeling hungry?
6 Is your mobile phone ringing?
7 Are you writing this with a black pen?
8 Is your watch / the clock showing the right time?
9 Are you listening to any music?

MY TEST!

Circle the correct option.

1 .... well, so I want to stay in bed. a I amn't feeling b I aren't feeling c I'm not feeling
2 A: .... the guitar? B: Yes, he is. a Is Diego playing b Diego is playing c Is playing Diego
3 Everyone at the party .... a are danceing b dancing c is dancing
4 A: Is Bianca wearing a yellow dress? B: Yes, ... a she wears b she are c she is
5 Mark .... to Monica. a isn't listening b not listening c don't listen

My Test! answers: 1c 2a 3c 4c 5a

6 Present continuous and present simple

I'm walking – I don't have a car.

Excuse me, **do** you **speak** English?
Yes, I do.
I'm going to the Eiffel Tower but I'm lost.
Are you **walking** or **driving**?
I'm walking – I **don't have** a car.
Good. I never **drive** in Paris. The traffic is terrible.

? Underline the correct option: Paris is a *bad* / *good* place for cars.

Answer: bad

Present continuous and present simple

1 **Use the present simple to talk or ask about things that are always or usually true.**
*Do you **speak** English?*
*We **don't have** a car.*

2 **Use the present simple to talk or ask about regular or repeated events and habits.**
*Sandra **phones** her mother every day.*
***Do** you **drink** coffee in the morning?*

3 **We often use the present simple with adverbs of frequency (*always, never, sometimes*, etc.).**
*It never **snows** here in summer.*
*I sometimes **dream** about you.*

4 **Use the present continuous to describe an activity in progress now / around now, or an unfinished activity.**
***Are** you **reading** this page.* (= now)
*They **are building** a shopping centre.* (= it is not finished yet)

5 **We rarely use the present continuous for verbs which are about states, not actions, e.g. *believe, know, like, love, need, seem, understand, want*. See Unit 39.**
*I **know** English.* NOT ~~*I'm knowing ...*~~
*Do you **need** a pen?* NOT ~~*Are you needing ...?*~~

present simple	present continuous
He usually **walks** to work.	He's **walking** to work today.
It **doesn't rain** on the moon.	It **isn't raining** at the moment.
Do you ever **read** comics?	She's **reading** a comic now.
I **have** two brothers.	I'm **having** a shower.
Charles **plays** the piano.	Charles **isn't** at home. He's **playing** in a concert.
A: What **do** you **do**? B: I'm a taxi driver.	A: What **are** you **doing**? B: I'm **driving** to the airport.

TIP

The present simple is much more common than the present continuous, and in most cases you should use the present simple.

*I **think** it's nice.* NOT ~~*I'm thinking ...*~~
*She is Turkish and **she comes** from Istanbul.*
NOT ~~*... she's coming ...*~~

▶ **See Units 3 and 5 for more information on the present simple and present continuous.**

Practice

A Underline the correct option.

1 They *play / are playing* rugby twice a week.
2 *Are you having / Do you have* breakfast every morning?
3 It *snows / is snowing* so we can't go skiing.
4 Your guide *speaks / is speaking* three languages.
5 We *don't know / aren't knowing* the way.
6 The DJ *plays / is playing* my favourite song.
7 *Do you like / Are you liking* the food?
8 I'*m not laughing / don't laugh*, I'*m crying / cry*.

B Match the pairs.

1	She speaks French well	a	because the tourist doesn't know Italian.
2	She is speaking French	b	because her mother is from Paris.
3	It rains a lot	a	in Mozambique.
4	It's raining a lot	b	and I'm wet.
5	She always has lunch	a	– please phone later.
6	She's having lunch	b	at school.
7	A: Do you buy computer games?	a	B: Yes, I'm in the shop.
8	A: Are you buying a computer game?	b	B: No, I download them from the Internet.
9	I don't work.	a	It's Sunday.
10	I'm not working.	b	I'm a student.
11	A: What is she doing?	a	B: She's reading.
12	A: What does she do?	b	B: She's a student.

C Complete the dialogues using the verbs in the box in the present simple or present continuous. Some are negatives or questions.

agree	carry	know	need	rain	~~understand~~	wait	wear

1 A: I ......*don't understand*...... these instructions.
B: Why not? They look clear to me.
2 A: London is a very expensive city.
B: Yes, I .... with you.
3 A: .... you .... any help?
B: No, I'm OK, thanks.
4 A: She .... a coat.
B: That's strange – it's very cold today.
5 A: They .... a piano up the stairs.
B: Help them – it's very heavy.
6 A: Where is the History Museum?
B: Sorry, I ....
7 A: .... Terry .... for me?
B: Yes – you're late.
8 A: It's a lovely day for a picnic.
B: We're lucky that it ....

D Complete this postcard with the present simple or present continuous of the verbs in brackets.

Hi, Rita,
I [1] ...*'m having*... (have) a lovely time in Manchester. The weather is nice and warm today, the sun [2] .... (shine) and everyone [3] .... (wear) T-shirts. Our teacher is great. He [4] .... (come) from Manchester too but he [5] .... (not speak) English with an accent. We [6] .... (study) three hours in the morning and [7] .... (go) on excursions in the afternoon. Now I [8] .... (sit) in a café on King Street. I [9] .... (not think) a king really [10] .... (live) here! How are you? [11] .... (work) this summer? Write soon.
Love, Julio

MY TURN!

You are on holiday. In your notebook, write a text message to your friend. Describe what you are doing and what you are wearing. Tell your friend what you do every day and what you like / don't like.

Example: *I'm lying by the pool. I swim every day.*

MY TEST!

Circle the correct option.

1 The tourist .... for the Eiffel Tower.
a is looking b look c are looking
2 He has a map, but he .... it.
a isn't understanding b doesn't understand c isn't understand
3 A: .... a car? B: Yes, but I never drive in Paris.
a Are you have b Do you have c Are you having
4 When we are in Paris, we always .... by metro.
a are go b are going c go
5 It is often sunny in Paris, but today it ....
a are rain b is raining c rains

My Test! answers: 1a 2b 3b 4c 5b

7 Imperatives

Stay calm!

People in California in the United States are always prepared for a large earthquake. The information below is for US teenagers.

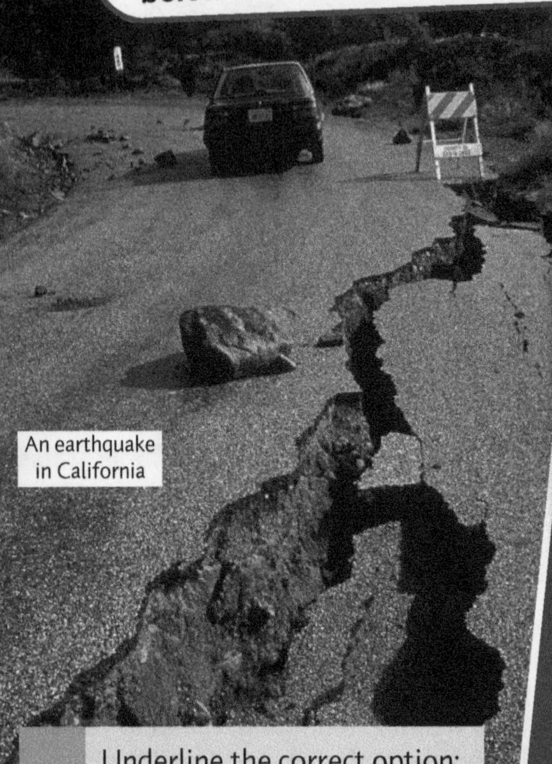
An earthquake in California

Stay calm!

Inside

Stay inside.
Sit under a table or **stand** against a wall.
Don't stand near doors or windows.
Never take an elevator.

Outside

Always stay where you are. **Don't run** inside.
Find a clear place away from buildings and trees.
Lie down on the ground until the earthquake stops.

In a car

Slow down and **stop** the car in a clear place.
Don't stop on a bridge.
Stay inside the car until the earthquake stops.

?

Underline the correct option:
A large earthquake is *possible / not possible* in California.

Answer: possible

Imperatives

1 Use imperatives for:
- instructions
Answer the questions.
- advice
Stay inside the car.
- orders
Be quiet!
- invitations
Come in and have a coffee.
- requests
Please put your bag over there.

TIP

Requests with imperatives often sound not very polite to English speakers, even if you add 'please'. It's better to use other structures, e.g:
Could you put your bag over there?
Would you mind putting your bag over there?

▶ See Unit 21 for the use of *can* and *could* for requests.

2 Use the infinitive without *to* for imperatives. There is usually no subject.
Lie down on the ground. NOT ~~*You lie down on the ground.*~~

3 Make negatives by adding *don't* (*do not*) in front.
Don't / Do not stand near windows.

4 *Always* and *never* can be used at the beginning of the imperative phrase.
Never take an elevator.
Always stay where you are.

A What do you do if there is a fire in the home? Underline the correct option.

1 *Panic!* / *Don't panic!*
2 *Leave* / *Don't leave* the house quickly.
3 *Take time* / *Don't take time* to collect your things.
4 *Close* / *Don't close* all doors behind you.
5 If a door is hot, *open* / *don't open* it. Go to the window.
6 *Go back* / *Don't go back* inside.
7 *Phone* / *Don't phone* the fire fighters.

B Complete the dialogues with the imperative or negative imperative forms of the verbs in the box.

forget go shopping have pick up put take turn left ~~turn down~~ worry

1 A: ...Turn... that music ...down!...
B: I can't hear you. The music's too loud!
2 A: It's my exam today.
B: .... It'll be OK.
3 A: I feel really bored. What can I do?
B: .... ! That's what I do when I'm bored!
4 A: Please .... your feet on the seat.
B: Sorry.
5 A: These cakes are lovely.
B: .... two!
6 A: I'm ready to go now.
B: .... a great holiday!
.... to send a postcard.
7 A: Look at that snake! Can I take it home?
B: No! Never .... a snake!
8 A: This is the road. .... now!
B: What did you say?

C You are visiting a friend this weekend. Complete your friend's advice with an appropriate verb in the imperative or negative imperative.

1 ...Go... to bed early tonight.
2 .... late. The train always leaves on time.
3 The station is always busy. .... your ticket before you come.
4 .... a sandwich on the train – they're very expensive.
5 The train arrives at platform 2. .... down the stairs and .... out of the main entrance.
6 .... left and .... to the car park.
7 .... in the car park. I'll meet you there.

MY TURN!

You work in a tourist information office in your town. Give some advice to tourists. Write three imperative sentences and three negative imperative sentences in your notebook.

Examples:
Bring a big coat.
Don't drive into the centre.

MY TEST!

Circle the correct option.

1 .... ! It's 8 o'clock and you're late. a You get up b Gets up c Get up
2 A: Can I go to a party tonight, Mum? B: OK, but please .... noisy when you come home.
a you aren't b be not c don't be
3 .... across the road. a Don't never run b Never run c Don't running
4 A: Excuse me? Where is the toilet? B: .... up these stairs and turn left. It's there.
a Go b Going c You going
5 A: Sorry. I can't help you today. I'm very busy. B: .... a Don't worry b Don't be worry c Doesn't worry

My Test! answers: 1c 2c 3b 4a 5a

R1 Review: present simple and present continuous

A Complete the sentences with the correct form of the verb. Be careful with spelling.

1 My sister ....plays.... (play) tennis every week and always ....watches.... (watch) tennis matches on TV.
2 Look at that cat! It .... (run) very fast. I think it .... (try) to catch that bird.
3 My uncle .... (work) in a factory. He .... (fix) broken computers.
4 The baby .... (cry) again. She always .... (cry) when she's hungry.
5 Look! Everyone .... (have) a great time at the party. Some people are .... (dance), and some .... (chat).
6 Mark usually .... (study) very hard for exams, but he .... (not study) tonight. He .... (make) a model.
7 Alice really .... (not want) her yoga course to end. She .... (say) it's great.
8 Daniel .... (have) an easy life. He just .... (relax) all day and .... (go) to parties at night.

B <u>Underline</u> the correct option.

Chris: Hello?
Sue: Hi Chris. It's Sue. [1] *<u>Are</u> / Do* you at home?
Chris: No, [2] *I'm not / I don't.* I'm at school. Why?
Sue: [3] *Are / Do* you have my Biology book?
Chris: Your Biology book? I think I have it but [4] *I'm not / I don't remember* where. Just a moment ... no, it [5] *isn't / doesn't* in my bag.
Sue: [6] *Is / does* it on your desk at home?
Chris: Ah, yes. Sorry. [7] *Are / Do* you need it?
Sue: Yes, I do. We have a big Biology test tomorrow. [8] *I'm not / I don't* understand Biology, so I need to study.
Chris: No, you [9] *aren't / don't.* Mrs Williams [10] *isn't / doesn't* at school this week. She's ill.
Sue: Really?
Chris: Yes. So the test [11] *isn't / doesn't* tomorrow. It's next Thursday. You [12] *aren't / don't* need to study tonight.

C Change the statements into negatives and the negatives into statements.

1 I'm very good at sports, but I don't like watching sport on TV.
I'm not very good at sports, but I like watching sport on TV.
2 My brother plays the guitar, but he isn't very good at singing.
....
3 We are very happy. Our team is winning.
....
4 Ann and Robert like London and they're planning to stay there.
....
5 Lucy is very good at dancing. We enjoy her shows.
....
6 Marcus is playing a computer game at the moment. He plays computer games every night.
....
7 That song is very good. I want to listen to it again.
....
8 Tony doesn't eat hamburgers. He doesn't eat a lot of meat.
....
9 Joanna has a swimming competition next week, so she is practising very hard today.
....
10 I don't go to school by bus – I walk. So I don't have time to read magazines on the way.
....

D Complete the email with the present simple or the present continuous of the verbs in brackets.

Delete Reply Reply All Forward Print

Hi Luis

Thanks for your email. I'm really pleased that you [1] ....'re enjoying.... (enjoy) your English course in the UK. [2] .... (your English / get) better?
We're all fine here – as always. I [3] .... (not / have) much free time at the moment. I [4] .... (practise) hard for the tennis competition – only three weeks to go and I'm really nervous about it. I really [5] .... (want) to win the competition this year. Brian [6] .... (think) I'm playing well, but I [7] .... (not think) I am.
[8] .... (you / remember) my 'baby sister' Maria? Well, can you believe she's 13 now? We [9] .... (still / think) of her as a little child, but she's very grown-up now. She [10] .... (learn) to play the violin, and she's already quite good. She [11] .... (play) right now, while I [12] .... (write) this email.
Right, time to stop writing. I have loads of work to do! See you soon.

Angela

E Cross out all the wrong options.

1 Carl ~~work~~ / *works* very hard most days, but he ~~don't~~ / *doesn't work* / ~~works~~ at the weekend. He ~~relax~~ / *relaxes.*
2 My cat *sleep / sleeps* all day and *go / goes* out all night. She never *catch / catches* birds – she's too slow.
3 A: *Do / Does* Caroline *go / goes* to your school?
B: No, she *don't / doesn't.* She *go / goes* to a private school in the city.
4 Sam and Leo *play / plays* tennis every week, but Sam never *win / wins.* Leo always *beat / beats* him.
5 A: *Do / Does* you *know / knows* Frances?
B: Maybe. *Do / Does* she *have / has* long blonde hair?
A: Yes, she *do / does.*
6 We always *visit / visits* our grandmother in the winter. She *live / lives* on a farm.
7 It *don't / doesn't snow / snows* very often here, but sometimes it *rain / rains* non-stop for weeks. I *don't / doesn't like / likes* it.
8 A: *Do / Does* Stuart and Paula *like / likes* dancing?
B: Well, Stuart *love / loves* dancing, but Paula *don't / doesn't enjoy / enjoys* it.
9 A: *Do / Does* your computer *stop / stops* very often?
B: Yes, it *do / does.* I *want / wants* to buy a new one.

F What do the people say in these situations? Complete the sentences with the imperative or negative imperative of the words in the box.

be late	be quiet	bring	come	drink	go out	look at	touch	wait	~~wash~~

1 It is lunchtime. What do you say to your young sister?
....Wash.... your hands before you eat.
2 Your young sister wants to help with the cooking. What do you say?
.... the pot – it's hot!
3 You are sitting in the exam room. Everyone is talking before the exam. What does the teacher say?
Please ....
4 A student is trying to see his friend's answers. What does the teacher say?
.... your friend's work.
5 You receive an invitation to a friend's party. What does the invitation say?
.... to my party on Saturday.
6 Your friend wants everyone at the party on time. What does the invitation say?
The party starts at 8 – .... !
7 If you enter Australia, there are some things you can't have with you. What does the sign in the airport say?
.... fresh fruit into the country.
8 You need to show your passport at the airport. There are a lot of people there. What does the sign say?
Please .... here.
9 You are ill. What does the doctor say?
Stay at home – ....
10 The doctor wants you to have more water. What does he say?
.... three glasses of water every day.

8 Past simple 1: *was / were*

He was a popular hero.

ROBIN HOOD

is a famous hero. He is the subject of stories and films. But **was** he a real man?

Who was Robin Hood?

Nobody knows. In the film, *Robin Hood: Prince of Thieves*, Robin **was** rich – but this probably **wasn't** true. We know that he **was** a popular hero in the 13th century. It's possible the real man **was born** before then.

Who were the Merry Men?

Little John and Will Scarlet **were** famous Merry Men. Robin Hood **was** the leader of this group of men (and women).

Why were Robin Hood and his Merry Men famous?

They **were** famous for robbing rich people. But Robin Hood and his Merry Men **weren't** robbers – the money **was** for poor people.

? Complete this sentence: There are many .... about Robin Hood.

Answer: stories and films

Past simple 1: *was / were*

1 ***Was*** **is the past of** ***am*** **and** ***is*****.**

*He **was** the leader.*
***Was** I asleep?*
*Who **was** Robin Hood?*

2 ***Were*** **is the past of** ***are*****.**

*They **were** famous for robbing rich people.*
***Were** you there?*
*Who **were** the Merry Men?*

3 **Use** ***wasn't*** **(*was not*) and** ***weren't*** **(*were not*) for the negative.**

*This **wasn't** true.*
*They **weren't** robbers.*

	statement ✓	negative ✗
I / He / She / It	**was**	**was not (wasn't)**
You / We / They	**were**	**were not (weren't)**

4 **Make questions and short answers as follows:**

question ?		short answer ✓✗
Was I / he / she / it	a robber?	Yes, (he) **was**. No, (he) **wasn't**.
Were you / we / they	famous?	Yes, (they) **were**. No, (they) **weren't**.
Who **was** he? Where **were** you?		

TIP

was / were born

*Shakespeare **was born** in 1564 and died in 1616.*

Practice

A Complete the sentences using *was, wasn't, were* or *weren't*.

1 Chiara and her sister ....were....... here a moment ago.
2 It .... a holiday last week and we .... at my uncle's house. My cousins .... at home, so it was quiet.
3 A: You're here at last! I .... worried about you.
B: The train .... late.
4 A: .... it a good film?
B: No, it .... It .... the worst film of the summer!
5 A: .... Ben at football practice on Monday?
B: No, he .... ! And where .... you?
6 A: .... your parents angry?
B: No, they ....

B Robin Hood's enemy, the Sheriff of Nottingham, is asking him some questions.
Complete the questions and the short answers.

Sheriff: Where [1] ....were you....... born?
Robin: I'm not telling you!
Sheriff: Were you at home yesterday?
Robin: No, I [2] ....
Sheriff: Were you with your friends?
Robin: The Merry Men? Yes, I [3] ....
Sheriff: [4] .... in the forest?
Robin: No, we [5] ....
Sheriff: Where [6] .... yesterday?
Robin: We [7] .... in your castle!
Sheriff: Where's my money?
Robin: I'm not telling you!

C Complete the sentences using *wasn't* or *weren't* and an appropriate adjective from the box. Sometimes more than one answer is possible.

afraid clean friendly hot hungry in a hurry very big

1 The town was pretty but it ....wasn't very big....... .
2 The restaurant was nice but I ....
3 The food was good but the waiters ....
4 The dog was very big, but the children ....
5 The weather was sunny but it ....
6 The beach was great but it ....
7 The hotel was nice but the rooms ....
8 The shop was busy but we ....

D Complete the text with *is, are, was, were, wasn't* or *weren't*.

Sherwood Forest [1] ....was....... home for Robin Hood and his Merry Men. In the 13th century the forest [2] .... a safe place for most people, but Robin and his friends [3] .... happy there. Their home [4] .... a camp near a large tree. Today the forest [5] .... a popular place for tourists to visit, and the tree [6] .... still there. Some people say that Robin Hood and Maid Marian [7] .... lovers. In fact, Robin [8] .... already married! But do you prefer to believe the stories? Then you can still see St Mary's Church where they [9] .... married. St Mary's Church and Sherwood Forest [10] .... near the city of Nottingham in the centre of England.

MY TURN!

In your notebook, write sentences using *was, were, wasn't* and *weren't* about a place you have visited.

I we it the town the streets the shops the weather the people

Example: *We visited Bath. The town was beautiful.*

MY TEST!

Circle the correct option.

1 A: Where .... all yesterday evening?
B: At the cinema.
a were you b was you c you were
2 The film .... very good, but Kevin Costner was excellent.
a wasn't b were not c weren't
3 Both Shakespeare and Galileo .... in 1564.
a were born b was born c are born
4 A: Mum, where .... born?
B: In Nottingham.
a I was b were I c was I
5 A: Were the Merry Men very rich?
B: No, ...
a they weren't b were not c they wasn't

My Test! answers: 1a 2a 3a 4c 5a

9 Past simple 2: regular past forms

She lived in a tree.

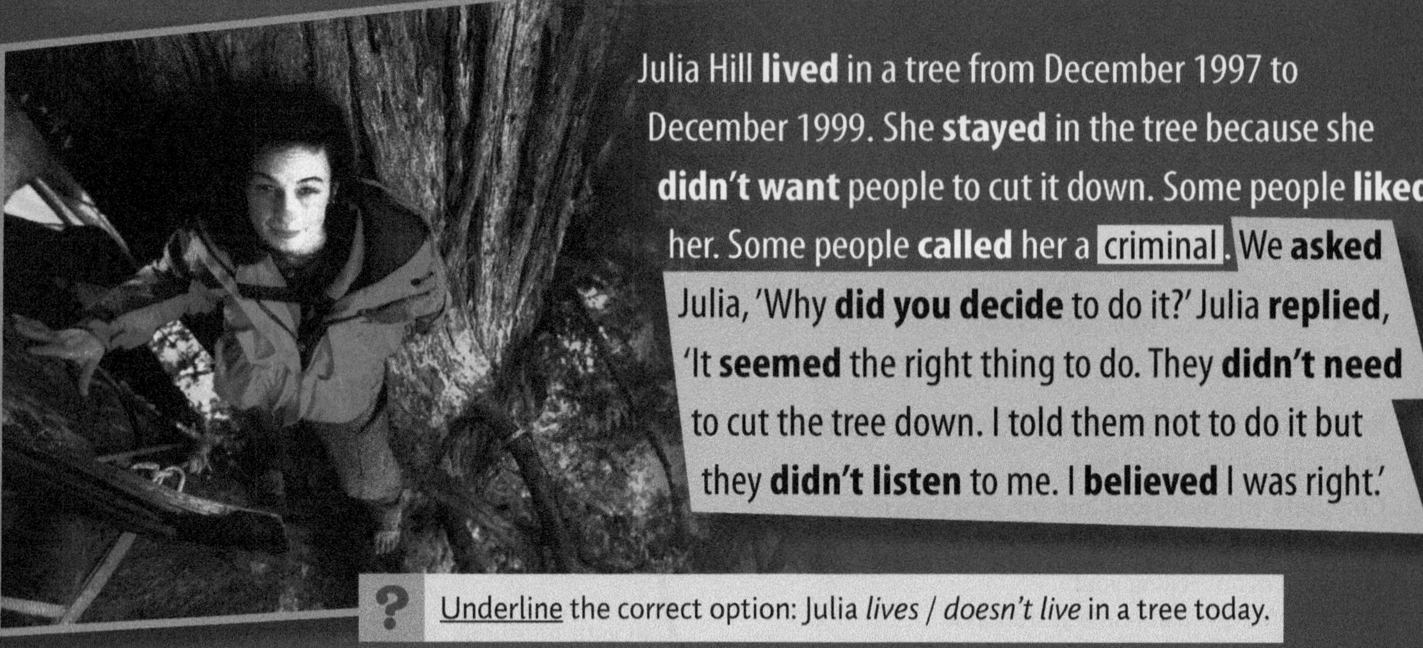

Julia Hill **lived** in a tree from December 1997 to December 1999. She **stayed** in the tree because she **didn't want** people to cut it down. Some people **liked** her. Some people **called** her a criminal. We **asked** Julia, 'Why **did you decide** to do it?' Julia **replied**, 'It **seemed** the right thing to do. They **didn't need** to cut the tree down. I told them not to do it but they **didn't listen** to me. I **believed** I was right.'

? Underline the correct option: Julia *lives* / *doesn't live* in a tree today.

Answer: doesn't live

Past simple 2: regular past forms

1 **Use the past simple for past actions, states and general truths.**
*I **phoned** Julia yesterday.*
*Did you **stay** at the party long last night?*
*Once people **didn't believe** the world was round.*

2 **The past time could be recent or distant.**

*We **finished** one minute ago.*

past — present — future

*The Chinese **invented** paper.*

3 **Add *-ed* to make the past simple (regular) for all persons. Use *did not* and the infinitive without *to* to make the negative and use *did* to make a question. We usually say and write *didn't* instead of *did not* in informal situations, e.g. an email to a friend.**

	statement ✓	negative ✗
I / You / He / She / It / We / They	**started**	**did not (didn't) start**

question ?	short answer ✓✗
Did I / you / he / she / it / we / they **start**?	Yes, (I) **did**. No, (I) **did not (didn't)**.

4 **Past time expressions, e.g. *yesterday*, *last* (*night* / *week* / *year*), (*a few minutes* / *two months* / *10 years*) *ago*, are sometimes used with the past simple.**
*She **didn't arrive** yesterday.*
***Did** you **clean** the car last weekend?*
*Colombus **discovered** America 500 years ago.*

Spelling

When a verb ends in *-e*, add *-d*.
die → *died*
love → *loved*

When a verb ends in a consonant (*b, t, m,* etc.) and *-y*, delete the *-y* and add *-ied*.
copy → *copied*
try → *tried*

When a verb ends in a single vowel (*a, e, i, o, u*) and a single consonant, double the last consonant.
stop → *stopped*
prefer → *preferred*

▶ **See page 182 for more spelling rules.**

Practice

A What was Margaret's life like in 1970 when she was young? Write past simple statements (✓) and negatives (✗) using the information below.

1 ✓ work in a shop — 1 She worked in a shop.
2 ✗ like her job — 2 She didn't like her job.
3 ✓ live in a flat — 3 ....
4 ✗ want a house — 4 ....
5 ✓ prefer flats — 5 ....
6 ✗ watch TV much — 6 ....
7 ✓ enjoy dancing — 7 ....
8 ✓ dance the Salsa — 8 ....
9 ✓ learn Spanish — 9 ....
10 ✗ stay at home much — 10 ....

B Complete the sentences with an appropriate verb in the past simple. Some are negatives or questions.

1 I was tired, so I d i d n 't w a l k to work.
2 _ _ _ you w _ _ _ _ _ the match last night on TV?
3 Yesterday she w _ _ _ _ _ _ all day in the factory.
4 The rain s _ _ _ _ _ _ _ , so the tennis started.
5 Tony was very quiet. He _ _ _ _ ' _ t _ _ _ to anyone.
6 Last summer we t _ _ _ _ _ _ _ _ _ _ around Europe by train.
7 A: _ _ _ Jane p _ _ _ _ the test?
B: No, she failed.
8 I l _ _ _ _ _ _ _ _ to the concert as a podcast.
9 A: _ _ _ the children f _ _ _ _ _ _ all their breakfast?
B: Yes, they were hungry.
10 The party was terrible, I _ _ _ _ ' _ l _ _ _ it.

C Complete the text using the past simple of the verbs in brackets.

Travis Carter [1] ......lived...... (live) in a fridge for 40 days from December 1998 to February 1999 – a world record. A reporter [2] .... (ask) Travis later, '[3] .... you .... (celebrate) New Year in the fridge?' Travis [4] .... (reply), 'No. I [5] .... (not know) that it was New Year: my watch [6] .... (not work) because it was so cold!' Two years ago, Travis [7] .... (try) another world record – 60 hours in a freezer. This time he [8] .... (fail). 'The freezer was just too cold. I [9] .... (not like) it,' Travis said. 'I [10] .... (prefer) the fridge.'

MY TURN!

A hundred British teenagers answered a questionnaire about technology. Change their answers into past simple sentences. Some are negative.

Question	Answer
Did you watch a DVD last Saturday night?	87 yes 13 no
Did you use the Internet yesterday?	70 yes 30 no
Did you download a song last week?	19 yes 81 no
Did you play a computer game yesterday?	35 yes 65 no
Did you email a friend last week?	58 yes 42 no
Did you like computers five years ago?	90 yes 10 no

1 87 teenagers watched a DVD last Saturday night.
2 13 teenagers didn't watch a DVD last Saturday night.
3 30 teenagers ....
4 19 teenagers ....
5 35 teenagers ....
6 58 teenagers ....
7 10 teenagers ....

Now answer the questionnaire in your notebook.

1 I didn't watch a DVD last Saturday night. / I watched a DVD last Saturday night.

MY TEST!

Circle the correct option.

1 She .... in the tree for 737 days.
a stayed b was stayed c is stayed
2 She .... when she finished her protest.
a cryed b cried c cry
3 .... to journalists?
a Did she talked b Talked she c Did she talk
4 A: Did she save the tree? B: Yes, she ....
a saved b save c did
5 A: Julia, was it boring?
B: Yes, it was. I .... TV for two years.
a didn't watched b don't watched
c didn't watch

My Test! answers: 1a 2b 3c 4c 5c

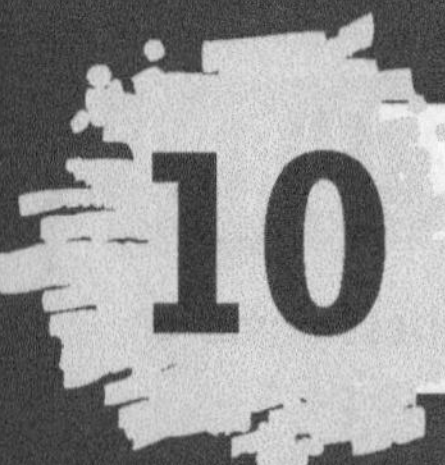

10 Past simple 3: irregular past forms

They spoke Celtic languages.

Where did English come from?

Old English	he on þa duru eode
Modern English	he went to the door

The ancient Britons **spoke** Celtic languages like Welsh. The Romans **made** Britain a colony in 43 AD but Latin **didn't become** the language of the common people. Not many of the ancient Britons **knew** Latin and they **didn't feel** happy with a new language.

In the 5th century AD, the Romans **left** Britain because they **had** problems at home. The Angles, Saxons and Jutes then **went** to England from Denmark and Germany. They **brought** their own Germanic languages. These languages **became** Old English. The story of English **began.**

True or False? English is a Latin language.

Answer: False

Past simple 3: irregular past forms

1 **Many past simple verbs do not end in *-ed*. They have irregular forms. For negative and question forms, use *did* and the infinitive without *to*.**

*The Romans **made** Britain a colony.*
*They **didn't feel** happy.*
*Did they **speak** Latin?*

statement ✓	negative ✗
You **sang.**	You **did not (didn't) sing.**
She **told** her brother.	She **did not (didn't) tell** her brother.
The army **went** home.	The army **did not (didn't) go** home.

question ?	short answer ✓ ✗
Did I / you / he / she / it / we / they **sing?**	Yes, (I) **did.** No, (I) **did not (didn't).**

present	past
be	was / were
become	became
begin	began
bring	brought
buy	bought
come	came
do	did
eat	ate
get	got
give	gave
go	went
have	had
hear	heard

present	past
know	knew
leave	left
make	made
mean	meant
pay	paid
put	put
say	said
see	saw
speak	spoke
take	took
tell	told
think	thought

▶ **See page 181 for a list of irregular verbs.**

Practice

A Circle the 12 past simple forms in the wordsearch puzzle, then write their infinitive-without-*to* forms.

h	e	a	r	d	t	y	r	t	u
i	o	p	a	w	s	q	d	o	k
s	a	w	t	s	f	g	h	o	n
j	k	l	h	x	b	r	o	k	e
z	s	p	o	k	e	w	e	c	w
l	m	b	u	s	f	u	d	n	j
m	e	e	g	d	a	y	g	m	l
g	a	f	h	i	e	m	a	d	e
o	n	h	t	k	c	g	k	l	f
t	t	j	k	(c	a	m	e)	i	t

1 come
2 ....
3 ....
4 ....
5 ....
6 ....
7 ....
8 ....
9 ....
10 ....
11 ....
12 ....

B The most famous poem in Old English is *Beowulf*. Complete the text using the correct past simple form of the verbs in brackets.

Beowulf [1] was (be) a great fighter 1,000 years ago. He [2] .... (win) many battles against monsters and dragons. Grendel was a terrible monster from Denmark. He [3] .... (have) big teeth and he was very strong. Grendel [4] .... (not sleep) and [5] .... (not eat). He[6] .... (drink) blood. King Hrothgar of Denmark [7] .... (pay) Beowulf to kill Grendel. Beowulf [8] .... (go) to Denmark, [9] .... (fight) the monster and killed it. King Hrothgar [10] .... (give) Beowulf a lot of money. Beowulf [11] .... (leave) Denmark and [12] .... (not come) back. He [13] .... (become) a King. Finally, Beowulf died because a dragon killed him.

C Read the notes about a typical teenager's day in 1000 AD. Write full sentences in the past simple. Some are statements (✓) and some are negatives (✗).

A teenager in 1000 AD
✓ get up: 5.30
✓ breakfast (bread and water)
✗ go to school ✓ go to work
✓ work begin: 6.30
✓ lunch (meat)
✓ get home: 5.00
✓ make clothes: evening
✓ before bed: tell story to sister
✗ sleep in a bed ✓ sleep on the floor

She got up at 5.30 and ....
....
....
....
....
....

MY TURN!

What did you do yesterday? Answer the questions in your notebook using past simple short answers and sentences. Then write three more questions and answer them in the same way.

1 Did you get up early?
No, I didn't. I got up at 10 o'clock.
2 Did you speak English?
Yes, I did. I said 'Hello' to my English teacher.
3 Did you buy anything?
4 Did you go anywhere in the evening?
5 Did you forget anything?
6 Did you see any friends?

MY TEST!

Circle the correct option.

1 A: Did they feel happy? B: No, they .... very angry. a feled b fell c felt
2 Where .... from? a did the Saxons come b the Saxons came c did the Saxons came
3 A: Did Beowulf speak Old English? B: Yes, he .... a did b spoke c does
4 The Ancient Britons .... pens and pencils. a hadn't b didn't have c didn't had
5 Beowulf .... sorry to the King. a sayed b said c saw

My Test answers: 1c 2a 3a 4b 5b

Past continuous

Everyone was talking about the alligators.

Urban legends are stories about strange things that happen in everyday life. But they are probably not true. Or are they?

Years ago in Florida and Georgia, you could buy baby alligators. But they are difficult pets, so people set them free. Where did these alligators go?
While we **were studying** English, my wife and I **were living** in New York. At that time everyone **was talking** about the alligators in the sewers. A friend told me that one day a man **was working** in the sewers. It was five o'clock and he **was** just **finishing** for the day. His friends **were waiting** for him in the street. They heard a scream. When they pulled the man out of the sewer, he was scared and he **was shaking**. There was an alligator in the sewer!

What do you think? Is this story true?

Past continuous

1 **Use the past continuous to talk about events which were in progress at a particular time in the past.**
At that time everyone ***was talking*** *about the alligators in the sewers.*

2 **Use the past continuous to set the background to a story – to talk about what was going on when an event happened. The main events are usually in the past simple.**
His friends ***were waiting*** *for him in the street. They heard a scream.*

3 **Use** ***when*** **or** ***while*** **to link past simple and past continuous. We can use** ***when*** **before the past simple or the past continuous.**

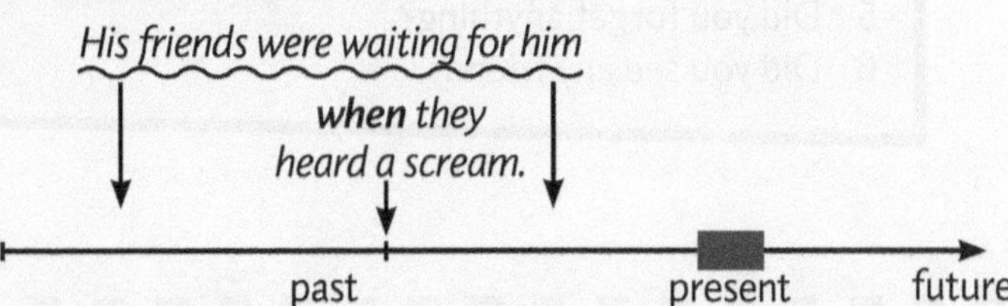

His friends were waiting for him
when they
heard a scream.
past
present
future

When *his friends were waiting for him, they heard a scream.*

We can also use ***while*** **before the past continuous.**
While *his friends were waiting for him, they heard a scream.*

4 **Use** ***while*** **with the past continuous in both parts of a sentence to talk about two situations going on at the same time.**
While *we* ***were studying*** *English, my wife and I* ***were living*** *in New York.*

TIP

When ***when*** **and** ***while*** **come at the beginning of a sentence, put a comma in the middle of the sentence.**
While I was falling, I closed my eyes.

5 **Use the past continuous to give the reason for a past event.**
I ***forgot*** *about the bath because I* ***was talking*** *on the telephone.*
She ***shouted*** *at me because I* ***was driving*** *fast.*

6 **Make the past continuous using the verb** ***was / were*** **+ verb + -*ing* form.**

	statement ✓	negative ✗
You / We / They	were working	were not (weren't) working
I / He / She / It	was working	was not (wasn't) working

question ?			short answer ✓ ✗
Were	you / we / they	working?	Yes, (you) were. No, (you) weren't.
Was	I / he / she / it	working?	Yes, (I) was. No, (I) wasn't.

▶ See page 182 for spelling rules.

Practice

A What was Grace doing this time last week? Look at the picture and complete the sentences with the correct past continuous forms of the verbs in the box.

drink feel read shine ~~sit~~ wear

'Can you believe it? This time last week I was on holiday ...

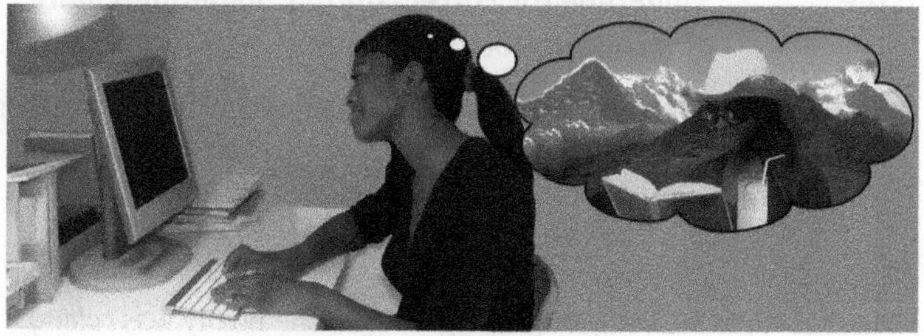

1 I ......was sitting...... in a café. 2 The sun ....
3 I .... my sunglasses. 4 I .... my book.
5 I .... lemonade. 6 I .... relaxed.'

B Write full sentences using the words in the same order. Change the verbs to the past continuous or past simple. One or both verbs should be in the past continuous.

1 He / sit / in the kitchen / when / the fire / start
......He was sitting in the kitchen when the fire started......
2 It / get late / and / the man / work / quickly.
....
3 The pencil / break / while / I / writing down / her phone number.
....
4 It / snow / but we / not wear / warm clothes.
....
5 A cat / run / in front of the car / when / I / drive / home.
....
6 The lights / change / while / she / still cross / the road.
....
7 You / still sleep / when / I / get up.
....
8 They / not build / the stadium / when / I / live / in the city.
....

C Complete this urban legend. Use past continuous or past simple forms of the verbs in brackets.

A TV team in Alaska 1 ......was making...... (make) a film about the life of salmon. They 2 .... (catch) a salmon in the sea and very carefully 3 .... (put) a radio transmitter on it. The radio transmitter 4 .... (send) messages to the TV team. They 5 .... (follow) the salmon's journey for two months. One day the cameramen 6 .... (camp) at the side of the river and they 7 .... (follow) the salmon as usual. Suddenly the fish 8 .... (leave) the river and 9 .... (go) through a forest. The team 10 .... (take) their cameras and followed. In the forest a group of boys 11 .... (camp). When the TV team 12 .... (find) the boys, they 13 .... (sit) around a fire. They 14 .... (cook) the salmon on the fire.

MY TURN!

In your notebook, copy and complete the replies with your own ideas using the past continuous.

1 A: Did you hear the phone?
B: ......No, I was listening to music......
2 A: Someone just knocked at the door.
B: Who was it?
A: I don't know ....
3 A: What was the weather like when you left home?
B: Terrible! ....
4 A: Did you catch a cold yesterday?
B: Yes, I did ....
5 A: Were you at school on Monday?
B: No, I wasn't ....
6 A: Did you hear me?
B: No, sorry, ...

MY TEST!

Circle the correct option.

1 He was working in the sewer .... he saw the alligator. a then b when c while
2 They .... television when they saw a cow in their garden. a are watching b watching c were watching
3 I was wearing sunglasses because the sun .... very brightly. a was shining b is shining c shone
4 A: .... raining when you arrived? B: No. It was very sunny. a Was it b It was c It is
5 A: Were you wearing a helmet when you fell off your bike? B: .... a No, I weren't b No, I wasn't c No, I'm not

My Test! answers: 1b 2c 3a 4a 5b

R2 Review: past simple and past continuous

A Complete the story by matching the phrases in the box to the correct places.

a while it was running
b and showing me his photos while we were eating
c when John was speaking
d because we were hungry
e it ran away
f when it happened

1 I was visiting my friend John in Australia [1] ......f......... .
2 We were having dinner early [2] ....
3 He was telling me about his family [3] ....
4 Suddenly, a kangaroo jumped through the window [4] ....
5 While we were thinking what to do next, [5] ....
6 He took a photo of the kangaroo [6] ....

C Underline the correct option. Sometimes more than one option is possible.

1 I *was having / had* a shower when my friend called.
2 While Sally *was walking / walked* to the station, she met Harry.
3 Tom went to bed and *was saying / said*, 'Goodnight.'
4 Did you get angry when she finally *was telling / told* you?
5 We danced while the music *was playing / played*.
6 I *was meeting / met* David many years ago.
7 *Were the Romans using / Did the Romans use* paper?
8 When she *wasn't watching / didn't watch*, I took another biscuit.

B Match each picture to the correct sentence.

a

1 She was running when she saw him. [a]

2 She ran when she saw him. [b]

b

c

3 We went home while it was raining. [ ]
4 When it started raining, we went home. [ ]

d

e

5 We talked about it when we got home. [ ]
6 We talked about it while we were going home. [ ]
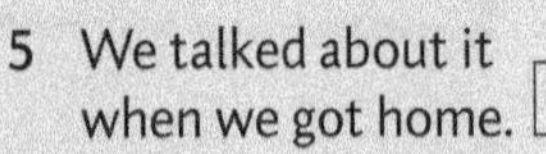

f

g

7 When he finished his lunch, Dad read the paper. [ ]
8 Dad read the paper while he was finishing his lunch. [ ]

h

D Complete these stories using the correct past simple or past continuous forms of the verbs in brackets.

The clock [1] ......broke...... (break) while the children [2] .... (play) football in the house. The clock [3] .... (fall) when the ball [4] .... (hit) it. The accident [5] .... (happen) while their parents [6] .... (come) home.

Jill [7] .... (drink) her coffee when she [8] .... (hear) her phone. It was her mother. While they [9] .... (speak), a man [10] .... (run) to the table and [11] .... (give) Jill some flowers.

E Circle the correct option.

Police officer: What [1] ...... when you saw the elephant?
Driver: I [2] ...... through the park.
Police officer: [3] ...... quickly?
Driver: No, I [4] ...... fast because there were a lot of animals. My wife [5] ...... out of the window and watching some lions. She [6] ...... to take some photos of them but while she [7] ...... the camera out of her bag, an elephant ran at the car!
Police officer: Why [8] ...... away while the elephant [9] ...... ?
Driver: The elephant was very fast. I only [10] ...... the elephant when it hit our car.

1 a do you do b was you doing (c) were you doing
2 a was driving b drove c were driving
3 a Did you go b Were you going c Was you going
4 a wasn't driving b weren't driving c didn't drive
5 a was looking b were looking c looked
6 a were wanting b was wanting c wanted
7 a got b was getting c were getting
8 a didn't you drive b wasn't you driving c weren't you driving
9 a ran b was running c were running
10 a were seeing b was seeing c saw

F Make sentences from the words and write them in your notebook. Put one verb in the past simple and one verb in the past continuous.

1 I / shop / when / meet / her
I was shopping when I met her.
2 While / we / eat / breakfast / the letter / arrive
3 Sarah / not go / because / she / not feel / very well
4 As / I / fall / my parachute / suddenly / open
5 you / have / a shower / when / I / phone?
6 Gavin / break / his arm / while / he / do / judo

G Make excuses for the following situations using the past continuous (and past simple, if you want). The excuses can be funny!

1 Why are you late for school?
I was taking my pet kangaroo for a walk and it ran away.
2 Why are your shoes dirty?
....
3 Why did you eat all the chocolates?
....
4 Why didn't you do your homework?
....
5 Why are you sleeping in class?
....
6 Why didn't you answer the telephone?
....

H Circle the correct option.

1 We went to the cinema last night and .... a film. It was excellent.
a watching (b) watched c were watching
2 She didn't understand the game. While I .... the instructions, she was writing a text.
a was explaining b am explaining c explained
3 The man took her bag and .... away with it. We never saw him again.
a run b ran c was running
4 She hurt her head when she fell off her bike. She .... a helmet.
a not wearing b didn't wear c wasn't wearing
5 A: What .... when you heard the noise?
B: I ran outside to help.
a did you do b were you doing c you were doing
6 Were you playing hockey when you broke your nose?
B: Yes, I ....
a did b were c was

Present perfect 1

They've already invented it!

The taxi's **just arrived**!
They**'ve already invented** it, Dad!
Sorry I'm late. I **haven't left yet**!
SCHOOL
TAXI
arbinventedortaarriveddtalreadyleftiedjustoopyeteom

?
Find six words from the cartoons in this word snake:

Answers: invented, arrived, already, left, just, yet

Present perfect 1

1 **Use the present perfect for a past event which the speaker feels is connected with the present.**
The taxi's ***arrived.*** (The taxi is here now.)

2 **We often use the present perfect to talk about a recent event. Use the adverb *just* to emphasise that the event is recent.**
The taxi's ***just arrived.***

3 **We can use the present perfect with *already* and *yet*. *Already* and *yet* mean 'before now'. We use *yet* in questions and negatives. *Already* comes after *has / have* and before the main verb. *Yet* comes at the end of the sentence or question.**
They've ***already*** *invented it.*
I haven't left ***yet.***
Have the boys arrived ***yet****?*

4 ***Still*** **with the present perfect negative stresses that the situation is continuing now.**
I ***still*** *haven't left home.*

5 **Make the present perfect using the verb *have* + past participle.**
I've just ***seen*** *her.*
I ***haven't visited*** *the museum yet.*

	statement ✓	negative ✗
I / You / We / They	**have ('ve) visited**	**have not (haven't) visited**
He / She / It	**has ('s) visited**	**has not (hasn't) visited**

question ?			short answer ✓✗
Have	I / you / we / they	**visited ...?**	Yes, (I) **have.** No, (I) **haven't.**
Has	he / she / it	**visited ...?**	Yes, (he) it **has.** No, (he) **hasn't.**

6 **Add *-ed* to form the past participle of regular verbs, e.g. *visited, arrived, tried.* (These are the same as the past simple verb forms.)**

▶ **See page 182 for spelling rules.**

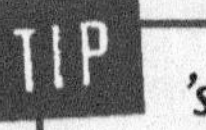
TIP
's = *is* and *has*
he's visited = he has visited
he's cold = he is cold

However, there are many irregular forms.

be ➜ *been*
break ➜ *broken*
come ➜ *come*
do ➜ *done*
go ➜ *gone*
give ➜ *given*
steal ➜ *stolen*
see ➜ *seen*
speak ➜ *spoken*
wake up ➜ *woken up*

TIP

Some irregular past participles are the same as the past simple form.

find ➜ *found* ➜ *found*
have ➜ *had* ➜ *had*
leave ➜ *left* ➜ *left*
lose ➜ *lost* ➜ *lost*
make ➜ *made* ➜ *made*
read ➜ *read* ➜ *read*
say ➜ *said* ➜ *said*
spend ➜ *spent* ➜ *spent*
tell ➜ *told* ➜ *told*
win ➜ *won* ➜ *won*

▶ **See page 181 for a list of irregular verbs.**

Practice

A Match the pairs of sentences.

1 She can't do sports. — c
2 He's still not feeling well.
3 She's crying.
4 I'm very happy.
5 The car won't start.
6 I have no money.
7 You're looking worried.
8 We can go now.
9 I'm not ready to go.

a She's lost her bag.
b He's just had flu.
c She's broken her arm.
d I haven't had a shower yet.
e I've spent it on CDs.
f I haven't left yet.
g The taxi has just arrived.
h My football team has just won.
i What has happened?

B Complete the sentences using the words in brackets in the correct form and position.

1 He can't find his keys. I think *he's lost* them. (lose)
2 Haven't you done your homework yet?
I .... it. (finish / already)
3 It's midnight and she .... home yet. (not / come)
4 .... lunch yet? (you / have?)
5 This is terrible. Someone .... my bike. (steal)
6 We .... a really cheap car! (just / buy)
7 Take your boots off before you come in. I .... the carpets. (just / clean)
8 .... the doctor yet? (you / phone?)
9 They .... the film. (see /already)

C It's Sunday night and Dad is asking Joe whether he is ready for school in the morning. Write Dad's questions and Joe's replies in your notebook

1 pack school bag [✓]
2 tidy your cave [✗]
3 do your science homework [✓]
4 have a bath [✗]
5 wash the dinosaur [✗]
6 make your sandwiches [✓]
7 buy the dinosaur food [✗]

1 *D: Have you packed your school bag yet? J: Yes, I have.*

What four things hasn't Joe done yet? Write sentences.

Example: *He hasn't tidied his cave yet.*

D Write reasons for each of these situations. Use the words in brackets and the correct form of the verb.

1 I don't have my glasses.
I still haven't found them. (find / still)
2 He's still asleep.
.... (wake up / yet)
3 The book looks very new.
.... (I / read / still)
4 She isn't here any more.
.... (go / just)
5 I don't have my old phone any more.
.... (give it to my dad)
6 She doesn't know.
.... (they / tell her / still)
7 I still haven't received the letter.
.... (postman / come / yet)
8 There's no more milk.
.... (I / finish / just)

MY TURN!

Imagine it's Sunday evening. In your notebook, write three things you have done and three things you haven't done.

Example: *I've cleaned my bike.*

MY TEST!

Circle the correct option.

1 The taxi hasn't arrived .... a already b just c yet
2 He's .... his new watch. a breaked b broke c broken
3 He left home four hours ago and he .... to say he's arrived. a still hasn't phoned b haven't phoned yet c hasn't just phoned
4 .... yet? a Have you eaten your vegetables b You have eaten your vegetables c Have you your vegetables eaten
5 A: Is Alex there? B: Oh sorry. He's .... a gone already home b just gone home c gone home yet

My Test! answers: 1c 2c 3a 4a 5b

13 Present perfect 2

Have you ever tried mustard ice cream?

Ingredients *food magazine*

Have you **ever** tried mustard ice cream?

Or chocolate on your vegetables? These are just some of the things you can eat at The Fat Duck restaurant near London. Some people **have called** The Fat Duck the best restaurant in the world. The chef, Heston Blumenthal, **has become** famous and **has been** on many TV shows.

John Willoughby of the New York magazine *Gourmet* says that The Fat Duck is possibly 'the most fun restaurant I**'ve ever eaten** in.' But what do you think?

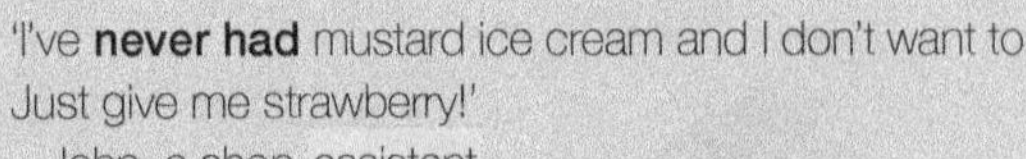

'I've **never had** mustard ice cream and I don't want to. Just give me strawberry!'
– John, a shop assistant

'I **haven't visited** the restaurant. It's too expensive for me!'
– Chris, a nurse

? Underline the answer which is **not** true: The Fat Duck restaurant is *famous / cheap / fun.*

Answer: cheap

Present perfect 2

1 **Use the present perfect when you do not know exactly when the past event took place, or it is not important.**
*He **has been** on many TV shows.*
*He **has become** famous.*

2 **We often use the present perfect with *ever, never* and *before*. *Never* and *ever* come after *has / have* and before the main verb. *Before* comes at the end of the sentence.**
*Have you **ever** tried mustard ice cream?*
*It was the most fun restaurant I've **ever** eaten in.*
*I've **never** had chocolate on my vegetables.*
*I haven't been to the restaurant **before**.*

▶ **See Unit 12 for the forms of the present perfect.**

TIP

***gone* or *been*?**
*My brother has **gone** to Croatia.*
(= My brother is travelling to Croatia or is there now.)
*My brother has **been** to Croatia.*
(= My brother went to Croatia but he is back home now.)

Practice

A Answer the questions with present perfect short answers.

1 Have you ever tried raw fish?
No, I haven't.
2 Have you ever used chopsticks?
....
3 Have you ever seen a banana tree?
....
4 Have you ever put sugar in a sandwich?
....
5 Have you ever made ice cream?
....
6 Have you ever eaten chips with sugar?
....
7 Have you ever drunk coconut milk?
....
8 Have you ever cooked a meal for your family?
....

B Which of these things have you done or not done? Complete the sentences using the present perfect of the verbs in brackets.

1 I haven't won a competition. (win)
2 .... to Cuba. (be)
3 .... a book in one day. (read)
4 .... rugby. (play)
5 .... an elephant. (see)
6 .... a famous person. (meet)
7 .... a leg. (break)
8 .... in a restaurant. (work)
9 .... ten kilometres. (run)

Do you know people who have done these things? Write true sentences about people you know.

Example: My brother has met a famous person.

....
....
....
....
....

C Complete the sentences using the present perfect of the verbs in the box.

~~break~~	ever forget	go	ever have	not meet
not play	see	not speak	never spend	write

1 I've broken my nose before.
2 He plays the guitar but he .... in a band before.
3 They .... Christmas away from home.
4 We .... our new neighbours.
5 My friends aren't here now, they .... home.
6 My sister .... an article for the local newspaper.
7 I .... to my parents about my exam results.
8 .... your teacher .... to give you homework?
9 We .... the new James Bond film.
10 She's the best friend I ....

D Complete the sentences with *gone* or *been*.

1 My grandparents have gone to Australia. They'll arrive tomorrow – the journey takes 22 hours.
2 They've visited the UK, but they haven't .... to Scotland.
3 My family loves travelling. We've .... to 10 different countries together.
4 They've .... out and left the lights on.
5 A: Where have you ....?
B: To post a letter.

MY TURN!

In your notebook, write three interesting things you have done in the past.

Example: I've been to Australia.

Now write three questions to ask a friend using *Have you (ever) ...?*

Example: Have you ever been to Australia?

Write about your friend.

Example: Betty has never been to Australia.

MY TEST!

Circle the correct option.

1 My sister .... sushi three or four times, but she doesn't like it. a tries b has tried c is tried
2 I've tried most things, but .... an insect. a I've ever eaten b I haven't never eaten c I've never eaten
3 A: .... on TV? B: Yes, he has. a Has Heston ever been b Has Heston been ever c Heston ever has been
4 It's our favourite restaurant. .... there many times. a We's been b We've gone c We've been
5 A: Have you ever been to The Fat Duck? B: .... a Yes, we've b Yes, we been c No, we haven't

My Test answers: 1b 2c 3a 4c 5c

Present perfect 3

They have lived there for centuries.

THE RICH AND FAMOUS IN LONDON

The rich and famous **have lived** in Marylebone **for** centuries. Past residents include Charles Dickens and the Beatles. Ringo Starr rented an apartment at 34 Montagu Square in Marylebone. Jimi Hendrix also lived there. There **hasn't been** a famous resident at 34 Montagu Square **since** the 1960s, but tourists still go to see the building.

Marylebone has been Madonna's favourite place in London for a few years now. The star owns four houses in the same street!

Complete the sentence: Marylebone is a place in ....

Answer: London

Present perfect 3

1 **Use the present perfect for a situation which started in the past and continues now.**

*Marylebone **has been** Madonna's favourite place in London for a few years now.*

past — present — future

2 **We can use *for* and *since* with the present perfect.**

*The rich and famous **have lived** in Marylebone **for** centuries.*
*There **hasn't been** a famous resident **since** the 1960s.*

3 **Use *How long ...?* to ask for how much time a situation has continued.**

***How long** has she lived in London?*
*She has lived in London **for a few years**.*

4 **We can use *always* with the present perfect.**

*I've **always** wanted to live in the city.* (= for all the time I can remember)

▶ See Units 12 and 13 for other uses of the present perfect.
▶ See Unit 12 for the forms of the present perfect.

5 **Use the present perfect + *for* to emphasise how long a situation has been going on, e.g. *for an hour, for a few days, for a week, for six months, for ages* (= for a long time).**

*They have lived there **for** centuries.*

6 **Use the present perfect + *since* to emphasise when a situation began, e.g. *since 12 o'clock, since Monday, since January, since last year, since the 1960s, since she got married.***

*The couple have been married **since** last year.*
*There hasn't been a famous resident **since** the 1960s.*

TIP

Use the present perfect, not the present, with *since* and *for*.

She has lived here for a few years.
NOT ~~*She lives here for a few years.*~~

Practice

A Complete each time expression with *for* or *since*.

1 ......for...... a long time.
2 .... two weeks.
3 .... 2003.
4 .... last year.
5 .... three years.
6 .... only a day!
7 .... Christmas.
8 .... I was 12.

Now answer the question.

How long have you lived in your house?
I've lived in my house ....

B Complete the sentences with the present perfect of the verbs in brackets. Use short forms where possible.

1 They ...'ve always wanted... to visit New York. (always want)
2 We .... my cousins since the beginning of last year. They are always very busy. (not see)
3 It .... a really good summer. I don't want it to end. (be)
4 They.................. in the same house all their lives. (live)
5 My sister and I share a bedroom. We .... our own rooms. (never have)
6 How long .... you .... your mountain bike? (have)
7 He .... his home town. (always love)
8 How long .... she .... ill? (be)
9 He .... in the same bank for years. (work)
10 I .... he was the best. (always think)

C Ask questions about the celebrities using *How long ...?* and the present perfect.

1 Michael Douglas and Catherine Zeta-Jones are married.
...How long have they been married?...
2 Madonna drives a Mini Cooper car.
....
3 Sienna Miller lives in Marylebone.
....
4 Paul McCartney plays the piano.
....
5 Ringo Starr is a vegetarian.
....
6 Jennifer Connelly speaks Italian.
....

MY TURN!

Make sentences with the words given and a time phrase which is true for you. Write them in your notebook.

1 I / be / hungry
...I've been hungry since 9 o'clock this morning....
2 I / not see / my cousin
3 I / be / at this school
4 I / know / my / best friend
5 I / not do / the washing-up
6 My family / live / here

MY TEST!

Circle the correct option.

1 .... to meet Madonna.
a I always have wanted b I've always wanted c I've wanted always
2 We've lived in Marylebone ....
a for ages b ages ago c since ages
3 They've had their flat in Marylebone since they .... married.
a get b got c have got
4 A: How long ....? B: For about six years.
a are they famous b have they been famous c they've been famous
5 She .... London since she was a child.
a isn't visit b didn't visit c hasn't visited

My Test! answers: 1b 2a 3b 4b 5c

15 Present perfect or past simple?

The company has invented the Mac and the iPod.

Steve Jobs **was born** in 1955 and **was** a multi-millionaire before the age of 30. He **is** dyslexic and one of his teachers at school remembers his 'different way of looking at things'.

In the 1970s, computers **were** large machines and only large companies **used** them. In 1976, Steve Jobs and Steve Wozniak **changed** all that. They **started** the company Apple Inc and **produced** the world's first personal computer, Apple I. Since then, Apple Inc **has** also **produced** Macintosh computers and the iPod.

Steve Jobs also **helped** to start Pixar Animation Studios. Some of the best-loved animated films **have come** from Pixar, including *Toy Story*, *Finding Nemo* and *Ratatouille*. Pixar **has won** many Oscars™ over the last 25 years.

Complete the sentence with three possible answers: Steve Jobs is famous for ....

Possible answers: Apple Inc, Apple I, Macintosh computers, the iPod, Pixar Animation Studios

Present perfect or past simple?

1 **Use the present perfect to talk about recent events or a past event which the speaker feels is connected with the present.**

TIP

Certain time expressions are common with this use of the present perfect. These include *already, yet, just, ever, never, before.*

*I **haven't eaten yet**.* (= I'm hungry now.)

***Has he left**?* (= He isn't here now.)

2 **Use the past simple to talk about a finished action. Certain time expressions may be used with the past simple. These include *yesterday, last week, ago, then, when, in* + year.**

*In the 1970s, computers **were** large machines.*

*When **did** Apple **invent** the iPod?*

3 **Use the present perfect to talk about an event or situation which began in the past and continues now.**

We often use time expressions with *since* and *for* with this use of the present perfect, e.g. *for a week, since yesterday, for a long time, since 2004,* and ask questions with *How long?*

***How long** have you worked at Pixar?*

*I've worked here **for ten years**.*

4 **The choice of the past simple or present perfect can sometimes depend on the point of view of the speaker, or on the context.**

***I didn't see** George this morning.* (The speaker is talking at the end of the day and *this morning* is finished.)

***I haven't seen** George this morning.* (The speaker is talking in the morning – *this morning* is still going on.)

Practice

A **Underline the correct option to complete the sentences about Tom Cruise.**

1. When he was a boy, Tom Cruise went / *has been* to fourteen different schools.
2. While he was at high school, he *acted / has acted* in school plays.
3. Since his first film in 1981, the actor *starred / has starred* in some very popular films, e.g. *Top Gun, Mission: Impossible* and *Jerry Maguire*.
4. He *worked / has worked* with some very famous film makers, including Kubrick and Scorsese.
5. He *was / has been* married to actress Nicole Kidman until 2001.
6. He *became / has become* a father in 2006, when his daughter Suri *was / has been* born.

Tom says:

7. 'I *had / 've had* a very interesting life.'

B **Complete these sentences using the past simple or present perfect of the verbs in brackets.**

1. My grandfather ..didn't have.. much money when he was a young man. (not have)
2. It .... difficult to get a good job then. (be)
3. .... you .... this song before? (hear)
4. What .... you .... about last night? (dream)
5. My uncle collects old motorbikes. He .... three. (buy)
6. When the teacher .... in the room, we stood up. (come)
7. There .... more accidents on the road last month than in the whole of last year. (be)
8. You .... that coat for a long time! (not wear)

C **Match the pairs.**

1. I've sent all the letters this morning. — a (It's four o'clock in the afternoon.)
2. I sent all the letters this morning. — b (It's eleven o'clock in the morning.)

3. She learnt to speak seven languages.
4. She has learnt to speak seven languages.

a (She is not still alive.)
b (She is still alive.)

5. He worked for the company for three years.
6. He has worked for the company for three years.

a (He still works there.)
b (He doesn't work there now.)

7. He has sold a lot of cars today.
8. He sold a lot of cars today.

a (It's 10 pm and he is not working now.)
b (It's 4 pm and he is still working.)

MY TURN!

Make past simple or present perfect questions from the words and write them in your notebook. Sometimes both tenses are possible.

1. you / ever / see a dolphin?
2. when / you / last / go swimming?
3. how many different schools / you / study at / before now?
4. what / you / yesterday / do?
5. how many exams / you / this year / take?
6. When your mother was young, where / she / live?
7. you / ever / live / another country?
8. what / your family / last weekend / do?

1 ..Have you ever seen a dolphin?..

In your notebook, answer the questions about yourself and your family. Use the past simple or present perfect in your answers.

MY TEST!

Circle the correct option.

1. A: How long .... a multi-millionaire? B: Since I was 30. **a** have you been **b** are you **c** you have been
2. A: Have you ever seen *Finding Nemo*? B: Yes, ... it on DVD last week. **a** I've watched **b** I've watching **c** I watched
3. .... her Apple I computer since 1977. **a** She has **b** She's had **c** She have
4. We've seen some Pixar films, but I .... *Ratatouille* yet. **a** don't see **b** haven't seen **c** haven't see
5. .... together for 20 years, from 1976 to 1996. **a** They work **b** They've worked **c** They worked

My Test! answers: 1a 2c 3b 4b 5c

16 Used to

Sick people often used to sleep in temples.

The Ancient Greeks **used to** think that they were ill because of bad magic, or because the gods were unhappy with them.

The Greeks **didn't use to** take medicine and they **didn't use to** go to the doctor. The first 'doctors' **used to** be witches or people with magic powers.

So, sick people often **used to** sleep in temples.

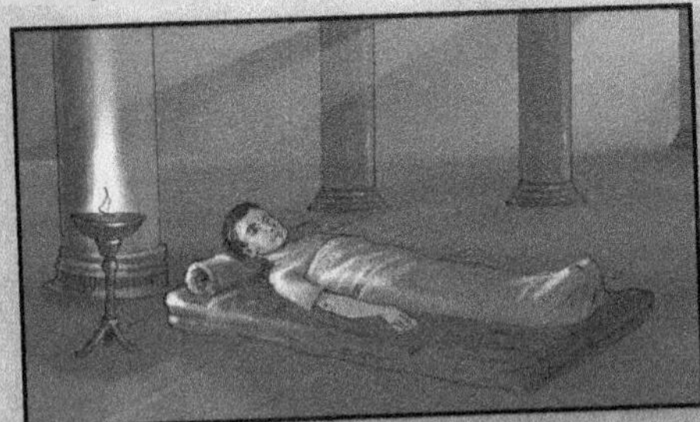

Some people **used to** eat flowers and herbs when they were ill but this **didn't use to** help everyone.

Hippocrates, born about 460 BC on the island of Kos, made medicine into a serious science. He is often called the father of medicine.

? Underline the correct option: The first doctors *were Greek / believed in magic / were women.*

Answer: believed in magic

Used to

1 ***Used to* is for habits and states which finished in the past. *Used to* often contrasts the past and the present.**
Jack ***used to*** *live in Brighton, but now he lives in Liverpool.*
Most people ***used to*** *believe in magic.*

2 **The past simple can usually replace *used to*.**
The Greeks ***used to sleep*** */* ***slept*** *in temples when they were ill.*
They ***didn't use to go*** */* ***didn't go*** *to doctors.*

3 **Use the past simple, not *used to*, when talking about single activities, how long they took or how many times they happened.**
I ***went*** *to the doctor yesterday.* NOT ~~*I used to go ...*~~
We ***didn't eat*** *for two days.*
NOT ~~*We didn't used to eat ...*~~
Jane ***visited*** *me in hospital twice.*
NOT ~~*Jane used to visit ...*~~

4 ***Used to* + infinitive without *to*. *Used to* has no present or continuous forms.**
Sick people often ***used to sleep*** *in temples.*

5 **Make questions with *Did* + noun / pronoun + *use to* ...?**
Did doctors use to *study science?*
Did you use to *eat a lot of sweets when you were young?*

6 **Make the negative with *did not* (*didn't*) *use to* or *never used to*.**
They ***didn't use to*** *take medicine.*
Operations ***never used to*** *be easy.*

TIP

In spoken English people often use *did* + *used* (instead of *use*) in questions and negatives.
Did *you* ***used*** *to play with dolls?*
I didn't used *to like him.*

Practice

A Charlie is now a millionaire but he used to be poor. In your notebook, write sentences about Charlie's life with *used to* and *didn't use to*.

Now	10 years ago
1 He gets up at 11.00.	~~7.00~~
2 He doesn't work.	supermarket
3 He has a very big house.	✗ big house
4 He plays golf.	✗ golf
5 He wears expensive clothes.	cheap clothes
6 He is unhappy.	happy

1 *He used to get up at 7.00*.

B <u>Underline</u> the correct option. Sometimes both options are possible.

1 I <u>*had*</u> / *used to have* a shower last night.
2 Kurt <u>*was / used to be*</u> a very good friend.
3 It *snowed / used to snow* a lot in winter.
4 I *met / used to meet* Janice yesterday.
5 Children didn't *watch / use to watch* so much TV.
6 It *wasn't / never used to be* very expensive.
7 My sister *went / used to go* to Mexico in 2007.
8 My sister *went / used to go* to Mexico every summer.

C Read these sentences about life 2,000 years ago. (Four are true, four are false.) If the sentence is true, rewrite it with *used to*. If the sentence is false, rewrite it with *didn't use to*.

1 Latin was an international language.
Latin used to be an international language.
2 People used to think that the world was round.
People didn't use to think that the world was round.
3 There were bears in England.
....
4 People ate a lot of meat.
....
5 Builders made houses out of wood.
....
6 Most people lived in towns.
....
7 Travelling by sea was dangerous.
....
8 Children learned English.
....

D Complete this advertisement with *used to* or the past simple of the verbs in the box.

not answer	be	change	criticise	do
~~get~~	lose	not listen	sit	not worry

[1] *Did you get* out of bed this morning and feel terrible?
[2] .... much fitter and healthier once?
If your answer is 'yes', you need *Powerflakes!*

Eva Clark (England): 'I [3] .... about my health but I never [4] .... exercise and my health got worse and worse. Then I tried Powerflakes! Now I feel like a new woman.'

Andrei Wojdylo (Poland): 'My friends [5] .... me all the time because I was so lazy and unfit but I [6] .... to them. I [7] .... in front of the TV all night and eat chocolates. If the phone rang, I [8] .... it! Last year everything [9] .... because I [10] .... my job and I needed to change my life. Now, I have Powerflakes and life is perfect!'

MY TURN!

In your notebook, write sentences about changes in your life with *used to, didn't use to* or *never used to*.

Example: *I used to do judo but now I do karate.*

MY TEST!

Circle the correct option.

1 She wants to be a vet now, but she .... want to be a doctor. a use to b used c used to
2 He .... eat healthy food, but now he only eats vegetables. a didn't used b didn't use to c doesn't used to
3 .... go to the doctor very often when you were young? a Did you use to b You used to c Did you used
4 My dad used to smoke, but he .... when I was born. a used to stop b stopped c used to stopped
5 My parents .... give us medicine when we were sick. a never didn't use to b didn't never use to c never used to

My Test! answers: 1c 2b 3a 4b 5c

R3 Review: present perfect and *used to*

A Complete the table with the missing forms.

infinitive without *to*	past simple	past participle
eat	ate	
		done
	fell	
		felt
		got
	had	
look		
	lived	
		made
play		
walk		
	wrote	

B Rewrite these sentences with *used to*, but only if it's possible.

1 I had a red bike when I was little.
I used to have a red bike when I was little.

2 Did you play computer games when you were a child?

3 I played tennis three times on holiday.

4 The Romans ate a lot of fish.

5 She played the violin at university.

6 He didn't go to the doctor yesterday.

7 Didn't they work hard at their old school?

8 This morning we made a cake for Grandma's visit.

C Make present perfect questions from the words.

1 your sister / live in Australia / how long?
How long has your sister lived in Australia?

2 ever / you / make a pizza?

3 start / yet / the film?

4 you / how many times / ride a horse?

5 all seven Harry Potter books / you / read?

6 be married / how long / Henry and Gloria?

7 ever / you / have a party in your house?

8 Tony / yet / say thank-you for the present?

9 study English / you / before?

10 clean her shoes / Maria / yet?

D Write present perfect or past simple answers to the questions in Exercise C, using the words given.

1 six months
She's lived in Australia for six months.

2 never

3 just

4 three times

5 four of them already / the other three not yet

6 two years

7 last year

8 already / four times

9 never

10 yesterday.

E Complete these dialogues using the present perfect, past simple or *used to*.

1 come A: Has the taxi come yet?
B: Yes, it came five minutes ago.

2 see A: .... you ever .... a UFO?
B: Yes, I .... one last year.

3 have A: How long .... you .... your cat?
B: About a year. We .... her since Christmas.

4 play A: .... you .... tennis every week?
B: Yes, I ...., but I hurt my leg.

5 write A: .... you .... a thank-you email to your aunt yet?
B: Yes, I .... to her this morning.

6 meet A: Lisa, ... you .... my cousin Alan before?
B: Yes, we .... at your birthday party last year.

7 decide A: .... you .... about your holiday yet?
B: Well, we .... to go skiing, but we .... where yet.

8 want A: When you were young, ... you .... to be a train driver?
B: Yes, when I was 12. Before that, I .... to be a circus clown.

9 watch A: .... you .... *Titanic* on TV last night?
B: No, I .... already .... it four times.

F Underline the correct option.

Lee Gould is in the middle of a tour of Europe … on a bike. We spoke to him in Portugal.

Interviewer: Hi Lee. Tell us about your tour of Europe.

Lee: Well, I've [1]*always / ever* wanted to visit different countries, and [2]*I was always / I've always been* good at cycling. So about two years ago I [3]*decided / have decided* to cycle around Europe. My plan is to visit every country in the European Union.

Interviewer: And how many countries [4]*did / have* you visited so far?

Lee: Only 11. I've [5]*been / gone* to all the countries in the south of Europe. I [6]*started / have started* in Cyprus last year, and then I [7]*took / have taken* a boat to Greece. Since then [8]*I cycled / I've cycled* about 5,000 km.

Interviewer: Have you been to Ireland [9]*still / yet*?

Lee: No, I [10]*didn't / haven't*. I haven't been to any countries in the north of Europe [11]*yet / already*, but I'm going to take a boat from Spain to Ireland next week.

Interviewer: Are you tired after cycling so far?

Lee: Yes, I am. I [12]*used / have* to get really tired at the beginning but it has got easier [13]*since / from* I left Spain.

Interviewer: [14]*Did / Have* you had any problems so far?

Lee: Well, [15]*I fell / I've fallen* off my bike many times, but I [16]*don't / haven't* really hurt myself. I've also lost my bike three times, but I've [17]*always / already* found it again. It's a very special bike for me – [18]*I have / I've had* it for six years, and it has been like a good friend for me.

Interviewer: Have you [19]*met / meet* any interesting people?

Lee: I [20]*didn't / haven't* had time to talk to people, but in every country the people have been very good to me. They have helped me a lot.

Interviewer: One last question. Why are you doing this?

Lee: I'm trying to collect money for a children's hospital. So far [21]*I collected / I've collected* almost £5,000.

17 *Will, shall, won't*

I hope you'll enjoy yoga.

easy yoga

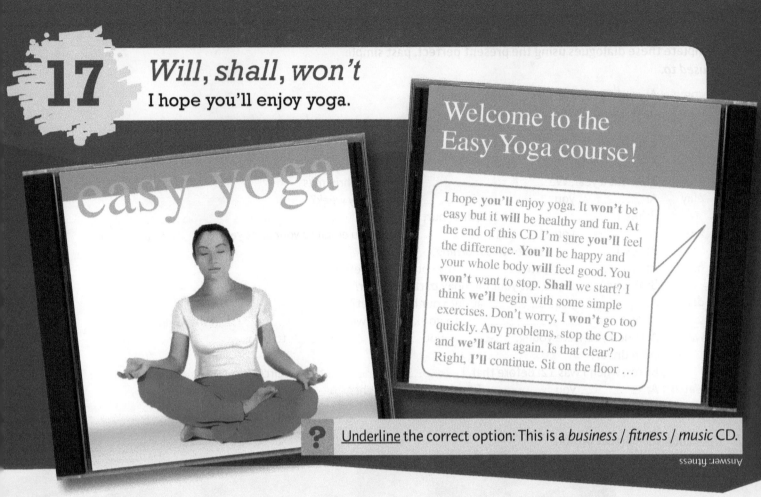

Welcome to the Easy Yoga course!

I hope **you'll** enjoy yoga. It **won't** be easy but it **will** be healthy and fun. At the end of this CD I'm sure **you'll** feel the difference. **You'll** be happy and your whole body **will** feel good. You **won't** want to stop. **Shall** we start? I think **we'll** begin with some simple exercises. Don't worry, I **won't** go too quickly. Any problems, stop the CD and **we'll** start again. Is that clear? Right, **I'll** continue. Sit on the floor ...

? Underline the correct option: This is a *business* / *fitness* / *music* CD.

Answer: fitness

Will, shall, won't

Will **is the most usual way to talk about the future in English.**

1 **Use *will* for general predictions based on what you think. Words like *think, hope* and *sure,* which show your opinion and attitude, are common with *will*.**
*It **won't** be easy but it **will** be healthy and fun.*
*I think the CD **will** be very popular.*
*I hope **you'll** enjoy yoga.*

2 **Use *will* for instant decisions made at the time of speaking.**
*Right, **I'll** continue.*
*I don't know, **I'll** check.*

Don't use *will* for plans or arrangements.
I'm going to have a yoga lesson tomorrow.
NOT ~~*I'll have a yoga lesson tomorrow.*~~
Are we meeting at 6? NOT ~~*Will we meet at 6*~~*?*

3 **Use *will* with the infinitive without *to*.**
*That **will be** nice.*
*I hope the lessons **will start** soon.*

▶ **See Units 18 and 19 for more future forms.**

4 **The short form *'ll* is used mainly with pronouns and in speaking.**
***I'll** go.*
*You'll be happy and your whole body **will** feel good.*

The negative short form *won't* is common in speaking and writing with nouns and pronouns.
*You **won't** want to turn this CD off.*

5 **Use *Shall I / we ...?* (NOT *will*) for offers and suggestions.**
***Shall** I open the bottle?*
***Shall** we start?*

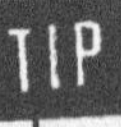

Shall **is occasionally used with *I* and *we* in very formal British English.**
*We **shall** be very happy to see you.*

	statement ✓	negative ✗
I / You / He / She / It / We / They	**will ('ll)**	**will not (won't)**

question ?	short answer ✓✗
Will I / you / he / she / it / we / they **go**?	Yes, (I) **will**. No, (I) **will not (won't)**.

Practice

A Write the short form of each full form. If no short form is possible, put ✗.

1 I will try yoga. ....I'll..........
2 Shall we sit down? ....✗..........
3 We will feel better. ....
4 Will she like it? ....
5 That will not be easy. ....
6 Shall I play it again? ....
7 I will not listen again. ....
8 Will the course be expensive? ....
9 I will stop the CD. ....
10 The instructor will not repeat it. ....
11 I hope it will be fun ....

B Read the text and make predictions about Victoria's new life. Complete the sentences with *will*, *'ll* or *won't*.

Victoria is from Russia. She moved to Vancouver last week with her parents. Victoria is 13 and she is a good student, but she doesn't speak much English. What do you think Victoria's new life in Canada will be like?

1 She ....'ll.......... learn English very quickly.
2 Victoria .... like Canadian food.
3 Her friends in Russia .... write to her.
4 She .... forget Russian.
5 The climate .... be a problem.
6 Her parents .... worry about her.
7 She .... feel homesick.
8 Victoria .... get lost in Vancouver.
9 Her grandmother .... visit her.
10 Her life .... be very different.

C Use the phrases in the box and *will* / *'ll* to make decisions.

buy some tomorrow	do it tomorrow	~~get my coat~~
give her some milk	have a swim	talk to him

1 I'm cold.
I'll get my coat.
2 The baby is hungry.
....
3 I don't have any eggs.
....
4 I'm tired.
....
5 The sea is lovely.
....
6 There's Tom.
....

D Underline the correct option.

Paul: What do you think, [1]*shall* / *will* Sunday be all right for the picnic?
Sue: Sunday [2]*will* / *won't* be fine for me. But, wait ... Sunday is my dad's birthday.
Paul: [3]*Shall* / *Will* we have the picnic tomorrow then?
Sue: [4]*Shall* / *Will* we have enough time to buy the food?
Paul: We [5]*will* / *won't* need much, just some snacks. My mum [6]*shall* / *will* probably make something nice.
Sue: [7]*Shall* / *Will* I call everyone or [8]*shall* / *will* you do it?
Paul: I [9]*'ll* / *won't* do it, it's no problem.
Sue: Great. It [10]*shall* / *will* be a lovely picnic.
Paul: I just hope it [11]*'ll* / *won't* rain.

MY TURN!

In your notebook, write predictions about the future with *will* and *won't*. Begin each sentence with *I* (*don't*) *think*, *I hope* or *I'm* (*not*) *sure*.

1 everyone / speak Chinese
I'm not sure everyone will speak Chinese.
2 we / live / on Mars
I hope we won't live on Mars.
3 robots / do / all the housework
4 children / drive / to school
5 everyone / have / a computer
6 people / live / until they are 120
7 I / rich
8 the world / be / very different

MY TEST!

Circle the correct option.

1 I hope my sister .... this yoga CD.
a will likes b will liking c will like
2 I'm sure .... time to do yoga.
a she won't has b she won't have
c she won't be have
3 A: .... to our new CD now? B: Yes!
a We shall listen b Shall we listened
c Shall we listen
4 A: Will I be good at yoga?
B: Yes, ...
a you will b you won't c you do
5 I think .... this yoga CD. It's too difficult.
a I'll stopped b I'll stop c I stop

My Test: 1c 2b 3c 4a 5b

18 Present continuous with future meaning

She's flying to Glasgow tomorrow.

Lucy Green is only sixteen but she is already a famous actress. Today is Monday and there is a busy week ahead. Look at her diary.

Tuesday
10:00 fly to Glasgow
13:00 make video

Wednesday
9:00 meet manager
11:00 see Jane
16:00 open new theatre

Thursday
8:00 fly back
all day with Mum & Dad!!

On Tuesday morning **she's flying** to Glasgow. She **isn't having** lunch because **she's making** a video. At 9:00 on Wednesday **she's meeting** her manager and **they're talking about** a new film. Lucy **is seeing** a friend at 11:00 and **she's opening** a new theatre in the afternoon. The next morning **she's going back** to Southampton. She **isn't working** on Thursday, **she's spending** time with her family.

True or False? Thursday is a free day for Lucy.

Answer: True

Present continuous with future meaning

1 Use the present continuous (*be* + verb + *-ing*) for plans in the future when we already know the time and place.
*On Tuesday morning she's **flying** to Glasgow,*
*We're **meeting** at two o'clock.*

2 We often use the present continuous to talk about a definite time in the future, e.g. ***tomorrow, six o'clock, on Friday.***
***I'm staying** at home tonight.*
*She **isn't working** on Thursday,*

TIP
We can often use *going to* instead of the present continuous with future meaning.
*She's **spending** time with her family.*
*= She's **going to spend** time with her family.*

▶ See Unit 5 for the present continuous and Units 17 and 19 for more future forms.

Practice

A Look at Lucy's diary for Friday, then complete the summary using present continuous statements.

Friday
7:00 get up
9:00 leave home
11:00 meet manager + sign contract
13:00 all have lunch together in theatre + read script
14:00 - 17:30 see Kate
18:00 - interview with journalists
21:00 take train home (Mum meeting me)

Lucy [1] *'s getting up early* on Friday morning. At 9:00 she [2] .... home. Her manager [3] .... her at 11:00 and they [4] .... the contract. Lucy [5] .... lunch with everyone in the theatre and they [6] .... the script. In the afternoon she [7] .... her friend Kate. At 18:00 some journalists [8] .... her. At 21:00 she [9] .... the train home. Her mum [10] .... her at the station.

B Here is part of Lucy's interview. Match the questions to the correct answers, then write both in full using the present continuous.

1 Lucy / you / go / to the Cannes film festival? [*c*]
2 you / have / a holiday / there? [ ]
3 you / fly / to Zurich? [ ]
4 where / you / stay? [ ]
5 your sister / travel / with you? [ ]

a No / I / do / a drama course
b No / we / not go / together
c No / I / spend / the spring / in Switzerland
d I / rent / a flat / in Geneva
e Yes / but / I / not stay / in Zurich

1 Question: *Lucy, are you going to the Cannes film festival?*
Lucy: *No, I'm spending the spring in Switzerland.*
2 Question: ....
Lucy: ....
3 Question: ....
Lucy: ....
4 Question: ....
Lucy: ....
5 Question: ....
Lucy: ....

C Complete this telephone dialogue with present continuous forms of the verbs in the box.

come do not do give ~~go~~ meet play play not spend not stay take

Angela: Hi, Stacy. [1] *Are* you *going* to the school disco tonight?
Stacy: No way! [2] I .... my Friday night at school. I [3] .... my brother at 8.
Angela: [4] .... he .... you with him to the hockey game?
Stacy: Yes, I'm so excited. He [5] .... against a very good team tonight. Steven Stamkos [6] ...., that guy from the NHL.
Angela: Steven Stamkos! [7] .... he .... too?
Stacy: No, he [8] .... the prizes. He [9] .... long. Anyway, what [10] .... you .... after the disco?
Angela: I [11] .... anything special.

MY TURN!

Imagine you are a famous person. What are you doing next week? First, write notes in your notebook, then write at least six present continuous sentences. Some can be negatives.

Examples:
I'm watching myself on TV.
I'm not getting up before 12 tomorrow.

MY TEST!

Circle the correct option.

1 .... my manager tomorrow evening.
a I'm meeting b I meeting c I meet

2 .... the new contract.
a He'll bringing b He's bringing c He's bring

3 .... coming to the theatre?
a You're b Will you c Are you

4 A: Are you making a video next week?
B: No, ... I made it last week.
a I don't b I won't c I'm not

5 We .... staying in a hotel.
a aren't b won't c don't

My Test! answers: 1a 2b 3c 4c 5a

19 Be going to

I'm going to use magic.

The dragon is very angry (and hungry!) now – **it's going to eat you**! You don't have a sword so you **aren't going to fight** an angry dragon! **Are you going to run away**?

I'm not going to fight. I'm going to run away.
➽ Turn to page 212.

I'm going to use magic.
➽ Turn to page 45.

I'm going to speak nicely to the dragon. **We're going to be** friends!
➽ Turn to page 170.

92

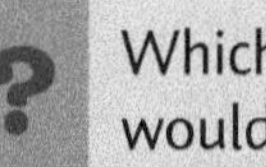

Which answer would you give?

Be going to

1 Use *be going to* + infinitive without *to* (e.g. *do, say, have*) for predictions about the future based on what we see or know now.
*The dragon is very angry – it's **going to eat** you!*
*The water is cold. **I'm not going to swim**.*

2 Often *be going to* + infinitive without *to* shows that something is going to happen immediately or very soon.
*Be careful, it's **going to fall**!*
*Julie is working too hard. She's **going to get** ill.*

3 Use *be going to* + infinitive without *to* for plans and decisions.
***I'm going to use** magic.*
***Are** you **going to clean** your shoes?*

4 We can also use the present continuous (*be* + verb + *-ing*) to talk about plans and decisions.
***I'm meeting** Fiona tonight. = **I'm going to meet** Fiona tonight.*

	statement ✓	negative ✗
I	am ('m) going to see	am ('m) not going to see
He / She / It	is ('s) going to see	is not (isn't / 's not) going to see
You / We / They	are ('re) going to see	are not (aren't / 're not) going to see

question ?	short answer ✓✗
Am I going to see ...?	Yes, I am. No, I am ('m) not.
Is he / she / it going to see ...?	Yes, (he) is. No, (he) is not (isn't / 's not).
Are you / we / they going to see ...?	Yes, (you) are. No, (you) are not (aren't / 're not).

▶ See Units 17 and 18 for more future forms.

TIP

Be going to **(NOT the present continuous) can be used for plans which have not been scheduled.**
*I'm **going to buy** a laptop tomorrow. = I'm buying a laptop tomorrow.* (A plan, I know when.)
*One day, I'm **going to marry** a prince.* NOT ~~*One day, I'm marrying a prince.*~~ (A plan but I don't know when.)

Practice

A What is (or is not) going to happen next? Look at the pictures and complete the sentences with *be going to* and a verb from the box.

break	~~buy~~	cry	finish	have	snow

1

2

3

4
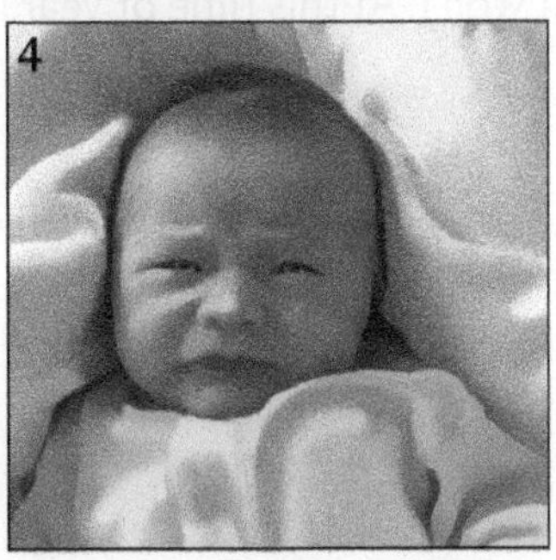
5

6
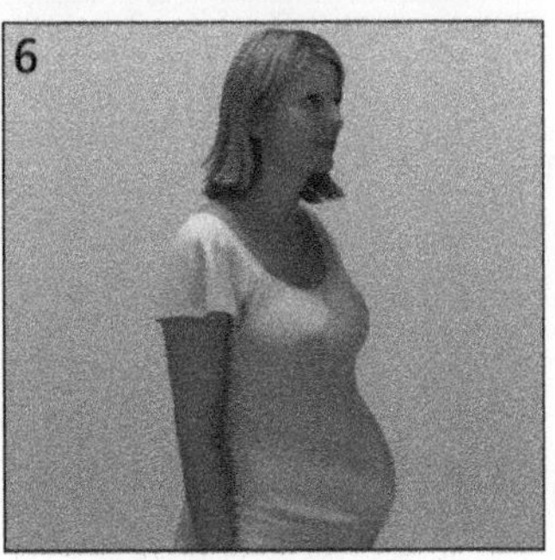

1 *She's going to buy a new dress.*
2 The ball .... window.
3 It ....
4 The baby ....
5 The manager .... work early.
6 She .... a baby.

B Complete the sentences with *be going to*. Some are negatives or questions.

1 I love science. *I'm going to* study Physics at university.
2 She feels hungry, so she .... have dinner.
3 The party is tomorrow. .... you .... come?
4 He's broken his leg, so he .... play tonight.
5 They like fast cars. They .... buy a Ferrari.
6 A: .... he .... win? B: I hope so.
7 We don't have tickets for the concert. We .... see it.

C Underline the correct option. Sometimes both options are possible.

1 We're *going to do / doing* it soon.
2 John is *going to do / doing* it tomorrow.
3 My son is *going to win / winning* an Olympic medal in 2020.
4 Are you *going to study / studying* hard at college next year?
5 My sister is *going to have / having* a baby in December.
6 We're not *going to finish / finishing* it soon, unfortunately.
7 Glenda is *going to write / writing* a book one day.
8 Is Dad *going to take / taking* you to the airport on Saturday?

MY TURN!

Read the sentences, make your own predictions with *be going to* and write them in your notebook.

1 The dog is hungry. It sees some meat on the table.
The dog's going to jump on the table and eat the meat.
2 Mike sees a nice jacket in the shop window.
3 I don't speak French well but I know the phone number of a private French teacher.
4 You like Biology and you are a good student.
5 Sally wants a car but her salary is very small.
6 They live in a town but they don't like the noise and pollution.
7 You find 100 euros in the street. You see a police officer.

MY TEST!

Circle the correct option.

1 Be careful! The dragon .... up. a be going to wake b is going to wake c is going to waking
2 .... to read this adventure book again. Do you want it? a I don't going b I'm not going c I won't going
3 A: Are they going to be friends? B: Yes, ... a they are b they going c they do
4 A: .... magic? B: No, she isn't. She's going to run away. a She is going to use b Is she going use c Is she going to use
5 Relax! The dragon .... you. It's a very friendly dragon. a aren't going to eat b isn't going to eat c not going to eat

My Test! answers: 1b 2b 3a 4c 5b

R4 Review: the future

A Match the questions to the answers.

1 Shall we go dancing tonight?
2 Will it be cold in Germany?
3 Are you meeting Rachel tonight?
4 Is the train going to be late?
5 Will they arrive on time?
6 Are you both going to watch the tennis match?
7 Will your sister want to come with us?
8 Is Dan cooking dinner tonight?

a Yes, they're never late.
b No, I'm not. She's on holiday, so I'm going to stay at home.
c Yes, she will. Is that OK?
d Yes, we are. I think it'll be really good.
e OK. That's a good idea.
f Yes, it is. Sue called to say she's still waiting at the station.
g Yes, he is. He's bought some pizzas.
h No, it won't. At this time of year it's usually warm.

B Read the reasons for using different future forms below. Find an example in Exercise A to match each reason.

1 *Will* for predictions based on what you think: Will it be cold in Germany?

2 *Shall* for offers and suggestions:

3 Present continuous for plans when we already know the time and place:

4 *Be going to* for predictions about the future based on what we see or know now:

C Change these sentences into questions (?) or negatives (x).

1 She's arriving at 10 pm tonight. (?) Is she arriving at 10 pm tonight?
2 This film will be very exciting. (✗) This film won't be very exciting.
3 We're going to be late. (?)
4 I'll need my passport at the hotel. (?)
5 Susan's going to the party, so I'll go. (✗)
6 You'll enjoy this book. (✗)
7 It's going to snow tonight. (?)
8 You're going to be sick. (?)
9 Your parents will be angry. (?)
10 We're going to win the match. (✗)

D Underline the correct option.

Jill: [1]*Will you go / Are you going* to Joe's Halloween party next week?
Kelly: Of course. I'm really excited about it. What about you?
Jill: Yes, [2]*I'll / I'm going to* go. But I don't know what to wear. Maybe [3]*I'll / I'm going to* be a witch.
Kelly: Oh no, please don't. [4]*I'll / I'm going to* be a witch. I've bought a black hat and [5]*I'll / I'm going to* have a green face.
Jill: Oh, right. OK, so I [6]*won't / I'm not going to* go as a witch. I know. [7]*I'll / I'm going to* put a white sheet on my head and be a ghost.
Kelly: Hmmm ... Sue and Chris and Sharon [8]*will all / are all going to* be ghosts. Sue told me yesterday.
Jill: OK, OK. [9]*I'll / I'm going to* buy some Dracula teeth. Is that OK?
Kelly: Yes, that's a great idea.
Rob: Hi Jill. Hi Kelly. [10]*Will you go / Are you going* to Joe's party?
Jill: Oh yes. Yes, and ... [11]*I'll / I'm going to* be Dracula.
Rob: Dracula? Oh no ... please don't. [12]*I'll / I'm going to* be Dracula too.

E **Match the pairs.**

1	We're going to Korea next month.	a	I think it's going to be hot.
2	It's a beautiful morning, with no clouds.	b	It'll probably be hot.
3	She's always late.	a	She probably won't be here on time today.
4	She phoned to say her bus didn't come.	b	She isn't going to be here on time.
5	Our football team is really good.	a	I'm sure we'll win today's match.
6	It's 6–1, with only 10 minutes to play.	b	We're going to win the match.
7	I've seen this film before. I know the ending.	a	Maybe she'll marry the doctor.
8	It's a great film. How will it end?	b	She's going to marry the doctor.
9	How many children are you going to have?	a	I don't know. Ask me again in 10 years' time.
10	How many children will you have?	b	Two. Next month.

F **Make predictions (using *will* and *be going to*) and plans (using *be going to* and present continuous) with the words given. Some are negatives.**

1 It / be very cold / tonight. (It's 8 o'clock in the evening, and already below zero!)
It's going to be very cold tonight.

2 It / be very cold / next week. (You think; you haven't seen the weather forecast.)
....

3 I / go to the cinema / tonight. (You're going with your sister; it starts at 8 o'clock.)
....

4 I / go to the cinema / next week. (You don't know when, who with or what film.)
....

5 My favourite football team / play a match / this weekend. (You have a ticket, the game starts at 3 o'clock.)
....

6 My favourite football team / win the cup / this year. (You think, but you don't know.)
....

7 We / go to a hot country on holiday / next week. (You have the plane tickets.)
....

8 We / go to a hot country on holiday / this summer. (You don't know which country or the date.)
....

20 Modal verbs: *can, could, be able to*

How can dogs help us?

How can dogs help us?

Dogs can hear and see much better than humans. They can also smell many things that humans can't.

During World War I, many soldiers went blind. Dogs **were able to** look after the blind soldiers.

In World War II, dogs **were able to** smell or hear survivors that people **could not** find.

Sony's Aibo. **Will** a robot ever **be able to** replace a dog?

? Why are dogs very good at finding people?

Answer: They can hear, see and smell much better than humans.

Modal verbs: *can, could, be able to*

1 Use *can* to talk about ability.
*Dogs **can** hear and see much better than humans.*

2 *Can* does not change. It is the same with all subjects.
***I can** swim. **He can** swim. **They can** swim.*

3 *Can* is followed by a second verb. The second verb is the infinitive without *to*.
*Dogs **can** hear much better than humans.*
NOT ~~*They can to hear ...*~~

4 The negative of *can* is *cannot*. The short form is *can't*. The short form is more common, especially in conversation.
*Emily **can't** swim very well.*

	statement ✓	negative ✗
I / You / He / She / It / We / They	**can** swim.	**cannot (can't)** swim.

5 Make questions and short answers as follows:

question ?			short answer ✓✗
Can	I / you / he / she / it / we / they	**swim**?	Yes, (he) **can**. No, (he) **can't**.
How **can** dogs **help** us?			

6 Use *could* (*not*) or *was* / *were* (*not*) *able to* for the past.
*In World War II, dogs **were able to** smell or hear survivors that people **could not** find.*

7 Use *will be able to* for the future. The negative form of the future is *will not be able to* or *won't be able to*.
*A robot **will** / **won't be able to** replace a dog.*
***Will** a robot ever **be able to** replace a dog?*

▶ See Unit 21 for *can* (request).
▶ See Unit 22 for *can't* (forbid).

Practice

A Underline the correct option.

1 Dogs *can / could* travel a long way to find food.
2 Most dogs *can't / couldn't* see the difference between red and green.
3 Often during World Wars I and II, people *were not able to / can't* find survivors.
4 However, dogs *were able to / will be able to* find them.
5 They *can / could* also carry messages.
6 In the future, scientists *will be able to / can* make better robot dogs.

B Make sentences by putting the words in the correct order.

1 bottle / I / open / can't / this
I can't open this bottle.
2 couldn't / name / her / remember / I
....
3 stand / child / able / The / wasn't / to
....
4 at / meet / we / Can / 7?
....
5 question / He / the / answer / couldn't
....
6 play / can't / I / tennis
....
7 truck / drive / Can / a / she?
....
8 able / come / friends / My / weren't / to
....

C Circle the correct option.

1 I ... use my mobile here – it doesn't work.
a can b can't c couldn't d wasn't able to
2 In 1998, 20% of the world's population ... not write.
a can b can't c could d was able to
3 The box was very heavy – I ... carry it.
a will be able to b won't be able to
c can't d couldn't
4 When I was younger, I ... read a book in one day.
a could b can c will be able to d can't
5 I ... take this to the post office. I haven't got enough time.
a can b can't c could d couldn't
6 I'm not busy. I ... go to the post office for you.
a can't b won't be able to c can d couldn't
7 Don't stay out late or you won't ... get up early.
a could b can c be able to d can't
8 The window was very small but my daughter ... climb in.
a wasn't able to b weren't able to
c won't be able to d was able to

D Complete the sentences using *can, can't, could, couldn't, will be able to* or *won't be able to* and a verb from the box.

come	have	hear	imagine
~~read~~	see	speak	understand

1 It's too dark in here. I ....can't read.... my book.
2 I want to learn Spanish. .... you .... another language?
3 When we move to the country next year, we .... a dog.
4 We don't really know what life was like in the past. We .... only ....
5 Bats .... very well but they have excellent hearing.
6 That film was really boring. .... you .... what it was about?
7 I couldn't sleep last night. I .... a strange noise.
8 If I go to Australia to study, I .... home very often.

MY TURN!

Make sentences about what you *can / can't* do now, *could / couldn't* do when you were younger or *will / won't be able to* do in the future and write them in your notebook. Use expressions from the box or your own ideas.

drive	run 10 kilometres	speak English
stand on my head	touch my toes with my nose	

Example: When I was four, I couldn't speak English.

MY TEST!

Circle the correct option.

1 My dog .... understand about 20 words in Spanish. a can to b can c is able
2 But he .... understand one word of English.
a doesn't can b can't c can not
3 When the people .... the survivor, their dogs helped them.
a couldn't find b can't found c couldn't found
4 My dog .... very fast.
a doesn't can run b can't run c cannot runs
5 A: Will the robot dog be able to swim?
B: No, it .... a can't b isn't c won't

My Test! answers: 1b 2b 3a 4b 5c

21 Modals for requests: *can, could, may*

Could we go on a safari?

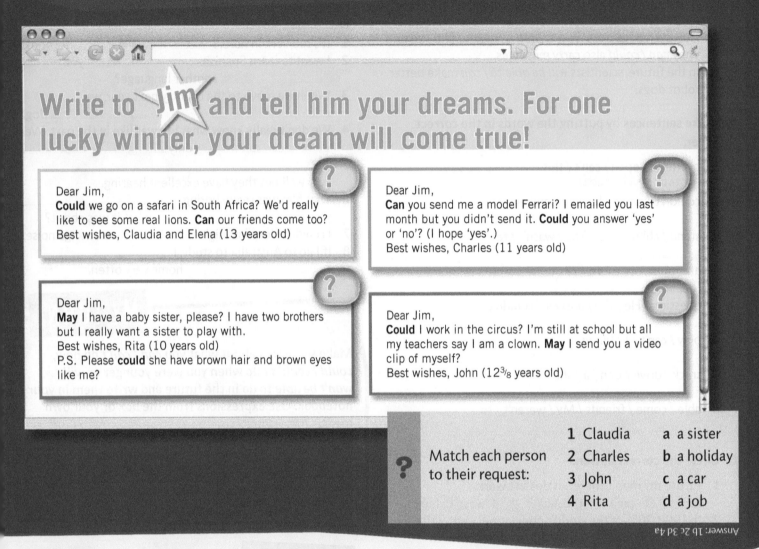

Write to Jim and tell him your dreams. For one lucky winner, your dream will come true!

Dear Jim,
Could we go on a safari in South Africa? We'd really like to see some real lions. **Can** our friends come too?
Best wishes, Claudia and Elena (13 years old)

Dear Jim,
Can you send me a model Ferrari? I emailed you last month but you didn't send it. **Could** you answer 'yes' or 'no'? (I hope 'yes'.)
Best wishes, Charles (11 years old)

Dear Jim,
May I have a baby sister, please? I have two brothers but I really want a sister to play with.
Best wishes, Rita (10 years old)
P.S. Please **could** she have brown hair and brown eyes like me?

Dear Jim,
Could I work in the circus? I'm still at school but all my teachers say I am a clown. **May** I send you a video clip of myself?
Best wishes, John (12 3/8 years old)

? Match each person to their request:

1 Claudia	a a sister
2 Charles	b a holiday
3 John	c a car
4 Rita	d a job

Answer: 1b 2c 3d 4a

Modals for requests: *can, could, may*

1 Use *can, could* and *may* to ask for something politely; *can* and *could* are more common than *may*.

Can you send me a model Ferrari?
Could I have a cake?
May I have a baby sister?

2 Use *can* and *could*, but not *may*, to ask people to do things.

Could she phone me when she's free?
Can you come here?

3 We can use *can, could* and *may* with the first person to ask for permission. *Could* is more polite than *can*. *May* is formal. We usually give permission with *can*, or we can just say *Of course* or *Sure*.

A: Can I leave the room? B: Yes, you ***can****.*
A: Could we have some more? B: No, you ***can't****!*
A: May I start? B: Of course.

TIP
Please + imperative is not very polite.
Please + *can* / *could* / *may* + the infinitive without *to* is polite.
Don't say *Please do it!*, say *Please can you do it?*

Practice

A Match each request to the correct reply.

1 May I come in?
2 Could you ring back later?
3 Can we meet on Saturday?
4 May I take your number?
5 Can your sister come?
6 Could they buy some bread on the way home?
7 Can I see your homework?
8 Could we try the cake?
9 Can you translate it?

a I'm not sure. I'll ask her.
b No, the shop is closed.
c Sorry, I don't know Italian.
d Sure, I'll phone again in an hour.
e Yes, take some. It's very good.
f No, I'm busy at the weekend.
g I haven't done it yet.
h One moment, I'll open the door.
i Sure. 737 – 52 – 25.

B Write sentences asking for permission.

1

I want to go out.

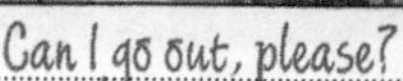

Can I go out, please?

2

I want to speak to Sarah.

3

We want to come home late tonight.

4

I want to ride your bike.

C In your notebook, write a request for each situation using *can, could, may* and the words in brackets. Use *may* when you need to be very polite.

1 You are in a very expensive cafe. You want a coffee. (I / have)
May I have a coffee?
2 You are lost. You see an old man with a mobile phone. (I / use)
3 Your computer won't work. Your friend is good with computers. (you / help)
4 You are late for class. You want to go into the room. (I / come in)
5 You want to see your friend after school. (we / meet)
6 You have invited your friend to a party. You like his CD. (you / bring)
7 It is cold. Your friend is in front of an open window. (you / close)
8 You are going to play tennis with a friend. You have the ball. (we / start)

D These emails to Jim are not polite. In your notebook, write polite versions of them using *can, could, may* and *please*.

1 Give me a Sony PlayStation ?
Could you please give me a Sony PlayStation? / Can you give me a Sony PlayStation, please?

2 Buy me a new bike ?

3 I want to visit London. ?
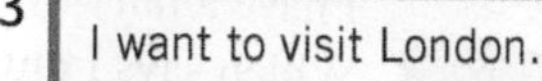

4 Translate this email from my friend in Mongolia. ?
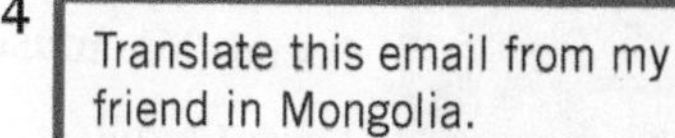

5 Do my Geography homework. ?
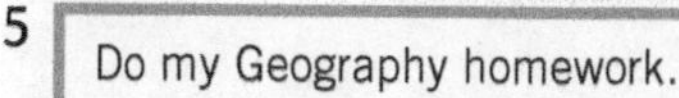

6 Send my sister a birthday present. ?

7 I want to go into space. ?

8 I want to be in the next Spider-Man film. ?

MY TURN!

In your notebook, write emails to Jim. Make them polite with *can, could, may* and *please*.

Examples: *Could I meet Roger Federer?*

MY TEST!

Circle the correct option.

1 Dear Jim. Can you .... my friend? a be b being c to be
2 A: Excuse me. .... your toilet, please? B: Yes, of course. a May I use b May I using c May I to use
3 .... for my sixteenth birthday? a May you give me a car b Could give you me a car c Could you give me a car
4 Dear Jim. Please .... a new mobile phone? a could have my sister b could my sister has c could my sister have
5 A: Mum? Can we have a dog? B: No, we .... a don't b haven't c can't

My Test! answers: 1a 2a 3c 4c 5c

22 Must, have to and can't

I have to stay here.

1

I love the first bit of the morning,
The bit of the day that no one has used yet,
The part that is so clean
You **must** wipe your feet before you walk
out into it.

Coral Rumble

2

I have a fairy by my side
Which says I **must not** sleep,
When once in pain I loudly cried
It said 'You **must not** weep'.

Lewis Carroll

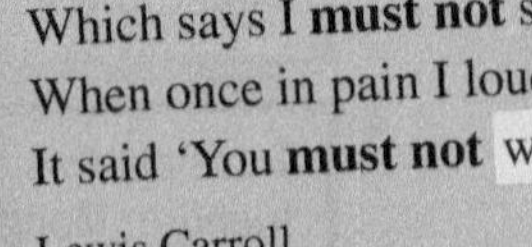

3

People tell you all the time,
Poems **do not have to** rhyme.
It's often better if they don't
And I'm determined this one won't.
Oh dear.

Wendy Cope

4

There's a bird that comes flying,
settles down on my knee,
and he carries a letter
from my mother to me.
Little bird, take the greeting,
take a kiss and a tear,
for I **cannot** go with you,
as I **have to** stay here.

German folk song, translated by
Gerda Mayer

? Which poem is about being far away from someone you love?

Answer: Poem 4

Must, have to and can't

1 Use *must*

– to talk about rules and laws
*All passengers **must** wear a seat belt.* (This is the rule.)
– to talk about something the speaker feels is necessary.
*You **must** phone me.* (The speaker feels that this is important.)

2 The negative form is *must not*. The short form is *mustn't*. Use *must not* or *mustn't* to talk about things we are not allowed to do.

*You **mustn't** smoke in the restaurant.*

3 We can use *can't* instead of *mustn't* to talk about things we are not allowed to do.

***I can't / cannot** go with you.*
***I couldn't** have sweets when I was a girl.*

4 Use *have to*

– to talk about rules and laws (a similar use to *must*)
*All passengers **have to** wear a seat belt.* (This is the rule.)
– to talk about obligation imposed on the speaker by others or circumstance.
*I **have to** stay here.* (The speaker can't change the situation.)

5 Use *don't have to* or *doesn't have to* to talk about something which is not necessary.

*Poems **do not have to** rhyme.* (The speaker doesn't think this is necessary.)

TIP

***Don't have to* is not the same as *mustn't*.**
You mustn't walk on the grass.
NOT ~~*You don't have to walk on the grass.*~~

6 The past of *have to* is *had to*.

***I had to** show my passport at the airport.*

The past of *don't / doesn't have to* is *didn't have to*.

***I didn't have to** get up early yesterday.*

7 There are no past or future forms of *must*. Use forms of *have to* to talk about obligation in the past or future.

***I had to** show my passport at the airport.*
***I will have to** leave early.*

8 *Must* does not change. It is the same with all subjects.

***I must** go. **He must** go. **They must** go.*

9 *Must* is a modal verb, and is followed by a second verb in the infinitive without *to*.

*You must not **weep**.*

10 Questions are more common with *have to* than *must*. Make questions and short answers as follows:

question ?	short answer ✓✗
Do I / you / we / they **have to** stay?	Yes, we **do**. No, we **don't**.
Does he / she / it **have to** stay?	Yes, he **does**. No, he **doesn't**.

▶ See Units 20, 21, 23 and 24 for more modal verbs.

Practice

A Complete the sentences with *have to* or *don't have to*. Make them true for you.

If you want to be my friend, ...

1 you .... be rich.
2 you .... be good-looking.
3 you .... be kind.
4 you .... like the same things as me.
5 you .... talk about your feelings.
6 you .... remember my birthday.

Example:
1 *you don't have to be rich.*

B Complete the sentences using *must*, *mustn't* or *can't* and a verb from the box.

be drink drive ride your bike ~~stop~~ talk

1
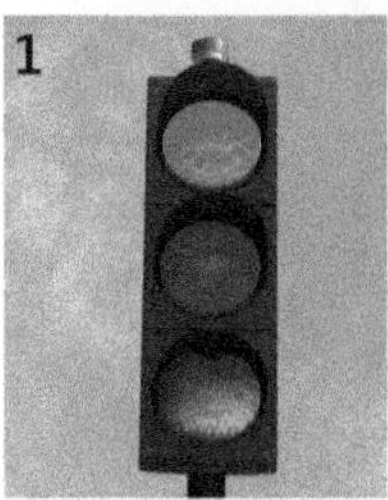
2

3

4

5

6

1 Drivers ....*must stop*............ .
2 You .... on your mobile phone.
3 You .... here.
4 Cars .... under 60 km per hour.
5 You .... the water.
6 You .... quiet here.

C Follow the instructions to complete the poem.

Think of something you need to **buy**. (Write the verb in 1 and the object in 2.) Think of someone you need to **talk to**. (Write the verb in 3 and the person in 4.) Think of something you want to **eat**. (Write the verb in 5 and the food in 6.) Now read your poem.

I must		1 ......*buy*......	2 ....
	and	3	4 ....
	and	5	6 ....
I must not		1 ......*buy*......	4 ....
	or	3	6 ....
	or	5	2 ....

MY TURN!

You are going on a camping holiday in the summer. In your notebook, write two things you *have to* do at the campsite, two things you *mustn't* do and two things you *don't have to* do. Choose from the verbs in the box.

arrive early bring a tent get up early have parties keep the campsite clean make a lot of noise pay in advance wear a uniform

Example: *I don't have to get up early.*

MY TEST!

Circle the correct option.

1 I .... remember it's my mum's birthday next week. **a** must to **b** has **c** must
2 .... write poems at school? **a** Have you **b** Do you have to **c** Do you must
3 Please don't tell my parents I had a hamburger. They .... know. **a** mustn't **b** have not to **c** doesn't must
4 I .... my poem to the class yesterday. **a** had to read **b** must read **c** must to read
5 .... travel a lot when you were a pop singer? **a** Had you to **b** Must you **c** Did you have to

My Test! answers: 1c 2b 3a 4a 5c

23 *Should, ought to*

You should take off your shoes.

Here are some things you should remember if you go to different countries.

If you go to a restaurant in South Korea, you **should** take off your shoes. This is polite.

You **should not** touch somebody on the head in Thailand. The head is a special part of the body in Thai culture.

In Russia, you **shouldn't** whistle inside a house. (No one knows why!)

Guests in Mexico **should** always leave a little bit of food on their plate. This shows they are not hungry.

You **ought to** knock loudly on doors in Nicaragua – knocking softly is not polite.

In Taiwan, you **shouldn't** give somebody an umbrella as a present. An umbrella will bring people bad luck.

? True or False? It is a bad idea to wear shoes in a restaurant in South Korea.

Answer: True

Should, ought to

1 ***Should*** **has a similar meaning to** ***must*****, but is not so strong.**

*You **should** eat healthy food.*
*In Taiwan, you **shouldn't** give somebody an umbrella as a present.*

2 **Use** ***should*** **to ask for and give advice.**

*What **should** I do now?*
*A: I don't feel well. B: You **should** go home.*

3 ***Should*** **is a modal verb so it has no** ***-s*** **in the third person singular. It is followed by the infinitive without** ***to*****.**

*Simon **should come** with us.*
NOT ~~*Simon should to come with us.*~~

4 **We make questions by putting** ***should*** **before the subject.**

***Should** we buy a guidebook?*
*What **should** I do?*

5 **We make negatives with** ***not*****. The short form of** ***should not*** **is** ***shouldn't*****.**

*You **should not** touch somebody on the head in Thailand.*
*Children **shouldn't** play here.*

6 ***Ought to*** **=** ***should*** **but it is much less common.** ***Ought to*** **is very rare in questions and negatives.**

*You **ought to** be polite.*

Practice

A Match the correct advice to each sentence.

1 It's raining. — c
2 I'm tired.
3 It's my birthday.
4 I'm worried about this test.
5 My tooth hurts.
6 My phone is ringing.
7 It's important information.
8 It smells strange.

a You shouldn't think about it.
b You should remember it.
c You should take an umbrella.
d You ought to see a dentist.
e You should answer it.
f You shouldn't eat it.
g You should not work so hard.
h You should buy a nice cake.

B Complete the sentences using *should* and the verbs in the box.

buy ~~come~~ eat give kiss meet open say

1 Guests ...*should come*... late to parties in Switzerland.
2 You .... flowers for women on 8 March in Romania.
3 In Ukraine, you .... guests with bread and salt.
4 If you get a present in Thailand, you .... it at home.
5 When you answer the phone in Germany, you .... your name.
6 In Belgium, friends .... three times when they meet.
7 Guests .... everything on their plate in Bolivia.
8 If you have a house party in New Zealand, you .... a key to guests.

C Tick ✓ the correct option.

1 You should not wear in wet weather

a It is necessary to wear the hat if it's raining.
b You can wear the hat if it's raining.
c It isn't a good idea to wear the hat if it's raining. ✓

2 Subject / Remarks / English — *Mike ought to spend more time on grammar*

a Mike is not interested in grammar.
b Mike should do more grammar.
c Mike has no time for grammar.

3

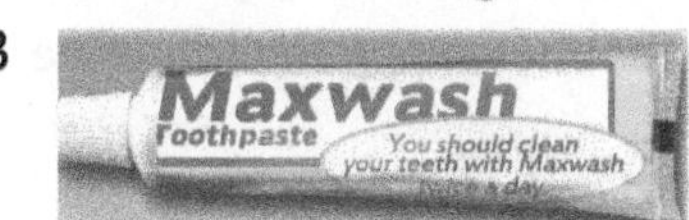

a It is a good idea to clean your teeth.
b This toothpaste is the best for cleaning your teeth.
c It is a good idea to use the toothpaste two times a day.

Maxwash
Toothpaste
You should clean your teeth with Maxwash

4 Geoff, Should I buy flowers? Liz.

a Liz doesn't know if she needs to buy flowers.
b Liz wants Geoff to buy flowers.
c Liz thinks it is necessary to buy some flowers.

5

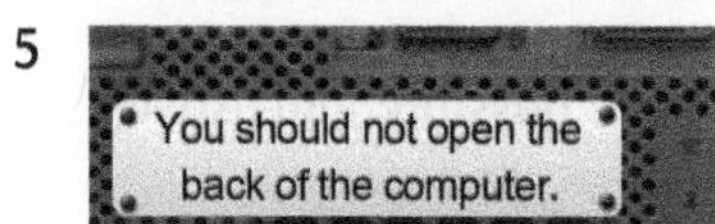

a It is necessary to open the back of the computer.
b It is impossible to open the back of the computer.
c It is a bad idea to open the back of the computer.

6 TEST SHEET PAGE 1 — You should not begin before you read the instructions.

a You ought to begin reading the test.
b Read the instructions first.
c This is not a test for beginner students.

D Give advice in the following situations using *should* or *ought to*.

1 You are always tired in the mornings.
You should go to bed early.
2 Your neighbour plays loud music at night.
....
3 You have nothing nice to wear to a party.
....
4 You don't know what to buy your father for his birthday.
....
5 You are waiting for a friend but he is very late.
....
6 There are mice in your house.
....
7 You want to be a pop star.
....
8 Your mum says you can't go to the party.
....

MY TURN!

What advice would you give to tourists coming to your country? In your notebook, write six sentences using *should, shouldn't* or *ought to*.

Example: *You ought to come in summer.*

MY TEST!

Circle the correct option.

1 Children should .... in the bus, so that older people can sit down.
a stand up b standing up c to stand up
2 You .... wear a hat in somebody's house.
a don't should b shouldn't c not should
3 .... take off my shoes in the house?
a Should I b Do I should c I should
4 When a man meets another man, he .... his hand.
a should shakes b should shake c should to shake
5 You .... a thank-you email for the present.
a should to write b ought to wrote c ought to write

My Test! answers: 1a 2b 3a 4b 5c

24 Modals of possibility: *may, might*

We may never know …

In 1925 a Greek photographer saw a strange thing in the Himalayas. It was like a man but much bigger. Since then many more people say they have seen it; they call it the Yeti. Is the Yeti real? It's possible, but we don't know for sure.

You **might** see a Yeti if you go to the Himalayas. There **may** be many Yetis or there **might not** be any. The Yeti **may** live very high in the mountains. It **may** be very shy. It **might not** want to meet people. It **mightn't** be very glad to see you (and you **mightn't** be very glad to see it!).

? What is the Yeti? **a** A man **b** An animal **c** We don't know.

Answer: c

Modals of possibility: *may, might*

1 Use *may* or *might* to talk about the chance of something being true.
*The Yeti **may** live in the mountains.*
*It **might not** want to meet people.*

2 Use *might* instead of *may* if you think the chance is less certain.
*It **may** snow in the Himalayas next week.* (It's cold in the mountains.)
*You **might see** a Yeti there.* (if they exist ...)

3 We can also use *could* to talk about possibility (see Unit 20).
*We **could** go in summer.*
*Where **could** the Yeti be?*

4 *May, might* and *could* are followed by the infinitive without *to*.
*We **may** / **might** / **could go** by helicopter.*

5 The negative of *might* is *might not*, or (sometimes) *mightn't*. The negative of *may* is *may not*.
*It **might not** / **mightn't** be very glad to see you.*
*Many people **may not** return alive.*

TIP

Maybe is not the same as **may be**.
Maybe (one word) means 'possibly' and usually begins a sentence.
Maybe the Yeti is friendly. Maybe it lives in the mountains.
may be is two words: a modal (like *can* and *must*) + verb.
*The Yeti **may be** friendly. It **may be** in the mountains.*

Practice

A Match facts 1–8 to the possible reasons / consequences a–h.

1 The sky is dark. — b
2 She speaks English.
3 The tourists are lost.
4 You don't want to go to that hotel.
5 She is beautiful.
6 You aren't at school.
7 I can't find my keys.
8 The baby is crying.

a She might be a model.
b It may rain.
c He might be hungry.
d You may be ill.
e She might be American.
f They may be in the car.
g It might be expensive.
h They may not have a good map.

B You are going on an expedition to find the Yeti. Use *may* (*not*) or *might* (*not*) and the information in the box to complete the sentences.

✓	✗
1 ~~snow~~	2 ~~not work~~
3 get lost	4 run away
5 not find the Yeti	6 not have enough food
7 follow	8 not attack
9 write a book	10 not survive

1 It ___*might snow*___ very hard.
2 The camera ___*may / might not work*___ in the cold.
3 We ______ in the mountains.
4 The Yeti ______ .
5 We ______ .
6 We ______ .
7 Animals ______ us.
8 The Yeti ______ us.
9 I ______ after the expedition but ...
10 We ______ !

C Captain Oakes is on an expedition to find the source of the river Ganges. Read his email and complete it with *may* (*not*) or *might* (*not*) and the words from the box.

be be find ~~get lost~~ have like need see work write

... I'm taking a good map because we [1] ___*might get lost*___ . We [2] ______ a compass too. I'm worried that we [3] ______ enough food but we can't carry more. I have my camera but it [4] ______ in the cold. So, we [5] ______ the source of the river but not get any pictures. This [6] ______ a good thing because the people who live there [7] ______ it if we take pictures. Well, we [8] ______ the source of the river, but if we do I [9] ______ a book about our expedition. We [10] ______ famous one day!
Captain Oakes

MY TURN!

Think of a possible explanation for each fact or situation using *may* or *might*. Write them in your notebook.

1 You feel bad.
You might be ill. / You may have a cold.
2 Your steak tastes terrible.
3 A dog follows you home.
4 You hear somebody knocking loudly at your door early in the morning.
5 Your phone rings. You answer in English. The other person doesn't answer.
6 You see a strange light in the sky.
7 Your father has a free ticket to the opera but he doesn't want to go.
8 A good friend hasn't spoken to you for two weeks.

MY TEST!

Circle the correct option.

1 The photographer's story ______ true.
a may don't be b not may be c may not be
2 My uncle's going to the Himalayas next year. He ______ a yeti.
a may see b may sees c mays see
3 Yetis ______ able to speak.
a might to be b might be c are might
4 Are you sure you saw a Yeti? ______ was just a big man.
a Maybe it b Might be it c May be it
5 You ______ this, but I saw a Yeti yesterday in your garden.
a might not to believe
b might not believed
c mightn't believe

My Test answers: 1c 2a 3b 4a 5c

R5 Review: modals

A Complete the sentences using the words in the box. Sometimes two or three answers are possible.

can could have may might must mustn't ought should

1 When you travel by bus, you ...must... have a ticket.
2 When I was a young man, I .... run 10 kilometres, but now I'm too old.
3 My mum says I .... to come home before 10 o'clock.
4 .... I go home early today, please?
5 You .... to read this book – it's very interesting.
6 I'm going to take an umbrella because it .... rain later.
7 She .... speak French and Spanish, but her English is terrible.
8 What do you think? .... I do the exam this year or next year?
9 You .... watch television, but please keep it quiet.
10 Don't worry. You don't .... to buy me a present.
11 .... you give me some money, please? I've left my bag at home.
12 At the zoo, you .... give food to the animals. It's very bad for them.

B Match the sentences in Exercise A to these reasons for using modal verbs.

a talking about present ability (Unit 20) ...7...
b talking about past ability (Unit 20) ....
c asking people to do things (Unit 21) ....
d asking for permission (Unit 21) ....
e giving permission (Unit 21) ....
f talking about rules and laws (Unit 22) ....
g talking about things we are not allowed to do (Unit 22) ....
h talking about an obligation imposed by others (Unit 22) ....
i talking about something which is not necessary (Unit 22) ....
j asking for advice (Unit 23) ....
k giving advice (Unit 23) ....
l talking about the possibility of something being true (Unit 24) ....

C Complete the sentences using the modal verbs from the boxes.

~~could~~ will be able to can

1 Last year I ...could... run 1500 metres in 5½ minutes.
2 Now I .... run 1500 metres in 5 minutes.
3 Next year I .... run 1500 metres in 4½ minutes.

must / have to will have to had to

4 Yesterday you .... wash the windows.
5 Today you .... wash my car.
6 Tomorrow you .... wash your clothes – they're very dirty.

will be able to, won't be able to could, couldn't can, can't

7 When I was 5 I .... climb trees but I .... ride a bike.
8 Now I'm 14 I .... ride a bike but I .... drive a car.
9 50 years from now I .... drive a car but I .... climb trees.

didn't have to, had to have to, don't have to won't have to, will have to

10 When I was small I .... do homework, but I .... go to bed early.
11 Now I .... do homework, but I .... go to bed early.
12 In 10 years I .... do homework and I .... go to bed early, but I .... get a job.

Write three more similar sentences about yourself.

....
....
....
....
....
....

D Complete each sentence b so that it means the same as sentence a. Use two to four words including the correct form of the word in brackets

1 a It's a good idea to eat fruit and vegetables every day. (ought)
  b You ....ought to eat............ fruit and vegetables every day.

2 a Maybe Sharon will know the answer. You should ask her. (might)
  b You should ask Sharon. She .... the answer.

3 a She'll be very good at playing the piano next year. (able)
  b Next year she will .... the piano very well.

4 a I want to open the window. Is that OK? (may)
  b .... the window, please?

5 a You must have clean hair before you go in the swimming pool. (have)
  b Your hair .... clean before you go in the swimming pool.

6 a Bob will be ready in five minutes. Please wait in the garden. (could)
  b .... for Bob in the garden, please? He'll be ready in five minutes.

7 a It's possible that Anna isn't asleep. I'll phone her. (may)
  b I'll phone Anna. She .... asleep.

8 a Don't worry. It's not necessary to wear a tie at the opera. (have)
  b Don't worry. You .... a tie at the opera.

E Tick ✓ the odd one out.

1 a You mustn't speak in the exam.
  b You don't have to speak in the exam. ✓
  c You can't speak in the exam.

2 a We may go home now.
  b We should go home now.
  c We ought to go home now.

3 a It might be sunny tomorrow.
  b It may be sunny tomorrow.
  c It has to be sunny tomorrow.

4 a May I sit here?
  b Must I sit here?
  c Can I sit here?

5 a I can't understand her.
  b I wasn't able to understand her.
  c I couldn't understand her.

6 a Could you be quiet?
  b Can you be quiet?
  c Should you be quiet?

F Complete the dialogue with the modals from the box. Sometimes there is more than one correct answer.

be able to	can / can't	could	have to	may	might	must	ought	should

Alice: Where are you going on holiday?
Brad: To Switzerland. We're going skiing.
Alice: Really? [1] ......can...... you ski?
Brad: Well, I [2] .... ski quite well when I was a child, but that was 10 years ago. I think I [3] .... have some problems.
Alice: No, you'll be fine. You'll [4] .... be careful on the first day, but after a day or two of lessons you'll [5] .... ski quite fast.
Brad: Lessons? [6] .... I have an instructor?
Alice: Hmm ... yes, I think you [7] .... to have some lessons. You don't [8] ...., but it's a good idea.
Brad: I don't know. It [9] .... be expensive.
Alice: It [10] .... be. Just a second, my friend is a ski instructor. He [11] .... know a cheap instructor in Switzerland. You [12] .... call him.
Brad: Great. [13] .... I have his number, please?
Alice: Er ... I [14] .... remember it. But my mum [15] .... know it.
Brad: Great. [16] .... you ask her?
Alice: Of course.

25 Yes / no questions and short answers

Are beetles important? Yes, they are!

sciencemagazinesciencemagazinesciencemagazine

This week Dr Stephen Elliot answers your questions about beetles.

Q Are beetles important?

A People often ask me this, and the answer is, **yes, they are!** Beetles are important because they feed on dead plants and animals.

Q Do beetles lay eggs?

A **Yes, they do.** Then the eggs change into larva, pupa and adult beetle. This is called metamorphosis.

Q There are 350,000 species of beetle. Is this true?

A **No, it isn't** – there are probably more! We just haven't found and named them all yet!

Q Do beetles live everywhere?

A **No, they don't.** Beetles don't live in the sea. But beetles were living on Earth before dinosaurs were here – and they have adapted to almost every habitat.

Q Have beetles adapted to the Arctic?

A You may not believe this – but **yes, they have!** The Arctic beetle can live in temperatures of –40°C!

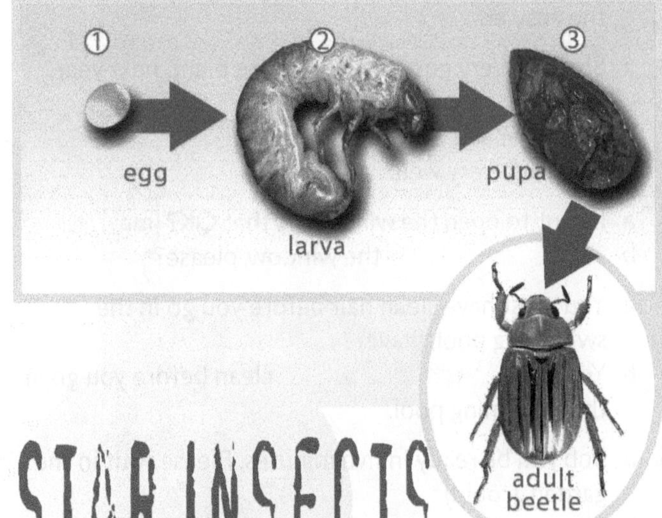

STAR INSECTS

? True or False? Beetles only live in warm countries.

Answer: False

Yes / no questions and short answers

1 **To make a yes / no question, put the auxiliary verb (e.g. *am, is, are, has, have*) before the subject.**
*Is this true? **Have** beetles adapted to the Arctic?*

auxiliary verb	subject	...?
Is	he / she / it	OK?
Am	I	happy?
Are	you / we / they	living here?
Has	he / she / it	arrived?
Have	I / you / we / they	found it?

TIP

Yes / no questions in English always have an auxiliary verb.
Do you come from here? NOT ~~*You come from here?*~~

2 **If there is no auxiliary verb, use *do* or *does*.**
***Does** it have wings? **Do** beetles lay eggs?*

auxiliary verb	subject	...?
Does	he / she / it	look good?
Do	I / you / we / they	have a question?

3 **Make a yes / no answer with just the subject pronoun and the auxiliary verb.**
*A: **Is** it true? B: Yes, it **is**. / No, it **isn't**.*
*A: **Are** you cold? B: Yes, I **am**. / No, **I'm not**.*
*A: **Has** she arrived? B: Yes, she **has**. / No, she **hasn't**.*
*A: **Have** beetles adapted to the Arctic?*
*B: Yes, they **have**. / No, they **haven't**.*
*A: **Does** it look good? B: Yes, it **does**. / No, it **doesn't**.*
*A: **Do** beetles lay eggs? B: Yes, they **do**. / No, they **don't**.*

Practice

A **Match these questions about ladybirds to the correct answers. The verbs will help you.**

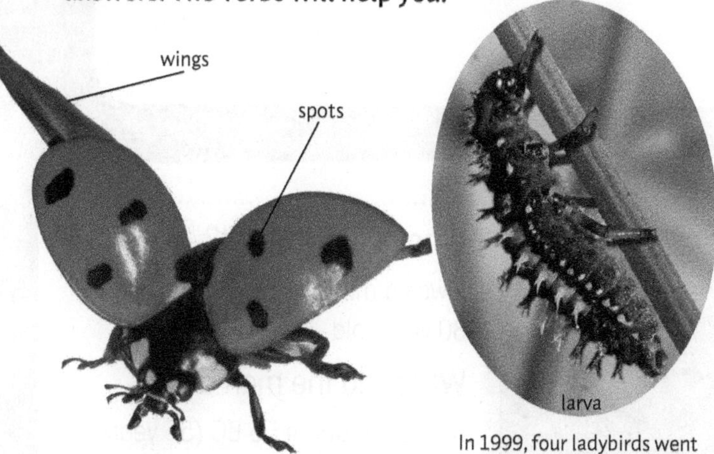

In 1999, four ladybirds went into space in a NASA space shuttle. They came back alive.

1. Are ladybirds beetles? — e
2. Are all ladybirds red and black?
3. Do ladybirds lay eggs?
4. Have ladybirds adapted to all habitats?
5. Is the ladybird larva red?
6. Does the ladybird larva have black spots?
7. Has a ladybird been in space?

a Yes, they do.
b No, they aren't.
c No, it isn't.
d No, they haven't.
e Yes, they are.
f Yes, it has!
g No, it doesn't.

B **Your aunt and uncle have a holiday house. You are going to stay there this summer, but you have some questions. Complete their answers.**

1. Is it close to the beach? ✓ *Yes, it is.*
2. Is it big? ✗ *No, it isn't.*
3. Does it have a swimming pool? ✗ ....
4. Is my cousin Silvia coming too? ✗ ....
5. Has Silvia been there recently? ✗ ....
6. Are the neighbours friendly? ✓ ....
7. Do the neighbours know we're coming? ✓ ....
8. Have you left the keys with the neighbours? ✓ ....

C **Use the words in the table to make eight or more different questions and write them in your notebook.**

Have Do Does	beetles a bee mosquitoes you	have ever seen ever picked up lay	eggs? wings? spots? a ladybird larva? a worm?
Is Are		important? black and yellow?	

Examples: *Do mosquitoes lay eggs?*
Are mosquitoes important?

MY TURN!

You are coming to visit your grandmother in the USA. At the airport, the immigration officer asks you some questions. Make the questions using the words in brackets and write them in your notebook.

1. (your name / Marco de Silva)
   Is your name Marco De Silva?
2. (over 18)
3. (more than one bag)
4. (live / in the USA)
5. (grandmother / living / in the USA)
6. (been / to the USA / before)
7. (staying / for more than a month)

Now answer the questions in your notebook using the information below.

NAME: Marco De Silva
AGE: 16
LIVES: Capri
REASON FOR VISIT:
Visiting grandmother. First visit.
LENGTH OF STAY: 2 weeks
NUMBER OF BAGS: 2

1 *Yes, it is.*

MY TEST!

Circle the correct option.

1. Sorry. .... late?
   a Do I b Are I c Am I
2. A: ....? B: Yes, some beetles eat dead fish.
   a Do beetles eat fish
   b Are beetles eat fish
   c Eat beetles fish
3. A: Are beetles very intelligent?
   B: No, ... They have very small brains.
   a it isn't b they don't c they aren't
4. A: Have you ever eaten a beetle?
   B: No, I ....
   a don't b didn't c haven't
5. A: Does your pet beetle have a name?
   B: Yes, he .... His name's Ringo.
   a has b does c have

My Test! answers: 1c 2a 3c 4c 5b

26 Question words: *Where? When? Why? How? Whose?*

How did he die?

In 1984 a farmer found a body in a field in Lindow Moss near Manchester. The farmer called the police. Scientists found that the person died 2,000 years ago. It was a very important archaeological discovery. They called it 'The Lindow Man'. There were many interesting questions for scientists and archaeologists to ask and answer.

Whose body was it?

It was a man's body. He was about 30 years old.

When did the man die?

He died in about 55 BC (55 years **B**efore Jesus **C**hrist was born).

How did he die?

The Celts – the people of Britain at that time – killed him with an axe.

Why did they kill him?

We don't know!

Where is the body now?

It is in the British Museum.

Underline the correct option: A farmer *found / killed* the Lindow Man.

Answer: found

Question words: *Where? When? Why? How? Whose?*

Where, When, Why, How **and** ***Whose*** **are question words.**

1 **Use *Where ...?* to ask about place.**
*A: **Where** is Lindow Moss? B: It's near Manchester.*
*A: **Where** are my shoes? B: Next to the door.*

2 **Use *When ...?* to ask about time.**
*A: **When** is your birthday? B: 7 July.*
*A: **When** did you get home? B: Ten o'clock.*

3 **Use *Why ...?* to ask about reason.**
*A: **Why** are you wet? B: It's raining.*
*A: **Why** did you become a teacher? B: I like children.*

4 **Use *How ...?* to ask about the way things are or the way people feel.**
*A: **How** did you get home? B: By taxi.*
*A: **How** are you? B: I'm fine, thank you.*

5 **Use *Whose ...?* to ask about who has something.**
*A: **Whose** is this? B: It's hers.*
*A: **Whose** army invaded Russia in 1812? B: Napoleon's army.*

6 **The word order is: question word + auxiliary (e.g. *is, did, will*, etc.) + subject + main verb.**

question word	auxiliary	subject	main verb
When	*will*	*they*	*understand?*
Where	*are*	*you*	*going?*
Why	*did*	*Jane*	*cry?*

7 ***Whose*** **can come before a singular or plural noun.** ***Whose*** **can refer to people, animals or things.**
*A: **Whose** bag is it? B: It's Barry's.*
***Whose** streets are cleaner – London's or Manchester's?*

▶ **See Unit 50 for more information on *whose*.**
▶ **See Units 27 and 28 for *Who ...?* and *What ...?* questions and Unit 30 for more *How ...?* questions.**

Practice

A Make questions by putting the words in the correct order.

1 did / he/ live / where *Where did he live?*
2 is / why / he / famous ....?
3 farmer / the / did / body / where / the / find
..................?
4 it / whose / farm / was
..................?
5 when / did / invade / the / Britain / Romans
..................?
6 did / the / Celts / why / him / kill
..................?
7 do / about / know / people / how / this
..................?
8 him / see / we / can / where
..................?

B Write *Where, When, Why, How* or *Whose*.

1 *How* was your trip?
2 .... is the British Museum?
3 .... do they know he died 2,000 years ago?
4 .... will the museum be open?
5 .... axe was it?
6 .... is the Lindow Man so famous?
7 .... did the farmer feel?
8 .... can you come with me to see the Lindow Man?

C Complete the questions with *Where, When, Why, How* or *Whose* and a form of *be* or *do*. Then choose the correct answers from the box.

An apple Brazil ~~Egypt~~ eleventh George Washington Greece horse Microsoft

1 Question: *Where are* the Pyramids?
Answer: They are in *Egypt*.
2 Question: .... the Normans invade England?
Answer: They invaded in the .... century.
3 Question: .... picture .... on an American $1 note?
Answer: It's a picture of ....
4 Question: .... the 1896 Olympics?
Answer: They were in...................
5 Question: .... Newton discover gravity?
Answer: .... fell on his head.
6 Question: .... Bill Gates leave university?
Answer: Because he wanted to create the .... company.
7 Question: .... national dance .... the *samba*?
Answer: It's the national dance of ....
8 Question: .... the Greeks enter Troy?
Answer: They hid in a wooden ....

D Write questions with *Where, When, Why, How,* and *Whose*.

1 *Whose birthday cake is it?*
It's my birthday cake.
2 *When is your birthday?*
It's tomorrow.
3 ....?
I usually celebrate it at home.
4 ....?
Because my family is there
5 ....?
Last year? Oh, I celebrated it with a big party!
6 ....?
That was my idea.
7 ....?
It started early, about 4 o'clock.
8 ....?
It started then because my gran goes to bed at 9.
9 ....?
I invited her because she's a great cook!

MY TURN!

Read the first paragraph of a detective story. In your notebook, write questions about it using all the question words *Where, When, Why, How* and *Whose* at least once.

Chapter 1

The man is alone. It is cold and wet but he isn't wearing a coat. He has been here a long time. He wants to leave but he can't. The police are not here yet. The man is afraid, very afraid. Suddenly, he hears a voice. He doesn't recognise the voice but he understands everything. The man runs back to his car. The car won't start. He sees a face in the mirror. He screams.

Examples: *Where is he?* *Why is he alone?*

MY TEST!

Circle the correct option.

1 .... body did the farmer find?
a Why b Whose c Where
2 How .... more about Lindow Man?.
a I learn b I can learn c can I learn
3 Why .... broken bones?
a did the body have b had the body c the body had
4 .... we going to the museum?
a When do b Where do c When are
5 A: I can't find my book. B: I'll help you. Where .... looked?
a did you b you have c have you

My Test! answers: 1b 2c 3a 4c 5c

27 Object and subject questions

Who studied at Hogwarts?

 Do you know the answers to any of these questions?

Facts Everyone Should Know

1 What happened on 24 August, 79 AD?

4 What did Sir Alexander Fleming discover in 1928?

5 Who lives at 1600 Pennsylvania Avenue, Washington D.C.?

2 Who did Romeo love?

3 Who studied at Hogwarts?

6 What happens in the ninth month of the Muslim calendar?

Answers: 1 Mount Vesuvius destroyed Pompeii. 2 Juliet. 3 Harry Potter. 4 He discovered penicillin. 5 The President of the United States. This is the official address for The White House. 6 Ramadan: Muslims do not eat during the day in Ramadan.

Object and subject questions

1 Object questions. In questions beginning with *who* or *what* and using the auxiliary verb *do, does* or *did*, the question word is the object.

*A: **Who** did John Lennon marry in 1969?*

*B: He married **Yoko Ono**.*

(*Who* / *Yoko Ono* = object)

*A: **What** does she want?*

*B: She wants **a new car**.*

(*What* / *a new car* = object)

2 Subject questions. If the question word is the subject, we don't use the auxiliary verb *do, does* or *did*.

*A: **Who** discovered penicillin?*

*B: **Alexander Fleming** discovered penicillin.*

(*Who* / *Alexander Fleming* = subject)

*A: **What** happens in November in the USA?*

(*What* / *Thanksgiving* = subject)

*B: **Thanksgiving**.*

TIP

In a subject question, the verb after the question word is in the third person singular, even when the answer is plural, e.g.
A: Who lives at number 42? B: Elena and Chris.

Practice

A Make questions by putting the words in the correct order.

1 Who / love / did / Scarlett O'Hara?
Who did Scarlett O'Hara love? .... [e]

2 What / on 4 April 1968 / happened?
.... [ ]

3 Who / *Around the World in 80 Days* / wrote?
.... [ ]

4 landed on Mars / What / in 1976?
.... [ ]

5 Who / Will Smith / marry / in 1997 / did?
.... [ ]

6 invent / did / What / Frank Whittle?
.... [ ]

7 in 1969 / What / Neil Armstrong / do / did?
.... [ ]

Now match answers a–g to questions 1–7.

a Jules Verne
b He walked on the moon.
c Viking 1
d Jada Pinkett
e Rhett Butler
f The jet engine
g The assassination of Martin Luther King, Jr.

B Write complete questions using the present simple or the past simple of the verbs in the box.

destroy invent live love paint sing about ~~write~~

1 What / Miguel de Cervantes?
What did Miguel de Cervantes write? .... *Don Quixote*

2 Who / at 10 Downing Street? ....
.... ? The British Prime Minister

3 What / most of San Francisco in 1906? ....
.... ? An earthquake

4 Who / Mary Jane Watson? ....
.... ? Spider-Man

5 Who / *Sunflowers*? ....
.... ? Vincent Van Gogh

6 What / Tim Berners-Lee? ....
.... ? The World Wide Web

7 Who / Elton John in his song *Candle in the Wind*? ....
.... ? Marilyn Monroe

C Read the texts and write a question for each answer.

There was an accident in our road yesterday. A driver was going down the road too fast. A bird hit the car roof and surprised the driver. The driver came off the road and hit a tree.

1 .... *What did the car hit* .... ? A tree.
2 .... *What hit the car* .... ? A bird.

Matt likes cats but Kelly likes birds.

3 .... ? Birds.
4 .... ? Matt.

My mum told my neighbour that I didn't like school. And my neighbour told my teacher!

5 .... ? My mum.
6 .... ? My teacher.

The world makes money and money makes the world go round.

7 .... ? Money.
8 .... ? Money.

MY TURN!

You have the chance to go on a sports activity course, but you are not sure if you want to go. In your notebook, write questions to ask the organisers, using *who* or *what* and the words in the box.

teach happen can come wear bring contact

Example: *What do you teach on the course?*

MY TEST!

Circle the correct option.

1 A: Who .... ? B: Tolstoy. a did write *War and Peace* b did *War and Peace* write c wrote *War and Peace*
2 A: What .... ? B: The Harry Potter books. a write J K Rowling b wrote J K Rowling c did J K Rowling write
3 A: What .... on 31 August 1997? B: Princess Diana died in a car crash. a happened b did happen c happens
4 A: Who .... on the left side of the road? B: British and Japanese people. a drive b drives c does drive
5 A: What .... every February or March? B: The Carnival. a happen in Rio b does happen in Rio c happens in Rio

My Test! answers: 1c 2c 3a 4b 5c

28 *Be like* and *look like*

What does Wolverine look like?

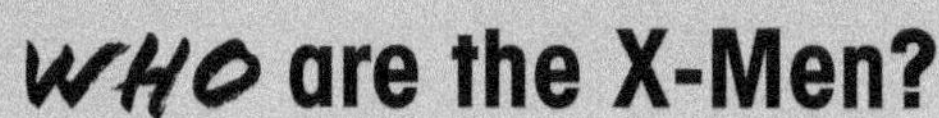

WHO are the X-Men?

The X-Men first appeared in comic books published by Marvel Comics in the 1960s.

WHAT are X-Men like?

X-Men are people who are born with superhuman powers.

WHAT do X-Men look like?

X-Men are very similar to humans but they are a little different. They may have strange-coloured skin, for example.

WHAT does Wolverine look like?

He has dark hair, blue eyes and claws.

WHAT'S he like?

Wolverine is good-looking. He is more than 100 years old, but he is still very strong. He can see and hear very well.

claws

Wolverine is one of the most popular X-Men.

What superhuman powers does Wolverine have?

Answer: He is very strong and he can see and hear very well.

Be like and *look like*

1 **Use the questions *What is ... like?* and *What does ... look like?* to find out about a person's looks.**

A: ***What does*** *Wolverine* ***look like****?* B: *He has dark hair and blue eyes.*

A: ***What is*** *Wolverine* ***like****?* B: *He is good-looking.*

2 **We can also use the question *What is ... like?* to find out about a person's character.**

A: ***What's*** *he* ***like****?* B: *He is still very strong. He can see and hear very well.*

3 **Use the question *What is / was it like?* to ask for a description of the weather, a place or an event.**

A: ***What was*** *the weather* ***like*** *yesterday?*

B: *It was really hot.*

A: ***What's*** *Mexico City* ***like****?* B: *It's very big and busy.*

A: ***What was*** *the football match* ***like****?* B: *It was great!*

TIP

What ... like? **is not the same as *How's ...?***

A: What's Jo like? B: He's really nice.

A: How's Jo? B: He's fine.

4 **The plural forms of the questions are *What are ... like?* and *What do ... look like?***

What	is	he / she / it	like?
What	are	you / we / they	like?
What	does	he / she / it	look like?
What	do	you / we / they	look like?

5 **Other verbs similar to *look like* include *feel like, smell like, sound like* and *taste like.***

What does *the coat* ***feel like****?*

What do *olives* ***taste like****?*

What does *the flute* ***sound like****?*

What does *the sea* ***smell like****?*

TIP

Generally, we don't include the word *like* in the answers to these questions.

A: What does he look like?

B: He ***is*** *tall and he* ***has*** *a beard.*

Practice

A Match the questions to the correct answers.

1 What does Batman look like? — d
2 What is Superman like?
3 What is Milan like?
4 What's the book like?
5 What do witches look like?
6 What are superheroes like?

a It's one of the largest cities in Italy and it's very fashionable.
b They're always strong and they usually have a good heart.
c They're usually ugly.
d He wears a black suit and a mask.
e It's funny, but also a little sad.
f He has short, dark hair and he wears a red and blue suit.

B Complete the questions using the verbs in the box.

feel like	~~look like~~	smell like	sound like	taste like

1 A: What ....do.... butterflies ....look like.... ?
B: Beautiful.
2 A: What .... sulphur .... ?
B: Very bad.
3 A: What .... honey .... ?
B: Very sweet.
4 A: What .... feathers .... ?
B: Very soft.
5 A: What .... drums .... ?
B: Very loud.

C In your notebook, write eight or more questions using *What ... like?, What ... look like?* and the words in the table.

What	do does did is / 's are was were	your grandparents the party Harry Potter Charlie Chaplin the weather Superman and Lois the first computers	like? look like? going to be like?

Example: ....What was Charlie Chaplin like?....

MY TURN!

Write appropriate questions for these dialogues, using *What ... like?, What ... look like?* and *How ...?*

1 A: ....What are your neighbours like.... ?
B: They're kind and friendly.
2 A: .... ?
B: She's tall and dark.
3 A: .... ?
B: She's feeling better now, thanks.
4 A: .... ?
B: It's an Italian island in the Mediterranean. It's very beautiful.
5 A: .... ?
B: It was by the sea and very modern. I had a lovely room.
6 A: .... ?
B: I'm fine, thanks.
7 A: .... ?
B: It was great. Everyone was there!
8 A: .... ?
B: They're quite old now but they are still good-looking!
9 A: .... ?
B: He's tall and he wears glasses.

MY TEST!

Circle the correct option.

1 A: What .... like? B: He is very friendly, but he worries a lot. **a** does Iceman look **b** is Iceman look **c** is Iceman
2 A: What does Iceman's skin .... like? B: It's cold and hard. **a** feel **b** smell **c** sound
3 A: .... like? B: It was really good. I loved it. **a** How was the film **b** What did the film **c** What was the film
4 A: How is your sister? B: She's .... **a** very pretty **b** friendly **c** fine, thanks
5 A: What does your brother look like? B: .... **a** He likes football **b** He's tall and thin **c** He's very nice

My Test! answers: 1c 2a 3c 4c 5b

29 *What?* and *Which?*

Which of them is the queen bee?

What kinds of bees do you know? There are many different kinds of bees, but which bees make honey? Honey bees, of course! Every family of honey bees has one - and only one - queen bee.

Look at the three pictures of bees. **Which** of them is the queen? Look carefully. **Which** one has the longest body? Yes, the bee in picture 2. This is the queen bee. Picture 1 is a drone and picture 3 is a worker.

What work does the queen do? She doesn't make honey - the workers do that. The queen bee is the mother of all the drones and workers. The workers give special food to the queen. **What** food is this? It is called 'royal jelly' and only queen bees eat it.

? Complete the sentence. .... makes honey.
a The worker bee **b** The drone **c** The queen bee

Answer: a

What? and *Which?*

1 **Use both *What* or *Which* + singular and plural nouns to ask questions.**
   What *colour is a honey bee?*
   Which *bees are dangerous?*
   What *food does a queen bee eat?*

2 **Use *What* + noun for general questions when there are many possibilities, and *Which* + noun when there is a small or limited number of possibilities.**
   What *language do they speak in Timbuktu?* (many possibilities)
   Which *language shall we use – Japanese or English?* (two possibilities)

3 **We say *What time ...?, What kind(s) of ...?* and *What size ...?***
   What time *is it?*
   What kinds of *bees do you know?*
   What size *are these jeans?*

4 **Use *Which of ...* + pronoun or *the*.**
   Which of them *is the queen?*
   Which of the *answers do you know?*

5 **We say *Which one(s) ...?***
   Which one *would you like?*
   Which ones *are worker bees?*

▶ See Unit 27 for how to make *What ...?* questions.

Practice

A Complete the questions using *Which* and a noun from the box.

bed car planet ~~team~~ telephone way

1 Which team .... is winning? 2 .... is mine? 3 .... shall I go?

4 .... am I on? Earth? 5 .... is ringing? 6 .... do you want?

B Complete the questions with *What* or *Which*.

1 A: What .... colour is it? B: It's blue.
2 A: .... season do you prefer: summer or winter?
B: Winter.
3 A: .... music do you like? B: I like jazz.
4 A: .... game are you playing? B: We're playing chess.
5 A: .... book is Janet reading?
B: She's reading *Charlie and the Chocolate Factory*.
6 A: .... school did you go to – Sheffield High or Sheffield Grammar? B: I went to Sheffield High School.

C Underline the correct option.

1 *What / Which* time do you go to bed?
2 *What / Which* one do you want?
3 *What / Which* size are you?
4 *What / Which* of the films have you seen?
5 *What / Which* kind of music do you like?
6 *What / Which* of her books is the best?
7 I don't know *what / which* time it is.
8 A: Here's your pizza, Sir.
B: *What / Which* pizza? I didn't order any!
9 A: *What / Which* university is older, Cambridge or Oxford?
B: Oxford.
10 A: Good morning, Jane Smith calling.
B: I'm sorry, I can't hear you. *What / Which* name was that?

MY TURN!

Write *What* or *Which* questions about bees in the correct places in the dialogue.

Beekeeper: Hello, nice to meet you.
1 What questions do you have about bees ?
You: I can see a lot of bees! 2 .... ?
Beekeeper: This one with the yellow spot.
You: 3 .... ?
Beekeeper: Honey bees live in many countries. You can find them on four continents.
You: 4 .... ?
Beekeeper: Antarctica. It's too cold! There are seven main types of honey bee but none of them live there.
You: 5 .... ?
Beekeeper: I have European honey bees. They make great honey.
You: 6 .... ?
Beekeeper: My honey, of course!

MY TEST!

Circle the correct option.

1 I don't know the difference between bees and wasps. Which .... is dangerous? a from them b of them c of they
2 A: .... food do wasps eat? B: Mostly they eat other insects. a Which b Which of c What
3 .... the flowers in your garden do the bees like? a Which b What c Which of
4 A: What .... ? B: Orange and black or brown and black. a are honey bees colour b colour are honey bees c colour honey bees are
5 A: .... homes do wasps live in? B: Paper nests. a What kind of b How kind c What kind

My Test! answers: 1b 2c 3c 4b 5a

30 *How ...?* questions

How cold is the Channel?

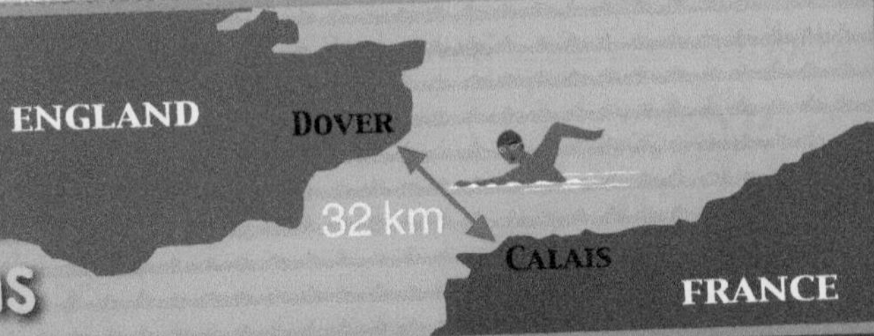

Swimming the Channel: Frequently Asked Questions

How many people have swum the Channel?
Around a thousand people have swum the Channel, the sea between England and France. The 'Queen of the Channel', Alison Streeter, has swum it 38 times.

How far is it?
The direct route is 32 kilometres from Shakespeare Beach, Dover to Cap Gris Nez, France.

How long does it take?
It takes 10–20 hours, depending on **how good** you are at swimming and the weather.

How cold is the water?
The water temperature is from 13–17° in summer. The cold is probably the biggest problem in swimming the Channel.

How much should I practise?
A lot! You will need to swim for one or two hours a day. Some of this training must be in open water.

How often should I eat during the swim?
Eat every half-hour. Eating in the water is not easy, so practise.

? Complete the sentence with the names of two countries:
The Channel goes between E.................. and F.................. .

Answer: England; France

How ...? questions

1 Use *How* + an adjective or an adverb in questions.
__How cold__ is the water?
__How hungry__ are you?
__How late__ did you get home?

2 Use *How far ...?* to ask about distance.
A: __How far__ is it from London to Paris?
B: One hour by plane.
A: __How far__ did you drive? B: 600 kilometres.

3 Use *How long ...?* to ask about time or length.
A: __How long__ is the film? B: It's two hours long.
A: __How long__ is the canal? B: About 200 kilometres.

TIP

Use *How long does it take?* to ask about how much time you need to go somewhere or do something.
A: There's a plane to Paris.
B: __How long does it take?__
A: One hour.

4 Use *How often ...?* to ask about frequency.
A: __How often__ do you go swimming?
B: Every day. / Twice a week.
A: __How often__ is Steven here?
B: He only comes on Tuesdays / Not very often.

5 Use *How many ...?* with plural countable nouns.
__How many__ people have swum the Channel?
__How many__ eggs do we need?

6 Use *How much ...?* with singular uncountable nouns.
__How much food__ shall we take?
__How much time__ do you need?

▶ **See Unit 40 for more information on countable and uncountable nouns.**

7 Use *How much ...?* without a noun to ask about the price or quantity of something.
A: __How much__ does it cost? B: Eleven euros.
A: __How much__ did she eat? B: A lot!

▶ **See Unit 26 for more information on *How* in questions.**

Practice

A Match the questions to the correct answers.

1 How wide is the Channel? — c
2 How important is it?
3 How deep is it?
4 How many types of fish live there?
5 How often are there big storms in the Channel?
6 How long does it take to get through the Channel tunnel?
7 How much does a ticket through the tunnel cost?
8 How popular is Dover Castle?

a Very. 400 ships cross the Channel every day.
b About 200 euros.
c Between 32 and 240 kilometres
d Rarely, the water is usually calm.
e 300,000 people visit it every year.
f It's about 120 metres in the middle.
g 20 minutes on most trains.
h There are about 1,000 different kinds.

B Complete the questions with the words in the box.

far fast good long much often ~~old~~

1 A: How ...old... is your grandmother?
B: She's 85 tomorrow.
2 A: How .... is your house from school?
B: It's about a ten-minute walk.
3 A: How .... is her English?
B: She speaks it almost perfectly.
4 A: How .... are you staying in Madrid?
B: We're only here for the weekend.
5 A: How .... does it cost?
B: Seven euros.
6 A: How .... does it go?
B: About 60 kilometres an hour.
7 A: How .... do you go to the cinema?
B: Once a month.

C Complete each question b so that it means the same as question a. Use one to three words.

1 a Does Alison Streeter train hard?
b How ...hard... does Alison Streeter train?
2 a Do you swim every day or every week?
b How .... swim?
3 a What is the temperature of the water in the Channel?
b How .... the water in the Channel?
4 a What is the distance from England to France?
b How .... from England to France?
5 a Did you swim the Channel quickly?
b How .... take you to swim the Channel?
6 a Did you eat a lot during the swim?
b How .... eat during the swim?

MY TURN!

Now write at least five questions with *How ...?* that you'd like to ask an Olympic athlete.
Example: How often do you train?

....
....
....
....
....

MY TEST!

Circle the correct option.

1 A: How .... were you when you first swam the Channel? B: I was 15 years old.
a old b many c age
2 A: How .... did it take you to swim the Channel?
B: About 18 hours.
a long time b many time c long
3 A: How .... water should I drink?
B: About 5 litres.
a much b many c often
4 A: How .... do they go swimming?
B: Five times a week.
a long b often c many
5 A: How .... to go swimming in your city?
B: Five euros.
a many it costs b much it costs
c much does it cost

My Test! answers: 1a 2c 3a 4b 5c

31 *So* and *neither*

Neither do I.

home | chat | message boards | contact us | links

THE 123 CHATROOM *for teens only*

SEND US YOUR COMMENTS.

Tell us things you don't need in your life.

[emma] Easy. My brother. Maths. Winter. Milk chocolate – I don't like it.
[nicko] **Neither** do I. Dark chocolate is the best.
[suzi and abi] Hello, Emma! You're right. Winter is so boring.
[todd] Hi, everyone. I think winter is OK.
[nicko] Me too. I love snow. And there's football …
I'm a Manchester United fan.
[todd] **So** am I. ☺
[emma] I hate football. ☹
[suzi and abi] **So** do we. And cabbage.
Does anyone like cabbage?
[emma] No.
[todd] Yuk!

? Who hates football?

Answer: Emma, Suzi and Abi.

So and *neither*

1 **Use *so* + auxiliary verb + subject to mean 'too' or 'also'.**
A: I'm a Manchester United fan.
*B: **So am I**!* (= I'm a Manchester United fan, too.)
A: I think winter is OK.
*B: **So do I**.* (= I think winter is OK, too.)
A: I hate football.
*B: **So do we**.* (= We hate football, too.)

2 **The negative is *neither* + auxiliary verb + subject.**
A: I don't like it.
*B: **Neither do I**.* (= I don't like it either.)

3 **Use the same auxiliary verb after *so* or *neither* as the auxiliary verb in the original statement.**
*A: I **am** a football fan.*
*B: So **am** I.*
*I've never been to Spain. Neither **has** my brother.*

4 **If there is no auxiliary verb in the original statement, use a form of *do*.**
*A: Nicko **likes** white chocolate.*
*B: So **does** Todd.*
*A: I **hate** football.*
*B: So **do** we.*

5 **After *so* and *neither* the auxiliary verb comes before the subject.**
*So **am I**.* NOT ~~*So I am.*~~
*Neither **does she**.* NOT ~~*Neither she does.*~~

6 **Instead of *So am I* or *So do I* we can say *Me too*. Instead of *Neither am I* or *Neither do I* we can say *Me neither*.**

TIP

You can pronounce *neither* with an /aɪ/ or an /iː/ sound. The first is more common in Britain, the second in the USA.

Practice

A Match each sentence to an appropriate reply.

1 I'm tired today.
2 I'm not working this weekend.
3 I don't come here often.
4 Frank plays tennis really well.
5 I haven't heard the new CD yet.
6 Isabel has been to the USA lots of times.
7 She can count to 20 in German.
8 My friends were on holiday last week.

a So can I.
b So was I.
c Neither do I.
d So has her sister.
e Neither am I.
f So does his brother.
g So am I.
h Neither have I.

B Suzi and Abi always agree. Write Abi's replies to what Suzi says (two replies each time).

	<suzi>	<abi>	
1	I am 16.	*So am I*	*Me too*
2	I chat on the website every evening.	....	....
3	I don't eat chocolate.	....	....
4	I am good at English.	....	....
5	I don't watch horror movies.	....	....
6	I hate football.	....	....
7	I'm not going out this weekend.	....	....
8	I think winter is boring.	....	....

C Write sentences about Suzi and Abi using the information in Exercise B.

1 *Suzi is 16 and so is Abi.*
2 ....
3 ....
4 ....
5 ....
6 ....
7 ....
8 ....

D Write replies to the following statements using *so* or *neither* and the subject in brackets.

1 A: We are ready!
B: (we) *So are we!*
2 A: Are your parents coming to the show?
B: No, they're not and (my friends) ....
3 A: Maria's studying medicine.
B: (her sister) ....
4 A: I didn't understand what he said!
B: (I) ....
5 A: My dad hasn't been here before.
B: (my mum) ....
6 A: I was up late last night.
B: (I) ....
7 A: I thought the film was great.
B: (we) ....
8 A: I can't see the board.
B: (I) ....
9 A: Mrs Jacobs isn't very polite.
B: (her husband) ....
10 A: They live in the city centre.
B: (my cousins) ....
11 A: I'm really cold.
B: (I) ....
12 You weren't listening!
B: (you) ....

MY TURN!

Complete the table with information about yourself. Which people have the same opinions? Write sentences in your notebook.

	Me	Emma	Todd	Nicko
likes cabbage		no	no	no
likes Maths		no	yes	no
is a Manchester United fan		no	yes	yes
thinks winter is boring		yes	no	no

Example: *Todd likes Maths and so do I!*

MY TEST!

Circle the correct option.

1 My cat is beautiful and so .... my dog.
a do b does c is
2 A: I've never used a chatroom. B: ....
a So have I b Neither have I c Neither I have
3 A: You shouldn't say bad things about your brother.
B: ....
a So shouldn't you b Neither shouldn't you c Neither should you
4 A: Robert isn't coming to the party.
B: Neither .... Paul and Jack.
a are b is c do
5 Emma chatted last night for four hours. So ....
a Todd did b did Todd c does Todd

My Test! answers: 1c 2b 3c 4a 5b

32 Question tags

Chocolate is bad for you, isn't it?

Q&A What do you know about your health?

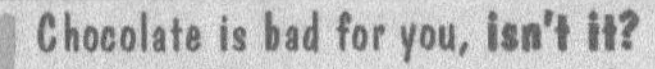

1 Chocolate is bad for you, **isn't it?**
Not really. Chocolate has a lot of calories but this is only a problem if you eat too much of it.

2 Coffee stops you sleeping, **doesn't it?**
Yes, it does. The caffeine in coffee is a stimulant, so it isn't a good idea to drink coffee before you go to bed.

3 Vitamin tablets aren't necessary, **are they?**
No, they aren't. Taking vitamins every day is definitely not a good idea.

4 Teenagers need to sleep more than adults, **don't they?**
Yes, they do. A 14-year-old needs eight or nine hours sleep a night. Seven hours is fine for most adults.

5 We shouldn't sunbathe, **should we?**
No, we shouldn't. Not in the middle of the day. Too much sunlight can be bad for you.

Underline the correct option: It is better to drink coffee in the *morning / evening.*

Answer: morning

Question tags

1 Use question tags in conversation to check information or to check that the listener agrees with you.

Chocolate is bad for you, ***isn't it****?*
You phoned the doctor, ***didn't you****?*
It's a lovely day, ***isn't it****?*

2 A sentence with a question tag has a main clause (*You know Simon ...*) and the question tag (*... don't you?*). The question tag has an auxiliary (e.g. *is, do, have*) or a modal (e.g. *will, can*) + a subject pronoun.

main clause	question tag
He's coming,	***isn't he****?*
They ***won't*** *go,*	***will they****?*

If there is no auxiliary or modal, use the correct form of *do*.

You know Dr Jones, ***don't you****?*
The doctor didn't phone, ***did she****?*

TIP

I'm in the main clause → ***aren't I*** in the question tag.
I'm right, aren't I?

3 Usually, if the main clause is affirmative, the question tag is negative.

She's a doctor, ***isn't she****?*
It could help, ***couldn't it****?*

If the main clause is negative, the question tag is affirmative.

You don't feel well, ***do you****?*
Mike won't be in hospital long, ***will he****?*

TIP

The intonation on the tag rises if it is a real question (i.e. if the speaker is not sure of the answer).

Canberra isn't the capital of Australia, is it? Sydney is bigger.

The intonation on the tag falls if the speaker is sure of the answer.

You're American, aren't you? You have an American accent.

4 Make a short answer with a subject pronoun and an auxiliary verb.

A: You're OK, aren't you? B: ***Yes, I am.***
A: Did you see the doctor? B: ***No, I didn't.***

▶ See Units 25 and 31 for more information on short answers.

Practice

A Match the sentence beginnings to the correct tags.

1 You don't like pizza, — e
2 It's a fact
3 The children know,
4 I'm not going,
5 His mum hasn't phoned,
6 They'll remember,
7 It didn't rain,
8 Simon can come,
9 I'm the winner,

a isn't it?
b aren't I?
c won't they?
d did it?
e do you?
f can't he?
g has she?
h am I?
i don't they?

B Complete the questions with the correct tags.

1 You're Mr Smith, *aren't you* ?
2 We aren't late, ... ?
3 I'm next, ... ?
4 He's having a meeting, ... ?
5 The dog won't bite, ... ?
6 You had fun at the party, ... ?
7 Your wife knows, ... ?
8 The workers made a mistake, ... ?
9 It hasn't snowed, ... ?
10 You don't have a brother, ... ?

C Write affirmative (✓) or negative (✗) short answers.

1 Is it 6 o'clock? (✓) *Yes, it is.*
2 Do you know Glenda? (✗) *No, I don't.*
3 Are you ready, Simon? (✓) ....
4 Is this my pen? (✗) ....
5 Did Dave tell you? (✓) ....
6 Have you two had dinner? (✗) ....
7 Can your cat swim? (✓) ....
8 Are the children coming? (✗) ....

D Sarah is a runner. She is talking to her doctor. Complete the dialogue with the correct question tags.

Doctor: Hello, you're Sarah, 1 *aren't you* ?
Sarah: Yes, I am. I'm not late, 2 .... ?
Doctor: No, don't worry. Now, your back isn't feeling good, 3 .... ?
Sarah: No, the pain is terrible. You don't have any aspirin, 4 .... ?
Doctor: Aspirin won't help. You've stopped training, 5 .... ?
Sarah: Almost. Jogging is all right, 6 .... ? Half an hour a day won't do any harm, 7 .... ?
Doctor: I suppose not.

E Change these statements into affirmative or negative questions with question tags.

1 *It's a dog, isn't it?*
2 ....
3 ....
4 ....

MY TURN!

In your notebook, write at least six questions with tags to ask a friend about a party he / she has been to. Ask about the guests, the music, the food, the time he / she left, etc.

Example: *The food was good, wasn't it?*

MY TEST!

Circle the correct option.

1 She eats a lot of chocolate, ... ? a isn't she b don't she c doesn't she
2 The doctor will tell me to do more exercise, ... ? a won't she b she won't c doesn't she
3 I'm getting very suntanned, ... ? Maybe I'm sunbathing too much. a am not I b aren't I c amn't I
4 You haven't been ill for a long time, ... you? a do b were c have
5 A: They shouldn't take vitamins every day, should they? B: No, ... a they should b shouldn't they c they shouldn't

My Test! answers: 1c 2a 3b 4c 5c

R6 Review: questions and answers

A Match the questions about Rosa to the correct answers.

1 Is Rosa beautiful? .... h
2 When is her birthday? .... ☐
3 Has she been to India? .... ☐
4 What does she like? .... ☐
5 What's she like? .... ☐
6 Why does she speak English well? .... ☐
7 Who likes her? .... ☐
8 Who does she like? .... ☐
9 Where does she live? .... ☐
10 How is she? .... ☐

a She's very nice.
b In February.
c We all like her. She's very popular.
d Yes, she has.
e Because her dad is from Scotland.
f She likes Brad Pitt. She thinks he's cool.
g She likes horses and dancing.
h Yes, she is.
i Not very well. She feels sick today.
j In the city centre.

B Make questions by putting the words in the correct order.

1 of / What / like / do / kind / music / you?
What kind of music do you like?
2 book / Who / favourite / wrote / your?
........?
3 your / are / How / parents / old?
........?
4 you / do / computer / Whose / use?
........?
5 are / friends / your / What / like?
........?
6 visited / How / have / many / you / countries?
........?
7 eyes / are / What / your / colour?
........?
8 games / you / How / do / often / computer / play?
........?
9 school / How / it / to / take / does / get / long / to?
........?

Now answer the questions for yourself.

C Complete the dialogues, using question tags, short answers and *so* or *neither*.

1 A You're 15, aren't you?
B No, I'm not. I'm 14.
A Really? So am I!

2 A You write poems, ...?
B No, ... I write songs.
A Do you? ....!

3 A You didn't go to Phil's party, ...?
B Yes, ... But I didn't go to Helen's party.
A Didn't you? ....!

4 A You can't speak Chinese, ...?
B Yes, ... But I can't speak Korean.
A Can't you? ....!

5 A You've lived here for eight years, ...?
B No, ... I've lived here for 11 years.
A Have you? ....!

6 A You don't like mushrooms, ...?
B Yes, ... But I don't like fish.
A Don't you? ....!

7 A Your sister is going on holiday to Peru, ...?
B No, ... She's going to Chile.
A Is she? .... my sister!

8 A Your brother has broken his arm, ...?
B No, ... He's broken his leg.
A Has he? .... my brother!

D Put the dialogue in the correct order. Write numbers 2–13 next to the lines.

1	a	A: Are you going to the concert tonight?
	b	B: Er ... no, I don't. Hey, the ticket has a photo of the band. Which one is your brother?
	c	A: No, he doesn't. He's a drummer. Have you heard him play?
	d	A: Because I prefer small concerts. I don't like it when hundreds of people are shouting.
	e	A: He's the one with long black hair and a big black hat. Do you think he looks cool?
	f	A: So do I. It's going to be really good. Did you know my brother is playing?
	g	A: Oh yes. He's fantastic. How many people will be there tonight?
	h	A: Heavy metal and hard rock. Do you like rock music?
	i	B: No, I haven't. Is he good?
	j	B: No, I didn't. Oh, I remember. He plays guitar, doesn't he?
	k	B: Neither do I. What kind of music does your brother play?
	l	B: Yes, I am. I love concerts.
	m	B: I don't know. Maybe 500. Why?
14	n	B: Er ... maybe.

E Complete each question with one word from Box A and one word from Box B.

A
~~How~~ How How How How What What What Which Whose

B
coffee ~~far~~ kind like long many much often one time

1 A: ...How far... is it from the Earth to the Moon?
B: 384,403 km.
2 A: .... does rabbit meat taste .... ?
B: It's a bit like chicken.
3 A: .... do you visit your grandparents?
B: About six times a year.
4 A: .... of computer games do you like?
B: I love fantasy games.
5 A: .... hats do you have?
B: Three. Two winter hats and a sun hat.
6 A: .... is this?
B: It's John's, he drinks about five cups a day.
7 A: .... were your shoes?
B: I paid 50 euros for them.
8 A: We have four different pizzas. .... do you want? B: Can I have that one, please?
9 A: .... is the journey from London to New York? B: About 7½ hours.
10 A: .... do you usually go to bed?
B: Between 10 pm and 11 pm.

F Read the text, then write a question for each answer.

Hi. My name's Tom and I'm 13 years old. I love computers. When I was 6 years old, I opened my mum's computer to see how it worked. She was very angry, because I couldn't put it back together. But I kept all the pieces and learnt about them, and when I was 8, I made a new computer for my mum. It was better than the old one, so she was very happy. Now I write computer games. I put my first game on my website when I was 10, and my friends all loved it. They said it was fantastic. I've written about eight games now, and they're all really good. Last week a man from a big software company wrote to me. He says he likes my new game, 'Ice Jungle', and he wants me to write games for them. So next week I'm going to London for a meeting. I'm very excited.

1 ...How old is Tom...? He's 13 years old.
2 ....? Computers.
3 ....? His mum's.
4 ....? Yes, she was. She was very angry.
5 ....?
Because he couldn't put it back together.
6 ....?
On his website.
7 ....?
About eight.
8 ....?
A man from a big software company.
9 ....?
His new one, 'Ice Jungle'.
10 ....?
To London.

33 *Have* and *have got*

Have you got a favourite crocodile?

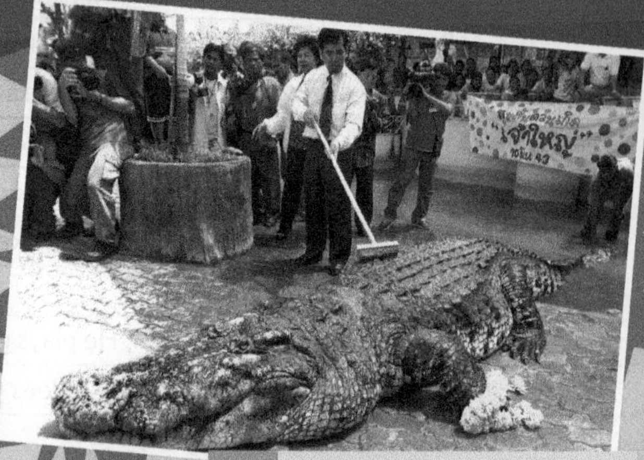

The Samutprakan Crocodile Farm (Thailand) **has got** over 60,000 crocodiles. The farm **has** a zoo, **it's got** a research centre and the shops, of course, **have** lots of crocodile souvenirs. Mr Utai **had the idea** of opening the museum in 1950. He **had some free time** yesterday to answer questions.

Question: **Does** the farm **have** any unusual crocodiles?

Mr Utai: **We've got** the biggest crocodile in the world. Come and see it **have breakfast** tomorrow morning!

Question: **Have you got** any plans for the future?

Mr Utai: I'm going to **have** a crocodile TV show. Crocodiles **haven't got** a good image. Hollywood films only show crocodiles trying to eat people! We need to **have** more information about crocodiles.

? Underline the correct option: Mr Utai *eats / likes / sells* crocodiles.

Answer: likes

Have and *have got*

1 We can say *have* or *have got*. *Have* is more common. We can use *have got* in conversation, especially in British English.

*The farm **has** a zoo.*
*It **has got** over 60,000 crocodiles.*
***Does** the farm **have** any unusual crocodiles?*

2 In the past and future, we can only use *have*.

*I'm going to **have** a crocodile TV show.*
*In 1950 the zoo didn't **have** many crocodiles.*
***Did** the shop **have** any crocodile T-shirts yesterday?*

3 We can use *have* + noun for many everyday activities. *Have* with activities can be in the continuous form.

*He didn't **have much free time** yesterday.*
*The crocodile **is having breakfast**.*

You can *have*:

an accident / a break / a rest / a sleep / a cold
tea / coffee; breakfast / lunch / dinner; a sandwich
a chat / a discussion / a talk
fun / a good time / a nice day / a holiday
a shower / a bath / a swim / a run / a walk

4 We do not use *have got* in the future or past. We use *have* instead.

I had a dog but it died. NOT ~~*I had got a dog ...*~~

5 Make questions and negatives with *have* using the auxiliary verb *do*.

***Do** you **have** a pen? She **doesn't have** it.*

	statement ✓	negative ✗
I / You / We / They	**have**	**do not (don't) have**
He / She / It	**has**	**does not (doesn't) have**

question ?	short answer ✓✗
Do I / you / we / they **have** ...?	Yes, (I) **do**. No, (I) **don't**.
Does he / she / it **have** ...?	Yes, (he) **does**. No, (he) **doesn't**.

6 Make negative forms of *have got* with *not*. Make questions with *Have / Has* + subject + *got* ...?

	statement ✓	negative ✗
I / You / We / They	**have ('ve) got**	**have not (haven't) got**
He / She / It	**has ('s) got**	**has not (hasn't) got**

question ?	short answer ✓✗
Have I / you / we / they **got** ...?	Yes, (I) **have**. No, (I) **haven't**.
Has he / she / it **got** ...?	Yes, (he) **has**. No, (he) **hasn't**.

Practice

A What do these people have? Use the information to make at least eight sentences with an appropriate pronoun and *have*, and write them in your notebook. Some sentences are negative.

	 dog	 sister	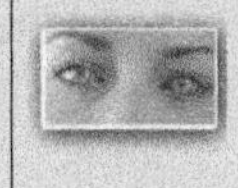 green eyes	 piano	 cold
Me	✓		✗		
Me and my brother		✗		✓	
Sarah			✓		✗
Brian		✗		✓	
Tom and Lucy	✗				✗

Examples: *I have a dog. We don't have a sister.* .

B A crocodile keeper is talking about his work. Underline the correct option. Sometimes both options are possible.

'I [1]*have / have got* a great job but it's very hard! The crocodiles [2]*have / have got* breakfast at 6 o'clock and some [3]*have / have got* special diets. After breakfast, we [4]*have / have got* a walk around the farm. Many visitors ask me, '[5]*Do crocodiles have / Have crocodiles got* fun in the farm?' I always answer, 'Of course!' They [6]*have / have got* a great time in the shows and we [7]*have / have got* lots of nice visitors. Last year I [8]*had / had got* a holiday in England and I went to London Zoo. The zoo [9]*had / had got* a lot of crocodiles but they [10]*didn't have / hadn't got* a special crocodile research centre. [11]*Do you have / Have you got* any questions?'

C Complete the sentences with the present or past of *have* or *have got* to make them true. Some sentences are negative.

1 Bill Gates *doesn't have / hasn't got* a university degree.
2 The English alphabet .... 26 letters.
3 Princess Diana .... a daughter.
4 Penguins .... wings.
5 Water .... vitamins.
6 The Romans .... a big empire.
7 Cats .... nine lives.
8 A beach volleyball team .... two players.

D Write sentences with *have* (*got*) in the present, past or future. Some are negatives or questions.

1 I *have* a dog; it's very nice.
2 We *haven't got* an uncle but we've got an auntie.
3 *Did you have* a cold last week?
4 She .... green hair. It looks strange!
5 All my friends .... mobile phones but I don't.
6 James couldn't run because he .... a broken leg.
7 France .... a King or Queen now.
8 I want to .... a holiday in Thailand.
9 .... Sharon .... your new phone number?
10 We .... a chat about it last night.
11 Are you going to .... a swim?
12 We .... time to .... coffee because we were late.
13 A: .... your new house .... a garden?
B: Yes, it ....

MY TURN!

In your notebook, write at least six questions, using *have* and *have got*, that you would like to ask a famous person.

Example: *Have you got a big house?*

MY TEST!

Circle the correct option.

1 How many teeth ....? a has a crocodile b has a crocodile got c a crocodile has got
2 When he was a child, he .... a baby crocodile as a pet. a had b has got c had got
3 A: Have crocodiles got cold blood? B: Yes, they .... a do b have got c have
4 They .... fish for breakfast. a usually have b usually have got c have usually got
5 .... a nice time at the farm? a Have you got b Are you having got c Are you having

My Test answers: 1b 2a 3c 4a 5c

34 Make, do and get

Do you get angry?

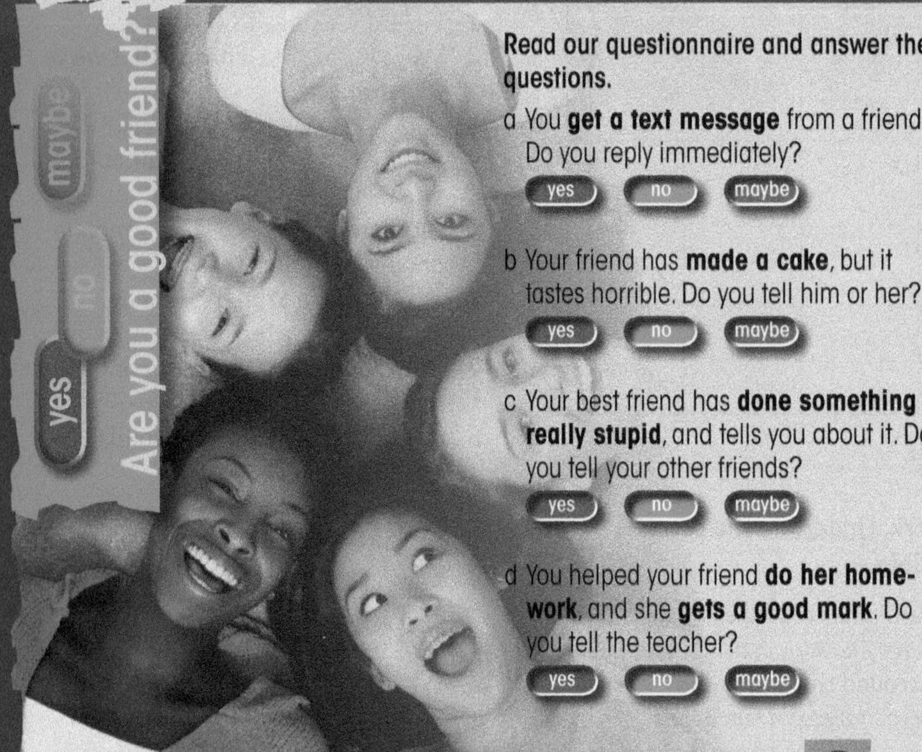

Read our questionnaire and answer the questions.

a You **get a text message** from a friend. Do you reply immediately?
yes no maybe

b Your friend has **made a cake**, but it tastes horrible. Do you tell him or her?
yes no maybe

c Your best friend has **done something really stupid**, and tells you about it. Do you tell your other friends?
yes no maybe

d You helped your friend **do her homework**, and she **gets a good mark**. Do you tell the teacher?
yes no maybe

e Your friend uses your phone and **makes a lot of calls**. Do you **get angry**?

f Do you always **get your friends a present** on their birthdays?

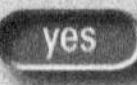  

Find out your score! **a** yes 5, maybe 3, no 0; **b** yes 0, maybe 3, no 5; **c** yes 0, maybe 0, no 5; **d** yes 0, maybe 0, no 5; **e** yes 3, maybe 3, no 5; **f** yes 5, maybe 3, no 3

KEY: 24–28 = You're a GREAT FRIEND! Your friends are lucky to know you.

13–23 = FAITHFUL FRIEND. You're a good friend, and you always think of others first. (But it's a good idea to tell your friends what you need, too.)

0–12 = You're NO FRIEND! (and soon you'll have no friends.)

What do you think? Are you a good friend?

Make, do and get

1 Use *make* to talk about producing something.

make a cup of coffee, make a cake, make a meal

When we say who we are making it for, we can say:

I made my dad a cake. OR *I made a cake for my dad.*
She makes them lunch. OR *She makes lunch for them.*

▶ **See Unit 37 for more verbs with two objects.**

2 Use *do* to talk about work and activities (which often end in *-ing*). You can *do*:

an exam	*the shopping*
exercise	*the washing*
(your) homework	*the washing-up*

3 *Make* and *do* are used in a number of expressions.

You can *make*:

the bed	*a mistake*	*a plan*	*sure*
a decision	*money*	*a phone call*	*a promise*
friends	*a noise*		

You can *do*:

your best	*nothing*	*well / badly*

4 *Get* can have different meanings. Use *get* + object to mean 'receive' or 'obtain'. You can *get*:

a bad / good mark
a letter
some milk from the shops (= buy)
a present
a text message

5 Use *get* + adjective to mean 'become'.

angry	*cold*	*late*
better	*dark*	*older*
bigger		

6 We can use *get* in other expressions. You can *get*:

on / off (a bus)	*dressed*
up	*to* (= arrive)
back (= return)	*lost*
a bus / train (= travel on)	*married*

TIP

We say *get to school* but *get home* (without *to*).

Practice

A Write each word / phrase from the box under the correct verb.

~~breakfast~~ a dress an exam exercise homework
a job a paper plane a salad the shopping the washing

do	make
....	breakfast
....	....
....	....
....	....
....	
....	

B Match the sentence beginnings to the most appropriate endings.

How to be a good friend ...

1 Text messages are fun but it's better to make — b
2 Don't be jealous if a friend makes new
3 Be happy when a friend does
4 And listen to her when she has done
5 Talk to your friends before you make an important
6 Say sorry if you make a
7 Nobody is perfect – just do
8 It's more important to make friends than make

a friends.
b a phone call.
c mistake.
d your best.
e well.
f money.
g badly.
h decision.

C Complete the sentences using a form of *get* and words from the box.

angry ~~a really bad mark~~ better dressed
late lost married some milk older
any text messages up

1 I'm going to stay home and study tonight. I got a really bad mark in my Maths exam.
2 My friend has been in hospital but she is slowly ....
3 It's OK to .... if you talk about it later.
4 It's .... We should go home.
5 My mobile phone isn't working. I don't like it when I don't ....
6 My brother is .... in February. Lots of people are coming to the wedding.
7 You will probably need to wear glasses when you ....
8 Could you .... me .... from the shop, please?
9 I didn't take a map and I soon ....
10 I .... late this morning. I .... and had breakfast in ten minutes!

MY TURN!

Make up the questions for a questionnaire and write them in your notebook. Use the options in brackets and *do, make* and *get*.

1 Your mum is feeling very tired. (a cup of coffee or a sandwich?)
Do you make her a cup of coffee or make her a sandwich?
2 You're hungry but the fridge is empty. (a pizza or the shopping?)
3 It's a sunny Sunday in the summer. (up early or up late?)
4 Your younger brother is really hungry but your mum and dad are not at home. (a snack or some lunch?)
5 You are late for school. (the bus or to school late?)
6 It's the summer holidays soon but you don't have any money. (a job or nothing?)

Now answer the questions.

MY TEST!

Circle the correct option.

1 It's my best friend's birthday, so I'm going to ....
a make a card her b make a card to her c make her a card
2 When you meet new people, is it easy to .... friends with them?
a make b do c get
3 My friend doesn't always get good grades, but he always .... his best.
a does b makes c gets
4 I'm sorry I'm late. I .... lost, and I couldn't find the café.
a made b did c got
5 Our plane was late, and we .... at midnight. It was terrible.
a got to home b made home c got home

My Test answers: 1c 2a 3a 4c 5c

35 Prepositional verbs

Think about it!

FOOD FACTS

Look at a menu in a restaurant in the United States and you'll find *French fries*. But don't **ask for** *French fries* when you go to France. The French call them *pommes frites* which means 'fried potatoes'.

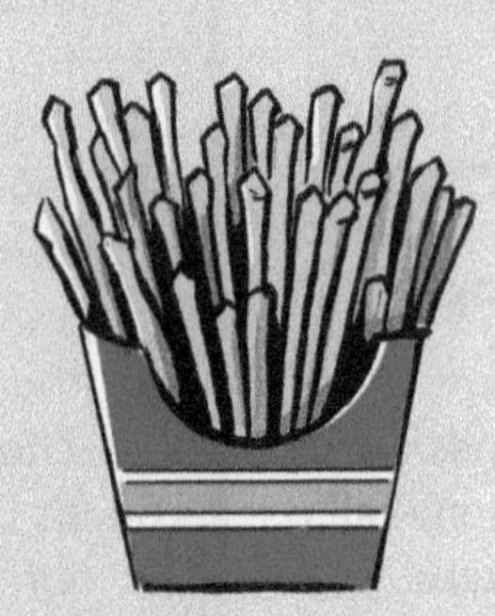

Do you **worry about** too much salt in your diet? Then listen to this – you need a little salt. Your body **depends on** salt for healthy blood pressure.

Think about it! Salmon **belongs to** a group of fish which have Omega-3. Omega-3 helps you think!

Why is salt good for you?

Answer: Your body needs it for healthy blood pressure.

Prepositional verbs

1 **Prepositional verbs have two words. The two words are: verb + preposition.**

Think ***about*** *it!*
Don't ***ask for*** *French fries.*
I'm ***listening to*** *some music.*

Other verbs include:

(dis)agree with	*depend on*	*learn about*	*suffer from*
believe in	*get off*	*look after*	*talk about*
belong to	*get on*	*look at*	*wait for*
come across	*go with*	*look for*	*worry about*
consist of	*laugh at*	*pay for*	

2 **Sometimes the meaning of the verb + preposition is very different from the meaning of the verb on its own.**

I didn't ***get*** *many birthday presents.*
Get off *the bus at the next stop.*

3 **Some verbs can be followed by a different preposition to give a different meaning.**

Look at *the menu.*
I'm ***looking for*** *my glasses – have you seen them?*
We ***looked after*** *my neighbour's dog last weekend.*

4 **Questions which begin with a *Wh-* word and use prepositional verbs often finish with the preposition.**

What are you looking ***at****?*

▶ See Units 26 and 27 for more information on forming questions.

Practice

A Complete these food facts with the correct form of the verbs in the box.

come across consist of depend on ~~go with~~ look after suffer from

1 Rosemary is the perfect herb to ....*go with*.... all kinds of meat.
2 Pineapples came to Europe in 1493 when Christopher Columbus .... them in the Caribbean.
3 An apple floats in water because it .... 25% air.
4 .... your body – eat at least five portions of fruit or vegetables every day.
5 A lot of people in my family .... high blood pressure.
6 Half of the world's population .... rice in their diets.

B Underline the correct option.

1 The politician agreed *with / on* everything the journalist said.
2 I want to go skiing this weekend, but it depends *on / of* the weather.
3 I'll ask *for / to* some help.
4 My parents are always worrying *in / about* something.
5 I was looking *for / after* my keys when he came in.
6 I'm not waiting *to / for* Flavia. She's always late.
7 I was just thinking *about / on* you.
8 He suffers *from / of* a lot of headaches.
9 That dog belongs *to / in* the waiter.
10 In this morning's History class we learnt *about / of* The Cold War.

C Complete the sentences with the correct verbs from the box.

believe come depend ~~get~~ get go look look

1 We don't ....*get*.... off here. It's the next station.
2 Do you .... in ghosts?
3 Nurses have to .... after some difficult people.
4 .... on the train! It's leaving!
5 .... at this photo in the paper.
6 That shirt doesn't .... with your trousers.
7 I've just .... across some old photos at the back of the cupboard.
8 Julia visits my grandparents every day. They really .... on her.

MY TURN!

Write appropriate questions for these replies. Use the verbs from the box in the correct tense.

~~agree with~~ belong to laugh at listen to look at pay for talk about ~~think about~~

1 A: *What are you thinking about?* B: Nothing much. I'm just really tired.
2 A: *Who agrees with Joe?* B: Me. We always like the same films.
3 A: .... B: My new CD.
4 A: ....
B: Colin just told me a really funny joke.
5 A: .... B: That jacket in the window.
6 A: ....
B: Oh, everything – their friends, their families, their jobs.
7 A: ....
B: Me. I forgot to take it home last night.
8 A: .... B: My brother. He's got lots of money!

Now use the verbs to make up your own questions and answers (at least five) about your friends. Write them in your notebook.

MY TEST!

Circle the correct option.

1 I'm looking .... the salt, but I can't find it. Have you seen it? **a** at **b** after **c** for
2 A: What ....? B: You. We didn't want to start eating without you.
a are you waiting for **b** you are waiting for **c** for are you waiting
3 A: Who does this 'Food Facts' book ....? B: It's Alan's. **a** depend on **b** consist of **c** belong to
4 I don't .... in diets. I think they're a waste of time and money. **a** believe **b** agree **c** worry
5 Sorry – I've forgotten my money. Could you ....? **a** for me pay **b** me pay for **c** pay for me

My Test! answers: 1c 2a 3c 4a 5c

Phrasal verbs

A friend to tidy up your room

Do you need a friend to welcome you home, **wash up** and **tidy up** your room? And never **tell** you **off** or need to **lie down**?
Sadly for you, that's still just a dream.
But things could get better with … Asimo.

Just some of the things Asimo can do:

- **turn** lights **on**
- carry things
- wave
- recognise ten different faces
- climb steps
- run (without falling over – not easy for a robot!).

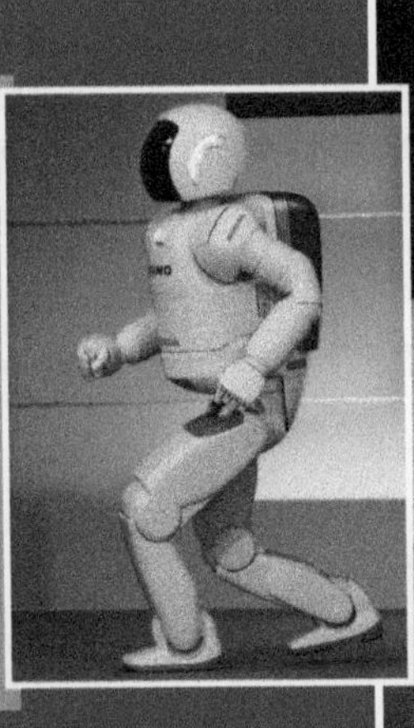

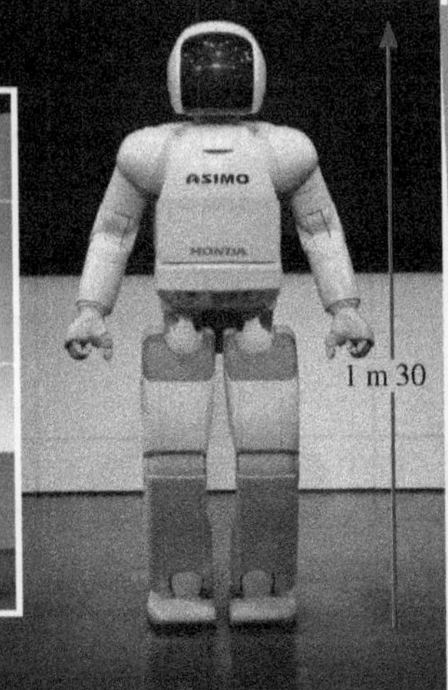

Honda's Asimo is the most advanced humanoid robot in the world. One day Asimo may help people or work in places which are dangerous for humans.

FACT

But it's not all good …
You need to **charge up** Asimo after only one hour.
Each Asimo robot costs nearly $1 million to make.

? What can Asimo not do?
a wave b run
c work all day d go upstairs

Answer: c

Phrasal verbs

1 Phrasal verbs have two words. The two words are: verb + adverb particle. Some phrasal verbs have an object and some don't.

Asimo can't ***tidy up*** *your room.*
Asimo doesn't need to ***lie down.***

2 Some phrasal verbs which we often use without an object are:

break down	*get up*	*run away*	*wake up*
find out	*hurry up*	*sit down*	*wash up*
get back	*lie down*	*stand up*	

3 Some phrasal verbs which we commonly use with an object are:

charge up	*put on*	*throw away*	*turn off / on*
look up	*take back*	*tidy up*	
pick up	*tell off*	*turn down*	

4 There are some verbs we can use in both ways, e.g. ***give up, take off, turn up.***

He's given up smoking.
Never give up!

Sometimes the verb has a different meaning in each case.

The plane has just taken off. (no object = *leave the airport*)
Take off your shoes, please. (with object = *remove*)
They turned up late. (no object = *arrive*)
Can you turn the music up? (with object = *make louder*)

5 If the phrasal verb takes an object, it can usually go before or after the adverb particle.

Asimo can ***turn*** *lights* ***on.***
Asimo can ***turn on*** *lights.*

But the object always comes before the adverb particle if it is a personal pronoun.

Asimo can turn them on.
NOT ~~*Asimo can turn on them.*~~

TIP

We often use prepositional and phrasal verbs in informal speech and writing and one-word verbs in more formal contexts. For example, ***We returned in the evening*** **is more formal than** ***We got back in the evening.***

TIP

Some verbs mean the same if they are used as one-word verbs, but then they sound more formal, e.g ***wake = wake up, tidy = tidy up, lie = lie down, sit = sit down.***

▶ **See Unit 35 for more information on prepositional verbs.**

Practice

A Complete the text using the phrasal verbs from the box in the correct tense.

break down find out get back lie down hurry up ~~run away~~ take off wake up

I hadn't seen Jason for six weeks. He [1] ......ran away...... after the fight with his brother. I got a postcard from New York and that was all I knew. Where was he? Was he OK? I had to [2] .... On the last night in November I [3] .... late. I [4] .... on the sofa and fell asleep right there. When I finally [5] ...., it was 10 o'clock the next morning. For a moment I couldn't think what day it was. And then I remembered – it was Sunday and today I was going to find Jason.
[6]'................, Jack,' I said to myself. 'The plane mustn't [7] .... without you.'
It was icy cold outside. I threw my bags in the car and started the engine. The car jumped forward and stopped. I couldn't believe it. This was not a good time for the car to [8] ....

B Rewrite each phrasal verb sentence using an appropriate noun object instead of the pronoun. Rewrite each sentence in two different ways.

1 My mum says I can't go out until I have tidied it up.
My mum says I can't go out until I have tidied my room up / until I have tidied up my room.

2 Take them off! The sun isn't shining in the house.
....

3 The beach is really dirty. People should pick it up when they go home.
....
....

4 It's too dark in here. Turn them on!
....

5 I can't ring Louie. I need to charge it up first.
....
....

6 Let's have a party! Turn it up!
....

7 They were writing on the wall. The policeman told them off.
....
....

8 When you sit in a car, you need to put it on.
....
....

9 You can't leave. I've locked the door and thrown it away.
....
....

C Complete the dialogues using the verbs in the box and appropriate adverb particles. Use the structure: verb + pronoun + adverb particle.

give look put ~~take~~ tell throw turn turn

1 A: I bought these shoes but they're too small.
B: *Take them back!*
2 A: What do you think of this hat?
B: It's great! Why don't you ....?
3 A: I don't know what this word means.
B: ....
4 A: The music is too loud.
B: Why don't you ....?
5 A: The little girl was really rude to me!
B: Why didn't you ....?
6 A: We've had these biscuits for weeks.
B: ....
7 A: The TV is boring.
B: Why don't you ....?
8 A: I don't enjoy learning to play the piano.
B: Why don't you ....?

MY TURN!

What activities would you like a robot to do for you? Write at least five sentences in your notebook using verbs from page 88.
Example: *I'd like it to tidy up my bedroom.*

MY TEST!

Circle the correct option.

1 I always leave my dirty clothes on the floor. Asimo .... and washes them.
a picks them up b them picks up c picks up them
2 Asimo can clean your shoes, but you have to .... them off first.
a turn b take c tell
3 This robot is broken, so I'm going to take .... to the shop.
a it back b back it c back
4 Asimo .... my T-shirt. He thought it was rubbish!
a ran away b broke down c threw away
5 Asimo always .... after a meal.
a looks up b picks up c washes up

My Test! answers: 1a 2b 3a 4c 5c

37 Verbs with two objects

Tell your friends the truth.

ARE YOU ASSERTIVE?

Answer the questionnaire to find out.

1 You **lend your friend €80**, but she doesn't give it back. Do you ...
a ask for the money back?
b never **lend money to her** again?
c forget about it?

2 Your uncle **gives you a book** for your birthday. You already have it. Do you ...
a tell him the truth?
b take it and give it away?
c say thank you and keep it?

3 A classmate **sells your young sister his bike**. It doesn't work. Do you ...
a ask for your money back?
b ask for a little money back?
c **buy your sister a new bike?**

4 A friend **sends an email to some classmates**. You see it. There is some information about you which is not true. Do you ...
a make sure your friend **tells your classmates the truth?**
b **send an email to your classmates?**
c not go to school for a week?

Mostly a answers: you're very assertive. No one worries you.
Mostly b answers: you're a diplomat, but is that always the best thing?
Mostly c answers: life is not easy for you. How can you change this?

? What do you think? Are you assertive?

Verbs with two objects

1 **Some verbs have two objects. Examples include *bring, buy, get, give, lend, make, offer, read, sell, send, show, tell, throw*.**

subject	verb	direct object	*to*	indirect object
You	lend	€80	to	your friend.
She	sends	an email	to	some classmates.

2 **We can also put the indirect object first and take out *to*.**

	verb	indirect object	+ direct object.
You	lend	your friend	€80.
NOT ~~*You lend to your friend €80.*~~			

TIP
With the verb *tell*, we prefer to say:
I told him the truth. NOT ~~*I told the truth to him.*~~

3 **Use *for* not *to* with *buy, get* and *make*.**
She bought lunch ***for*** *me.*
She got some milk ***for*** *him.*
We made a cake ***for*** *our parents.*

Again, we can put the indirect object first.
She bought me lunch. NOT ~~*She bought for me lunch.*~~
She got him some milk.
We made our parents a cake.

Practice

A Rewrite the questions without *to* or *for*.

1 Your friend has a new haircut. It doesn't look good. Do you tell the truth to your friend?
Do you tell your friend the truth ?

2 You were playing with your sister's phone and now it's not working. Do you get a new phone for your sister?
.... ?

3 Your cousin wants to go out on Saturday night. You don't want to go. Do you phone or send a text message to him?
.... ?

4 An old woman gets on the bus. There are no seats. Do you offer your seat to the old woman?
.... ?

5 Your mum is not feeling well and doesn't want to make lunch. Do you make lunch for your family?
.... ?

6 Your Maths teacher talks very fast and you don't understand the lessons.
Do you tell the problem to her?
.... ?

7 You want to learn to drive, but you have no money. Does your dad give driving lessons to you?
.... ?

B What are the people doing? Use the words in brackets and make sentences similar to the example.

1

He is showing the teenager / her the CDs.
(show the CDs)

2
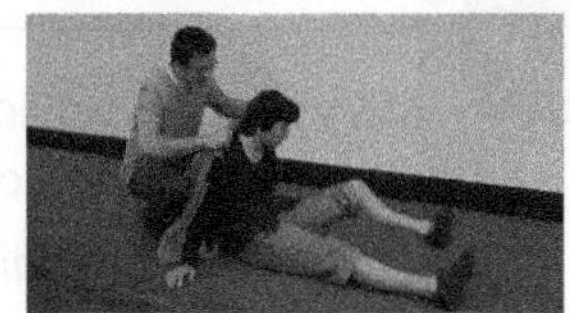
....
(lend his jacket)

3

....
(make a cake)

4

....
(give some flowers)

5
....
(throw the frisbee)

6
....
(buy some balloons)

C In your notebook, write at least six different sentences using these words.

the woman me her the boy I	made sold gave sent	a cup of tea a new bike a present a message	to for

Example: *The woman gave me a cup of tea.*

MY TURN!

What can you do for these people? In your notebook, write suggestions using the verbs in brackets.

1 It's your mum's birthday. (buy)
Buy her a present. / Buy a present for her.
2 Your little cousins are bored. (read)
3 A poor man needs help. (give)
4 Your little brother is hungry. (make)
5 I'm thirsty. (bring)
6 A friend doesn't know the answer to 12 x 12. (tell)
7 A friend needs to make a phone call. (lend)

MY TEST!

Circle the correct option.

1 Do you remember? I lent .... last week.
a €80 you b to you €80 c you €80
2 Why did you tell .... ?
a her my secret b to her my secret
c my secret her
3 I think you've got my phone in your bag. Can you show ...., please?
a me to it b it for me c it to me
4 I've .... these earrings for you. Do you like them?
a made b given c lent
5 When you go to the shop, you can buy ....
a to me a present b for me a present
c me a present

My Test! answers: 1c 2a 3c 4a 5c

38 Verb + *-ing* or verb + *to*-infinitive; *like* and *would like*

Learn to speak any language in two weeks!

Do you **like travelling**? Do you **enjoy meeting** people? Do you **want to communicate** with people easily? **Would you like to speak** other languages? If your answer is 'yes' to any of these questions then we have the product for you – **Super Lingo!**

Learn to speak any language in two weeks with our new **Super Lingo!** system. Yes, two weeks! And thanks to your big vocabulary, you won't **need to carry** a dictionary around with you.

If you **decide to try** **Super Lingo!** then telephone 095 973 2593 or send an email to i.smith@superlingo.net. We **promise to give** your money back if you're not happy.

We **hope to hear** from you soon!

? Underline the correct option: Super Lingo! is *a dictionary / a study programme / a language school.*

Answer: a study programme

Verb + *-ing* or verb + *to*-infinitive; *like* and *would like*

1 Some verbs, e.g. *enjoy*, take another verb with *-ing*.

*I **enjoy learning** English.*
*I **finished talking**.*

2 Some verbs, e.g. *want*, take another verb with *to*-infinitive.

*I **want to learn** English.*
*I **decided to try** the course.*

3 Some can take either *-ing* or *to*-infinitive.

*I **like helping** people.*
OR *I **like to help** people.*

Only *-ing*	Only *to*-infinitive		*-ing* or *to*-infinitive
avoid	*decide*	*plan*	*begin*
enjoy	*hope*	*promise*	*continue*
finish	*intend*	*refuse*	*hate*
mind	*learn*	*wait*	*like*
suggest	*need*	*want*	*love*
	offer		*prefer*
			start

TIP

***Very much* is an adverb, so it cannot go between the verb and the object.**

*I **like playing** tennis **very much**.*
NOT *~~I like very much playing tennis.~~*

▶ See Unit 56 for more information on the word order of adverbs.

TIP

When you learn a new verb, learn what comes after it.

decide /dɪ'saɪd/
▶ ***verb* 1** Ⓔ [I OR T] to choose something, especially after thinking carefully about several possibilities: *They have to decide by next Friday.* ○ *I don't mind which one we have – you decide.*
○ [+ **to** INFINITIVE] *In the end, we decided to go to the theatre.*

4 *Would like* (short form: *'d like*) is one way of saying *want* or *might want*. The negative is *would not* (short form: *wouldn't*). Use *Would you like* + *to*-infinitive for a polite invitation.

*I **would like to learn** Greek one day.*
*You **wouldn't like to be** in a strange town without any money.*
***Would** you **like to come** to the cinema with me?*

Practice

A Complete the sentences using the verbs in brackets in the *-ing* or *to*-infinitive form.

1 Do you promise ...to tidy... your room this weekend (tidy)?
2 I've always wanted .... a dog (have).
3 Would you mind .... the window, please (open)? It's too hot here.
4 Dogs don't enjoy .... at home all day (be).
5 Philip refused .... to my advice (listen).
6 Did the hotel offer .... your room (change)?
7 Children love .... to the circus (go).
8 We don't need .... an umbrella with us (take).
9 You should avoid .... too many sweet things (eat).
10 The workers finished .... the house (paint).

B Rewrite these sentences using the correct forms of *like* and *would like*.

1 Do you want a banana?
Would you like a banana?
2 I enjoy playing tennis.
....
3 My dream is to be a chef.
....
4 Do you want to see my paintings?
....
5 Going to the theatre is interesting for us.
....
6 Can I get you a drink?
....

C Underline the correct option.

Most teenagers like [1]*spend* / *spending* time in front of the TV, but is this a good thing? Is TV just a way of avoiding [2]*to do* / *doing* something more useful? Some people think that most TV programmes are not right for teenagers. 'Teenagers need [3]*to have* / *having* better programmes,' agrees TV producer Erica Johnson. 'Our TV company promises [4]*to make* / *making* educational programmes which teenagers will enjoy [5]*to watch* / *watching*.' Erica suggests [6]*to create* / *creating* a special channel for teenagers. 'Teenagers want [7]*to be* / *being* different, so a different channel is a good idea. TV is a great way of learning. Teenagers can learn [8]*to understand* / *understanding* the world through television.' What do teenagers think? Emily, 13, said, 'It's a bad idea. We have enough channels already. I wouldn't like [9]*to see* / *seeing* one more.' Erica said, 'We are planning [10]*to show* / *showing* the first programme on this new channel next spring.'

D Complete the email with the verbs from the box. The verbs should be *-ing* or *to*-infinitive forms.

buy ~~complain~~ get hear learn listen spend study teach write

To: i.smith@superlingo.net

I want [1] ...to complain... about Super Lingo. My wife and I decided [2] .... Super Lingo because we needed [3] .... Arabic very quickly for a business trip. You promised [4] .... us Arabic in two weeks. We started [5] .... a month ago and finished [6] .... to all the CDs last week. And now? We know nothing! Super Lingo is useless! The course was very difficult and boring. We certainly didn't enjoy [7] .... hours translating poems from Arabic into English.

I was very angry, so my wife suggested [8] .... this email to you. Please give us back our money immediately; we'd like [9] .... it this week. We hope [10] .... from you soon.

Jane & Peter Stevens

MY TURN!

In your notebook, write at least six true sentences about yourself using the verbs on page 92.

Examples: *I want to be a doctor.*
My uncle likes skiing very much.

MY TEST!

Circle the correct option.

1 If you want to learn a language, you need .... for years and years. a study b studying c to study
2 I've .... to learn Russian. a finished b decided c enjoyed
3 I .... studying every day. a don't mind b don't want c don't need
4 The Super Lingo! system didn't work, but they refused .... me my money back. a to give b to gave c giving
5 .... like to buy my Super Lingo! system? a Do you would b You would c Would you

My Test! answers: 1c 2b 3a 4a 5c

39 State verbs

Imagine a story.

Do you **know** that your brain is actually divided into two halves?

Scientists today **believe** that the two halves of your brain **have** different functions. When you **remember** things like words, numbers or lists, you are exercising the left side of your brain. When you **see** colours, **hear** the rhythm in your favourite song or **imagine** a story, you are using the right side of your brain.

When you are using only one side of your brain, it is similar to walking on only one leg. It **seems** learning is easier when you use both sides of your brain.

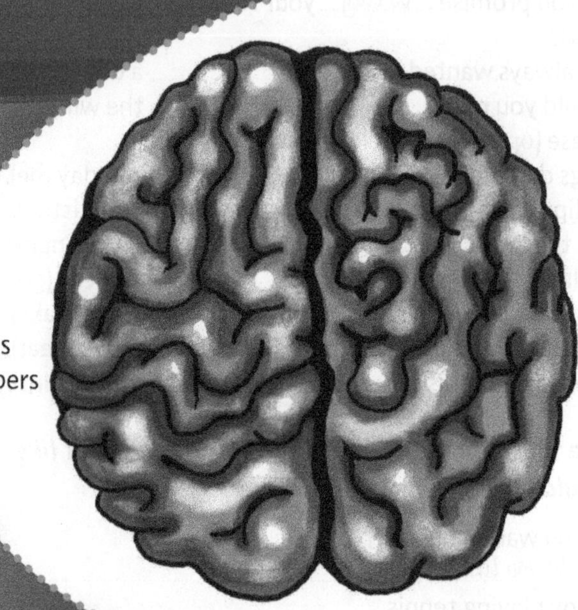

? True or False? The left and right sides of the brain are the same.

Answer: False

State verbs

1 **State verbs usually describe a state and not an action. We usually use them in the simple form, not the continuous.**

When you ***see*** *colours ...* NOT ~~*When you are seeing ...*~~

2 **Other state verbs include:**

verbs of thinking and knowing	verbs of the senses	verbs of feeling	verbs of possession
forget	*feel*	*believe*	*belong*
imagine	*hear*	*doubt*	*own*
know	*see*	*feel*	
mean	*smell*	*hate*	
realise	*sound*	*like*	
recognise	*taste*	*love*	
remember		*prefer*	
understand		*want*	

other

appear	*agree*	*contain*	*depend on*
be	*promise*	*fit*	*need*
seem		*include*	

3 **Some common state verbs can have a continuous form with a different meaning.**

He ***has*** *two brothers.* (state verb = *own* / *possess*)
He ***is having*** *a good holiday.* (activity)
That cake ***looks*** *nice.* (state verb = *seem*)
I'm ***looking*** *at these photos.* (activity)
I ***think*** *it's a great idea.* (state verb = *have the opinion*)
I'm ***thinking*** *about tomorrow.* (activity)

TIP

We often use the verbs of sense (*see*, *smell*, *hear*, *taste*) with *can*.

I ***can smell*** *coffee.*
He ***can't hear*** *you.*

▶ **See Unit 20 for more information on *can*.**
▶ **See Unit 28 for more information on verbs of the senses.**

Practice

A Match the beginnings to the correct endings.

1	Humans have	a	the brain has two halves.
2	The brain is	b	colours.
3	The left and right sides of the brain have	c	oxygen to survive.
4	Scientists think	d	75% water.
5	The brain needs	e	words and numbers.
6	With the right side of the brain, you see	f	different ways of working.
7	With the left side of the brain, you recognise	g	a very complex brain.

B Underline the correct option.

1. I *promise / am promising* I won't tell anyone.
2. I don't know this word. What *does it mean / is it meaning*?
3. I saw your daughter yesterday. She*'s growing / grows* up fast.
4. I *disagree / am disagreeing* completely with what you are saying.
5. Don't talk to Dad. He *watches / is watching* TV!
6. My parents *don't understand / are not understanding* why I want to stop piano lessons.
7. *Do you remember / Are you remembering* that day we spent in Capri?
8. *Do computers become / Are computers becoming* more difficult to use?
9. *It seems / It's seeming* a shame not to go.
10. I *don't doubt / am not doubting* that you are right.
11. Are you OK? You *don't listen / are not listening* to me.
12. He *believes / is believing* everything she says.

C Do these sentences describe states or activities? Complete the sentences with the correct forms of the verbs in brackets.

1. We ...don't have... very much money. (have)
2. A: Hi, Stan. You look worried!
   B: I .... about tomorrow's meeting – that's all. (think)
3. Where is Carlo? He .... a shower. (have)
4. That food .... great. (look)
5. They .... a baby. He is six months old. (have)
6. My dad .... the party is a good idea. (not think)
7. What .... you .... at? (look)

MY TURN!

Use your imagination to answer the questions with full sentences in your notebook. Use your own ideas or words from the box.

alone	birds	bitter	dry sand	excited
flowers	frightened	hard	the horizon	
insects	nothing	smooth	soft	
sweet	the wind			

You are in the ***jungle****.*

1. How do you feel? ...I feel excited.
2. What can you smell?
3. What can you hear?

You pick an exotic fruit.

4. What does it feel like?
5. How does it taste?

You are in the ***desert****.*

6. What can you smell?
7. What can you hear?
8. What can you see?
9. How do you feel?

MY TEST!

Circle the correct option.

1. This song .... really beautiful. Who is the singer? a is sounding b sounding c sounds
2. A: You're using the wrong side of your brain. B: Sorry. ....
   a I don't understand b I'm not understand c I'm not understanding
3. A: You're very quiet, Tom. B: Yes, sorry. .... about my holiday. a I think b I'm thinking c I'm think
4. It's very noisy here, and .... you. a I'm not hearing b I don't hear c I can't hear
5. You're very good with colours and stories. .... you're probably using the right side of your brain.
   a That's mean b That means c That's meaning

My Test answers: 1c 2a 3b 4c 5b

R7 Review: verb structures

A Match the sentence beginnings to the correct endings.

1 He used to play the violin but he had to give
2 Please turn the music
3 Please pick
4 I asked my mum
5 My teacher told me
6 She never stops talking
7 My phone was broken,
8 I wake
9 The plane took
10 I lent him
11 I phoned the theatre to find
12 I have to tidy up

a my pen, but he didn't give it back.
b off because I didn't do my homework.
c off at 7 pm, three hours late.
d up at 6 every morning, I hate it!
e so I took it back.
f out what time the show starts.
g my room before I go out.
h down, I'm trying to concentrate.
i up your clothes from the floor.
j about her daughter.
k for some money, but she said 'No'.
l it up when he broke his arm.

1 l 2 ...... 3 ...... 4 ...... 5 ...... 6 ...... 7 ...... 8 ...... 9 ...... 10 ...... 11 ...... 12 ......

B Make full sentences from the words.

1 I / love / listen / music.
I love listening to music.
2 Yesterday / David / suggest / go bowling tonight.
....
3 My mum / decide / throw away / my old trainers / yesterday.
....
4 We / want / make / a birthday card / Sharon.
....
5 Last night / I / finish / study / 10 pm.
....
6 I / not mind / wait / you.
....
7 She / promise / take / me / cinema
....
8 Last week / Duncan / offer / buy / me / a ticket.
....
9 I / need / speak / Jo / now.
....
10 Alison / refuse / pay / her dinner.
....

C Make questions from the sentences using the words in brackets.

1 Your sister would like ? for her birthday. (What ... ?)
What would your sister like for her birthday?
2 Steven has ? brothers. (How many ... ?)
....
3 I'm worried about ? (What ... ?)
....
4 This guitar belongs to ? (Who ... ?)
....
5 We've got a ? house. (What kind of ... ?)
....
6 The plane took off at ? (What time ... ?)
....
7 This word means ? (What ... ?)
....
8 Pauline would like to go ? (Where ... ?)
....
9 This sandwich tastes ? (What ... like?)
....
10 They were waiting for ? (Who ... ?)
....

D Complete the text using the words in the box.

bought getting getting ~~got~~ got had laughed looked made make offered planned prefer sat turned wait wanted

Yesterday I [1]..........got.......... really angry with Wendy. We [2]..........
to meet at 3 pm at the shopping centre. I [3].......... to buy some new shoes, and Wendy
[4].......... to help me choose. I always [5].......... shopping with a friend,
because I can never [6].......... a decision. Last time I went shopping alone I
[7].......... a mistake and bought a very ugly hat, and all my friends [8]..........
at me.
I started [9].......... worried about her when she still wasn't there at 5 pm. It was [10]..........
dark, but I couldn't phone her because her phone was broken. When she [11].......... up she
[12].......... terrible. She [13].......... down and explained. 'Sorry I'm late. I
[14].......... on the wrong bus. Then the bus [15].......... an accident and I had
to [16].......... for the police. It was terrible.' So I [17].......... her a coffee and
she told me the whole story.

E Complete the advert. Use one word in each gap.

Salsa Club

Do you love dancing? Do you want to get some exercise? Would you like to learn something new? Do you want to make friends? Do you enjoy listening [1]........to........ Latin American music? Then come [2].................. our Salsa Club!

Do you think you can't dance? Do you think people will laugh [3].................. you? Don't worry [4].................. that! You don't have to be a good dancer – just come and have fun. We can help you to be a great dancer, but it depends [5].................. YOU! Just do your best and you'll do well. The course consists [6].................. 20 lessons, so you have lots of time to get better and better.

So what are you waiting [7]..................? Put [8].................. your dancing shoes and come to Salsa Club!

F Cross out all the wrong options.

1. She ~~*had*~~ / *is having* / ~~*is got*~~ a good time at the moment.
2. We *had got* / *is having* / *had* an accident on the way home last night.
3. What time did you get *by* / *from* / *to* work?
4. He's looking *up* / *after* / *like* his baby brother while his parents are at work.
5. We looked *after* / *up* / *at* the long word in a dictionary.
6. She *is look* / *is looking* / *looks* like her grandmother.
7. Did you look *at* / *for* / *after* your keys in the kitchen?
8. I*'d like* / *liking* / *liked* to go out for dinner tonight.
9. They *like to* / *are liking* / *like* swimming in the lake.
10. *Think of* / *Think about* / *Think* coming with us tomorrow.
11. When did your visitors finally turn *over* / *up* / *down* last night?
12. The music was too quiet so I *turned it down* / *turned up it* / *turned it up*.

40 Countable and uncountable nouns

Where does sand come from?

Grains of sand are really very small pieces of rock. It takes a long time to change rock into sand. On beaches, waves hit the rock and break it up. The salt in the sea water also attacks the rocks. Rain, ice and wind are important too.

The sand on the beach can be many different colours. Tropical white sand usually comes from white limestone rock. Red sand means there is iron in the rocks. Sand from volcanic rock can be black or even green.

? Name three things that break up rock and make sand.

Answers: waves, salt in the sea, rain, ice, wind

Countable and uncountable nouns

1 Countable nouns are nouns we can count. They have singular and plural forms. Use the articles *a* or *an* before a singular noun.
a beach, an apple, a wave

Use words like *some, many, twenty* or nothing before a plural noun.
some beaches, many rocks, two apples, waves

2 Uncountable nouns often refer to liquids, materials, general concepts and abstract qualities. Uncountable nouns are singular – they don't usually have plural forms.
The homework is easy. NOT ~~*The homeworks are easy.*~~

Don't use *a* or *an* before uncountable nouns; use words like *some, any, no* or no article.
some sand, no rain, furniture, time

▶ See Unit 45 for more information on *some, any* and *no*.
▶ See Unit 47 for more information on *many*.

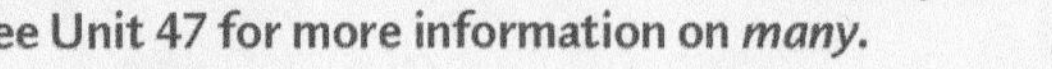

TIP

Some nouns which are uncountable in English may be countable in your own language. In English, these nouns are uncountable:

accommodation	*furniture*	*knowledge*	*music*	*traffic*
advice	*homework,*	*luggage*	*news*	*transport*
fruit	*information*	*money*	*pasta*	

Can I have some information? NOT ~~*Can I have some informations*~~?

3 Some nouns can be both countable and uncountable with a difference in meaning.

rock (uncountable = the material)

a rock (countable = a piece of rock)

coffee (uncountable = the substance)

a coffee (countable = a cup of coffee)

hair (uncountable)

a hair (countable = one hair)

4 Uncountable nouns can be countable if we use expressions such as:
a piece of advice / fruit / information / news
a slice of bread / toast / cheese
a bar of chocolate
a cup of coffee / tea
a grain of sand
a glass of water

Practice

A Which of these words can be used in the plural?

~~accommodation~~ ~~bag~~ beach bread car cotton cup furniture happiness job luggage melon piece room table traffic wave work

can be used in the plural: bag, ...

can't be used in the plural: accommodation, ...

B Complete the text by writing *a*, *an* or – (= no article).

Where does [1] – chocolate come from?
Next time you buy [2] .... bar of chocolate, think about where it came from. Did you know that it is made from [3] .... cocoa butter? This butter comes from the beans of [4] .... *cacao* trees. They grow mainly in South America and Africa.

Amazing Chocolate Facts

- ★ The Aztecs thought [5] .... cocoa beans were very important. They believed that the beans brought [6] .... wisdom.
- ★ The Aztecs and the Maya used the beans to make [7] .... hot drink.
- ★ The word 'chocolate' comes from [8] .... word in the Aztec language, *xocoatl*.
- ★ The Spanish brought [9] .... cocoa to Europe in the 16th century. They mixed the beans with [10] .... sugar.
- ★ There is [11] .... iron in cocoa.
- ★ There are 5 mg of caffeine in 25 g of milk chocolate. In [12] .... cup of coffee, there are about 100 mg of caffeine.

C Underline the correct option.

1. Did you show your *homework / homeworks* to Miss Elliot?
2. The woman gave me some useful *information / informations*.
3. Let's make some cheese *sandwich / sandwiches*.
4. Black sand *come / comes* from volcanic rock.
5. Can you give me some *advice / advices*?
6. He has long *hair / hairs* and dark *eye / eyes*.
7. Spaghetti *is / are* my favourite food.
8. There are a lot of *bus / buses* in the city centre.
9. Good *luck / lucks* in your new job.
10. The news *is / are* not very good.

MY TURN!

Complete the sentences using the words from the box. Use the countable nouns in either the singular or plural form.

car food friend good looks knowledge love money music weekend work

Examples:
Work is important to me.
A car isn't important to me.
Friends are important to me.

1. .... important to me.
2. I cannot live without ....
3. .... the best!
4. .... not essential in life.
5. .... all you need.
6. .... last forever.
7. Everyone needs ....
8. .... beautiful.

MY TEST!

Circle the correct option.

1. When I came home from the beach, my socks were full of ....
   a red grain of sand b red grains of sand c a red grain of sand
2. I found .... on the beach, so I picked it up and took it home.
   a beautiful rock b a beautiful rock c some beautiful rocks
3. I didn't eat my bar of .... because it fell on the sand. a bread b chocolate c pasta
4. I always listen to Paul when I need some good .... a informations b advice c knowledges
5. Could I have ...., please? a two coffees b two cup of coffees c two coffee

My Test! answers: 1b 2b 3b 4b 5a

41 Plural nouns

He ate 47 sandwiches in ten minutes.

Amazing people

Ron Hill (England) has run 115 **marathons**. He has run more than 290,000 **kilometres** – five **times** around the world.

Susan Baker (Australia) loves the colour orange. Her house is full of orange **things**, everything from **cups** and **knives** to **dresses** and **pyjamas**.

Joey Chestnut (USA) can eat 47 cheese **sandwiches** in ten **minutes**.

Mulai Ismail (Emperor of Morocco) had a lot of **children**. **Records** for 1703 show he had 342 **daughters** and 525 **sons**.

Enid Blyton (England) wrote more than 800 **books** and short **stories** for young people. You can read **translations** of her books in almost 90 different **languages**.

?

Match the numbers to the plural nouns:

1 47	a marathons
2 90	b sons
3 115	c languages
4 525	d sandwiches

Answers: 1d 2c 3a 4b

Plural nouns

1 There are countable and uncountable nouns. Countable nouns (e.g. *chair, apple*) can be in the plural (e.g. *chairs, apples*). Uncountable nouns (e.g. *advice, information*) cannot usually be in the plural (~~*advices, informations*~~).

▶ See Unit 40 for more information on countable and uncountable nouns.

In the plural we usually add *-s*.

banana → bananas, cat → cats, garden → gardens

If the word ends in *-s, -ch, -sh, -x*, we add *-es*.

dress → dresses
sandwich → sandwiches
wish → wishes
box → boxes

Many words ending *-f(e)* end in *-ves* in the plural.

knife → knives, loaf → loaves, wife → wives

If the word ends in consonant + *-y*, we change the *-y* to *-ie*.

story → stories, city → cities

But if the word ends in vowel + *-y*, we just add *-s*.

day → days, monkey → monkeys

Some words ending in *-o* take *-s*, but some take *-es*.

piano → pianos, photo → photos,
potato → potatoes, tomato → tomatoes

▶ See page 183 for more spelling rules.

2 Some common nouns have special plurals.

child → children	*person → people*
fish → fish	*sheep → sheep*
foot → feet	*tooth → teeth*
man → men	*woman → women*
mouse → mice	

3 Some nouns only have a plural form, e.g. ***glasses, jeans, pyjamas, scissors, trousers***. We can use ***a pair of*** before these nouns to mean one item, then we treat it as a singular.

*Susan wears orange **pyjamas**.*
*Can I have the **scissors**, please?*

 *There **are** some **glasses** on the table.*

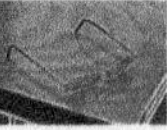 *There **is a pair of glasses** on the table.*

TIP

When talking about things in general, use a plural noun and no article.

*Enid loved **children**.*
*Ron doesn't run **marathons** now.*

▶ See Units 42 and 43 for more information on articles.

4 Some nouns, e.g. ***staff*** and ***police***, look singular but we use them like plural nouns.

*How many **staff work** in this school?*
*The police **are** here.*

5 Some nouns which refer to groups of people, e.g. ***team, family, company***, can be singular or plural.

*Her family **lives / live** in Verona.*

Practice

A Write the plurals.

1	a dog	– dogs	2	a girl	– ....
3	a table	–	4	a person	– ....
5	a leg	–	6	a beach	– ....
7	a tomato	–	8	a bike	– ....
9	a country	–	10	a sheep	– ....
11	a fox	–	12	a photo	– ....
13	a family	–	14	a wish	– ....

B Complete the sentences using the plurals of the words in the box.

bag bus child piano ~~runner~~ sandwich tooth wife wolf woman

1 There are four runners in a 4 x 100 m team.
2 You'll need some .... to carry the shopping.
3 She has two ....: a boy and a girl.
4 King Henry VIII of England had six ....
5 Humans usually have 32 ....
6 We need two .... for the concert.
7 There are bears and .... in the forest.
8 No .... or trains go to town on Sundays.
9 The decathlon is for men, the heptathlon is for ....
10 They had cheese .... for lunch.

C Underline the correct option.

1 I think snakes *is / are* very nice pets.
2 My house *has / have* mice.
3 Sheep *eat / eats* grass.
4 Your pyjamas *is / are* in the cupboard.
5 One of the students *come / comes* from Venezuela.
6 There *is / are* a pair of scissors on the desk.
7 *Do / Does* children learn Italian in England?
8 Not many people *understands / understand* my jokes.
9 Jack and Jill's best friend *live / lives* next to me.
10 *Is / Are* your jeans dirty?

D Complete the text with the plural forms of the nouns in brackets.

Peter Olsen from Aarhus in Denmark is an amazing collector. He collects everything! Peter started his collection with toy [1] cars (car) and he now has 870 different [2] .... (model). They fill two [3] .... (room) of his house. Then Peter began to collect [4] .... (clock) and [5] .... (watch). He is never late for [6] .... (meeting)! Peter has many collections but his favourite is probably his smallest: he owns 21 plastic Christmas [7] .... (tree). Peter's two [8] .... (child) think their dad is great. Tomas, 9 years old, says, 'Not many [9] .... (person) understand Dad but we do. OK, the house is full of [10] .... (box) and [11] .... (shelf) but we don't mind.'

MY TURN!

Do you like these things? Why (not)? Write your answers in your notebook, then write four sentences about other things you like / don't like.

1 mouse I don't like mice. I'm afraid of them.
2 Monday
3 black jeans
4 cheese sandwich
5 butterfly
6 hip-hop music
7 orange furniture

MY TEST!

Circle the correct option.

1 Mulai Ismail didn't know the names of all his .... a wifes and baby b wifes and babys c wives and babies
2 I'm hungry. Can you make me some ....? Just 40 or 50, please. a sandwiches with cheese and tomatoes b sandwichs with cheese and tomatoes c sandwiches with cheese and tomatos
3 I need to cut this paper. Do you have ....? a a pair of scissor b a scissors c a pair of scissors
4 .... very small teeth. a Mouse have b Mouses have c Mice have
5 While he was stealing the car, the .... filming him. a polices were b police was c police were

My Test! answers: 1c 2a 3c 4c 5c

42 Articles 1

Do you know the answer?

What happened?

Romeo and Juliet are in a room. They are in the middle of the room, on the floor. They are dead. Next to them there is some glass. The glass is broken. In the room you can also see an open window. It isn't a hot day but the window is still open.

How did Romeo and Juliet die?

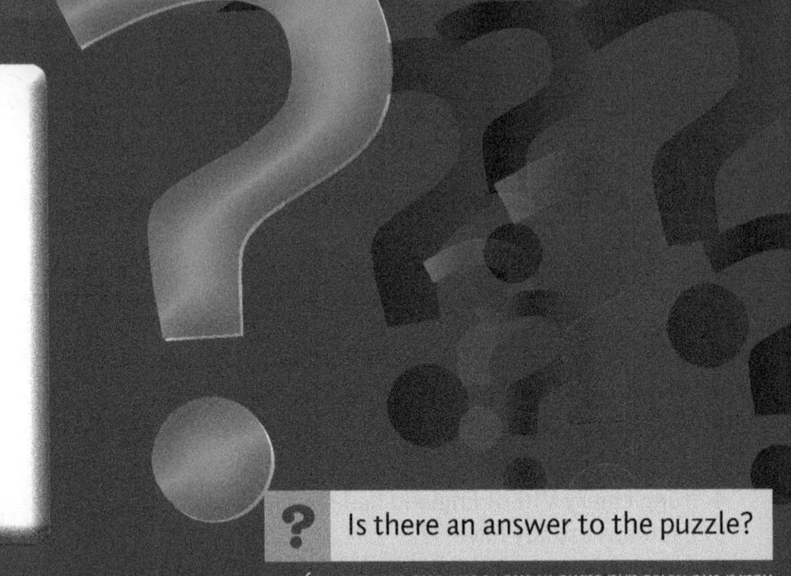

? Is there an answer to the puzzle?

Answer: Romeo and Juliet are fish. The glass is from a broken fish bowl. A hungry cat came in through the window. The cat broke the bowl. A man heard the noise and came in the room. The cat ran away.

Articles 1

1 **Articles (*a, an* or *the*) go before nouns. Sometimes, there is no article before a noun.**
*I saw **a** cat outside.*
*I gave some fish to **the** cat.*
I like cats.

2 **Names of people and places usually have no article.**
Romeo and Juliet lived in Verona.

3 **We don't use articles when we are talking about things in general with plural or uncountable nouns (e.g. *houses, information*).**
I like puzzles.
Cats drink milk.

4 **We use *a* or *an* with singular countable nouns when we are talking about only one person or one thing.**
*Juliet had **a** brother.*
*Do you want **an** apple?*

5 **Use *a* or *an* to talk about which job somebody has.**
*My mum is **an** engineer.*
*Shakespeare was **a** writer.*

6 **Use *a* before a consonant sound (/b/, /t/, /s/, etc.) and *an* before a vowel sound (/e/, /o/, /u/, etc.).**
*There is **a** room.*
*You can see **an** open window.*

TIP

***h* is a consonant, so use *a* with words which begin with *h* in sound and spelling.**
*It isn't **a** hot day.*
A hungry cat.
You say *an hour* and *an honour* because *hour* /'aʊə/ and *honour* /'ɒnə/ start with vowel sounds.

7 **Use *the* before singular and plural countable nouns and uncountable nouns.**
***The** window is open.*
*What's **the** news?*

8 **Use *the* when the speaker and listener both know what is being talked about.**
***The** glass is broken.* (= the glass was mentioned in the previous sentence)
*I saw **the** cat.* (= the cat we both know)
***The** bank is closed.* (= our bank)

TIP

Note the difference:
*I have **an** idea.* (= but I haven't told you what it is yet, so you don't know)
*I like **the** idea.* (= we both know which idea we're talking about)

▶ **See Unit 40 for article use with countable and uncountable nouns.**

Practice

A Underline the correct option.

1 I get *a same bus* / *the same bus* / *same bus* every morning.
2 John is *a nurse* / *the nurse* / *nurse* at Hope Hospital.
3 I'm busy. I'll feed *a cat* / *the cat* / *cat* later.
4 There are a lot of students in *a Manchester* / *the Manchester* / *Manchester*.
5 What is *a tomato* / *the tomato* / *tomato*? Fruit or vegetable?
6 Please give me *a scissors* / *the scissors* / *scissors*.
7 My dog loves *a chocolate* / *the chocolate* / *chocolate*.
8 *Frankenstein* is *a horror story* / *the horror story* / *horror story* by Mary Shelley.
9 Did you see *a game* / *the game* / *game* last night? It was great.
10 *A sport* / *The sport* / *Sport* is important.
11 I have *an older brother* / *the older brother* / *older brother*.
12 Where is *a Post Office* / *the Post Office* / *Post Office*? I can't find it.

B Complete the puzzle with *a, an, the* or – (= no article).

This puzzle is about [1] ....a.... town called [2] .... Darkville. It is [3] .... old town with [4] .... university and [5] .... history museum. [6] .... tourists often visit it. Now [7] .... dog is walking down [8] .... main road of [9] .... town. It is [10] .... black dog. There is no moon and [11] .... weather is bad. No lights are on in [12] .... streets. All [13] .... shops in [14] .... town are closed. Now [15] .... man is driving quickly from [16] .... airport. [17] .... headlights of his car are not on. He almost hits [18] .... dog. There is nearly [19] .... accident but he stops [20] .... car. Luckily, [21] .... dog survives. It doesn't die. It is [22] .... miracle – how did [23] .... man see [24] .... dog? You know, [25] .... life is sometimes very strange ...
(See [26] .... bottom of the page for [27] .... answer to [28] .... puzzle.)

C Make full sentences from the words, adding articles if necessary. Then mark them True or False.

1 Shakespeare / was / actor
Shakespeare was an actor. True.
2 colours / of / English / flag / are / red / and / blue
....
3 cats / have / nine / lives
....
4 there / is / town / called / Moscow / in / America
....
5 'musicals' / are / plays / or / films / with / singers / and / dancers
....
6 mile / is / longer / than / kilometre
....
7 Elvis / Presley / played / concert / in / London
....
8 original / name / of / New York / was / New Rome
....

MY TURN!

In your notebook, write six sentences about what you can see around you now.
Example: *I can see a cat. The cat is climbing a tree.*

MY TEST!

Circle the correct option.

A man and his son loved climbing [1] .... mountains. One day, they were climbing [2] .... mountain when [3] .... son fell and cut his head. The boy looked terrible – he had [4] .... blood on his face, his hair and his clothes – but he felt OK. The man phoned for help, and after about [5] .... hour, a helicopter came and took the boy to hospital. The man had to stay on the mountain. At the hospital, a doctor started to clean [6] .... blood from the boy's face. Suddenly the doctor said, 'Oh no! This is my son!'
How is this possible?

1 a the b an c a d –
2 a the b an c a d –
3 a the b an c a d –
4 a the b an c a d –
5 a the b an c a d –
6 a the b an c a d –

Answer to Exercise B: It is day, not night!

My Test! answers: 1d 2c 3a 4d 5b 6a The doctor was the boy's mother.

43 Articles 2

Play music and watch the birds.

Blogspot

The most famous guitar in the world is the Fender Stratocaster (Strat).
An American Standard Stratocaster is **a** classic guitar. **The** colour is beautiful. **The** sound is perfect.
People play guitars for many reasons: fun, money, interest. There is one reason why I play **the** Stratocaster: love.
What is happiness? Take **a** Strat, put it in **a** rucksack, go to **the** train station, buy **a** ticket to **the** seaside and stay there for **a** month. Play music on **the** beach, swim and watch **the** birds every day. This is happiness.

? Why do people play guitars?
a fun b money c interest d all of these things

Answer: d

Articles 2

1 **Use *the* before things in the world that we all know about. Examples are: *the desert, the mountains, the river, the sea* and *the town*.**
*Swim in **the** river.*
*The country is quieter than **the** town.*

2 **Use *the* before things that are the only ones around us, or that are unique.**
*Look at **the** moon.* (There is only one moon we can see.)
*She's the best singer in **the** world.* (There is only one world.)

3 **Use *the* with streets and hotels.**
*Walk across **the** road carefully.*

4 **Use *the* before superlatives (*smallest, most interesting*, etc.).**
***The most** famous guitar in the world.*
*It is **the best**.*

▶ See Unit 42 for the basic rules for articles.
▶ See Unit 40 for countable and uncountable nouns.

5 **Only use *the* with uncountable nouns (*music, air, furniture*, etc.) if they are specific things we know about. Note the difference:**
***Money** does not bring **happiness**.* (= money in general)
*Where is **the money**?* (= physical money you can touch)
***Coffee** is bad for you.* (= all coffee)
*Put **the coffee** on the table.* (= this cup of coffee)

TIP

We can talk about specific types and examples of things with *the* and a singular countable noun.
***The** guitar is very popular today.* (*the guitar* = a type of musical instrument)
*Marconi invented **the** radio.* (*the radio* = an example of technology)

6 **Use *a* or *an* with nouns to talk about something that the listener doesn't know about yet.**
*There is **a** concert tonight.*
*Listen to this, it's **a** true story.*

Practice

A Complete the sentences with *a, an* or *the*.

1 Do you play ..the.. guitar?
2 It's .... second house on the left.
3 Esperanto is .... language.
4 .... longest river is in Brazil.
5 When I was young I had .... dog.
6 Wear .... dress you bought last week.
7 I love .... sea.
8 That is .... interesting idea.

B Match the pairs.

1	I can see	a	money.
2	Everyone needs	b	the money.
3	Turn on	a	the light.
4	Plants die without	b	light.
5	The bread	a	is easy to make.
6	Bread	b	is in the kitchen.
7	I want to study	a	music.
8	Listen to	b	the music.
9	Football	a	is in the car.
10	The football	b	is a sport.

C Make sentences by putting the words in the correct order. Add *a, an* or *the* if necessary.

1 in / I / mountains / live
I live in the mountains.
2 where / tomorrow / is / party / ?
....
3 night / was / it / exciting
....
4 most / is / beautiful / who / ?
....
5 animal / is / horse
....
6 hot / nice / is / milk / on / cold / day
....
7 car / full / is / park / again.
....
8 music / need / people.
....

D Cross out the pictures in this story and write the correct words with *a, an, the* or – (= no article).

Billy wanted to play [1] the guitar  because he loved [2] . But there was a problem. He had no money to buy one. He lived near a big forest and every day he walked in [3] and dreamed about a guitar. One day Billy sat under [4] and listened to [5]. They sang beautifully. [6] was shining. Billy was thinking. 'Guitars are made of [7] 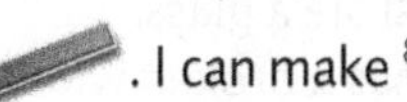. I can make [8] !' He walked back to [9], went home and got [10] and some string. He went back to [11]. Billy made his guitar. The birds sang and Billy played. He was happy now.

MY TURN!

In your notebook, answer these questions with *a, an, the* or – (= no article) and the noun.

1 What is a carrot? A vegetable.
2 What musical instrument would you like to play?
3 Where can you swim in salt water?
4 What do you put in coffee?
5 What was the Titanic?
6 What object can you see in the sky at night?
7 What plastic thing can you use in a shop?
8 Money cannot buy ...?

MY TEST!

Circle the correct option.

1 I'm sorry. I've broken your Stratocaster. I was playing music on the beach and it fell in .... sea. a a b the c –
2 .... most expensive Stratocaster costs about $12,000. a A b An c The
3 I usually play ...., but sometimes I play it for money.
a guitar for the fun b the guitar for a fun c the guitar for fun
4 My friend has just bought .... old guitar. It's 40 years old and it sounds fantastic. a an b the c –
5 Who invented .... electric guitar? a an b the c –

My Test! answers: 1b 2c 3c 4a 5b

R8 Review: nouns and articles

A Write the plurals of these nouns.

1 boy – *boys*
2 child – *children*
3 dog – ...
4 man – ...
5 shoe – ...
6 tomato – ...
7 box – ...
8 table – ...
9 computer – ...
10 mouse – ...
11 tooth – ...
12 banana – ...
13 knife – ...
14 house – ...
15 dictionary – ...

B Change the sentences into the plural. Be careful with words like *a, the, some* and *this*.

1 This boy has found a key. *These boys have found some keys. / These boys have found keys.*
2 That lady has a pretty baby. ...
3 The man is going to buy a new watch. ...
4 The woman found a mouse under the piano. ...
5 That girl stole a glass. ...
6 This bus has a broken window. ...
7 The child is eating a potato. ...
8 That farmer is buying a sheep and a fish. ...

C Put the nouns from the box in the correct places in the table.

advice air ~~chair~~ city family feeling fun furniture game garden help ice cream information luggage music problem soap soup tree trip ~~water~~ work

a / an	some
chair	*water*

D Underline the correct option.

1 Jill jumped into *a* / *some* water.
2 I have just read *any* / *a* book about it.
3 He did *a* / *some* good work.
4 He did *a* / *some* good job.
5 *A* / *Some* people like it.
6 Mr and Mrs Brown don't have *any* / *some* children.
7 Have you lost *any* / *a* money?
8 The police now have *some* / *an* information.
9 Would you like to come on *some* / *a* trip?
10 Please give me *some* / *an* advice.

E Match the pairs.

1 We need to talk about your plans for the future. Do you have ______ a time?
2 I've forgotten my watch. Do you have ______ b the time?

3 Do you often eat a a pizza?
4 Do you want to eat b pizzas?

5 I want to be a teacher because I love a children.
6 Dinner's ready. Please go and tell b the children.

7 Her house is in the middle of a a forest.
8 I love walking in b the forest.

9 Marconi invented a a radio.
10 My mobile phone doesn't have b the radio.

11 My sister never drinks a milk.
12 Ugh ... this coffee's disgusting. There's something wrong with b the milk.

F Write *a, an, the* or – (= no article) in each space.

Last year we went to Wales for 1 ...a... holiday and we stayed in 2 .... old house. 3 .... family of 4 .... mice was living in 5 .... house too. We never saw 6 .... mice, but we knew they were there, because they used to eat our bread. On 7 .... last day of 8 .... holiday we decided we wanted to see 9 .... mice, so we bought 10 .... smelly cheese. That night, we put 11 .... cheese in 12 .... bowl and put 13 .... bowl on 14 .... floor of 15 .... living room. We sat in 16 .... dark and waited for 17 .... mice to come. After 18 .... two hours of waiting, I was feeling hungry, so I went to 19 .... kitchen to make myself some 20 .... tea and 21 .... sandwich. I remembered there was some bread on 22 .... table. When I turned on 23 .... light I saw 24 .... mouse. It was sitting on 25 .... kitchen table and eating 26 .... bread.

G Complete each sentence b so that it means the same as sentence a. Use two to four words including the word in brackets.

1 a She teaches English at our school. (teacher)
b She's ...an English teacher... at our school.
2 a He's a violinist in an orchestra. (violin)
b He .... in an orchestra.
3 a I want a relaxing beach holiday this year. (beach)
b This holiday, I want to relax ....
4 a We had some cheese in the fridge this morning, but now it's gone. Who's eaten it? (all)
b Who's eaten .... from the fridge? It was here this morning.
5 a Kenny is Tom's only brother. (of)
b Kenny is .... Tom.
6 a I'm going out now. I'll be about 60 minutes. (hour)
b I'm going out now. I'll be back in ....
7 a Sorry I'm late. I had a meeting with my bank manager. (bank)
b Sorry I'm late. I went to .... meeting with the manager.
8 a She needs to travel to Italy on business. (trip)
b She needs to go .... to Italy.

44 This, that, these, those

This is me.

Hello – I'm Anusibuno and I live in Ghana.

These children are studying at school. We learn Kasenanankani, one of the languages of Ghana, and also English at school.

This is me at home. When I grow up, I want to be a photographer. I'd like to take photos of the people and children in my country. **That's** my dream.

I live in the north of Ghana where it's very dry. But not all of the country is dry. **This** photo is of the port of Accra, and **those** are fishing boats.

? True or False? Anusibuno speaks English as her first language.

False. She speaks Kasenanankani. She learns English at school.

This, that, these, those

1 Use *this* or *that* with a singular noun.
this photo, that girl

2 Use *these* or *those* with a plural noun.
these friends, those hills

3 We usually use *this* or *these* for people and things which are near.
This photo is of the port of Accra.
Are these your children?

4 We usually use *that* or *those* for people and things which are not near:
Who's that girl over there?
Those are fishing boats.

5 Use *this* for things which are happening now or will soon happen.
This TV programme is really interesting. (= the TV programme I am watching now)
You'll laugh when you hear this story. (= the story I am about to tell you)

TIP

On the phone, we usually use *this is* to say who is speaking.
Hello. This is Fatima.

6 Use *that* for things which happened in the past or have just finished.
That was a great holiday.
What was that noise?

7 Use *that* to say more about something that someone has just said.
I want to be a photographer. That's my dream.

A: She wants to be a photographer.
B: Really? I didn't know that.

8 We can also use *this, that, these* and *those* on their own.
This is me. (= This person in the photo is me.)
These are my friends. (= These people in the photo are my friends.)
Who's that? (= Who's that person in the photo?)

TIP

The short form of *that is* = *that's*. *This is, these are* and *those are* do not have short forms.

Practice

A Complete this letter with *this, that, these* or *those.*

[1] This .... is me at home with my family. [2] .... is our lunch. We are eating yams. [3] .... are our animals you can see outside.

You'll like [4] .... photo. [5] .... is me again and [6] .... are my friends. The photo shows the first day of school. [7] .... was a special day. We are wearing our school uniform. [8] .... building behind us is the school.

B Underline the correct option.

1 Can you give me *this / that* book on the top shelf, please?
2 Can you hold *this / that* for me? I need to put my hat on.
3 Come and look at *these / those* photos.
4 A: David failed his exam.
B: Really? I didn't know *this / that.*
5 Hello, *this / that* is Alice. Can I speak to Abe?
6 Look what I found! Do you remember *this / that* photo?
7 *This / That* film was amazing. Did you see it last night?
8 I love the painting over there in the corner. Just look at *these / those* flowers! I can't believe they're not real.

C Complete the speech bubbles using *this, that, these* or *those.*

1 How much is this?
€?
2 ....

3 ....?
4 ....'s my sister!

5 ....!

6 Excuse me, ...?
7 Excuse me, ...?

MY TURN!

Find a photo which includes you or someone you know and write a description of what you can see, using *this, that, these, those,* in your notebook.
Example: This is me and my cousin, Pavel.

MY TEST!

Circle the correct option.

1 A: Did you know they speak Kasenanankani in Ghana? B: No, I didn't. .... interesting.
a It's b This is c That's
2 Look at .... mountains! They're so far away, but they look really beautiful. a that b those c these
3 A: I lived in Ghana for eight months when I was a student. B: Really? I'm sure .... was an amazing experience.
a this b that c those
4 Mmm, ... food is delicious. Do you want to try some? a this b that c those
5 Can you help me with .... bags, please? They're really heavy. a this b those c these

My Test! answers: 1c 2b 3b 4a 5c

Some, any, no, none

There are no trains or buses.

Do you have **any** plans for your vacation? None? Good, then …

Visit Knoydart!

Knoydart is a beautiful place in Scotland. It's perfect for a holiday. You won't find **any** pollution in Knoydart and there are **no** cars. There are **some** boats to Knoydart but **none** of them carry cars. Don't worry, there are **some** roads but you'll have plenty of exercise because there are **no** trains or buses!

Knoydart has a post office, a school and **some** small hotels. The hotels are very nice but **none** of them are very big and **some** are only open in summer. Do you have **any** questions? The website at the bottom of the page has **some** useful information.

? Underline the correct option: Knoydart is a good place for people who like: *quiet holidays / driving / big luxury hotels.*

Answer: quiet holidays

Some, any, no, none

1 Use *some* and *any* to talk about a limited quantity of something. Use *not ... any*, *no* and *none* when there is nothing there.

*You can see **some** birds.*
*The beach doesn't have **any** cafés.*
*There are **no** tourists.*
*Are there any people swimming? No, **none**.*

2 Use *some* and *any* with countable plural nouns and uncountable nouns.

***Some** people like quiet holidays.* (*people* = plural noun)
*Do you have **any** news?* (*news* = uncountable)
*I need **some** information.* (*information* = uncountable)

▶ See Unit 40 for countable and uncountable nouns.

3 We often use *some* in statements.

*Knoydart has **some** roads.*

4 We usually use *any* in negative sentences. We also use *any* in questions instead of *some*.

*There isn't **any** pollution.*
*Do you want **any** milk with your coffee?*

5 We can use *some* in questions when we expect the answer 'yes', especially for offers, requests and suggestions.

*Do you have **some** good ideas? I'm sure you do!*
*Would you like **some** help?* (offer)
*Can I have **some** sugar?* (request)
*Shall I take **some** photos?* (suggestion)

6 We can use *any* in statements to mean 'it doesn't matter which one'.

*Use **any** colour.*

7 We can use *some* and *any* without a following noun when it is clear what *some* and *any* are referring to.

*There are hotels but **some** are only open in summer.*
*We have time for some questions. Do you have **any**?*

8 Use *no* with countable plural nouns and uncountable nouns. *No* is often more emphatic than *not any*.

*There are **no** trains.*

9 *None* = not any.

*I wanted some water but there was **none**.*

10 We can use *of* after *some*, *any* and *none*, before *the* or a pronoun.

*I read **some of** the website.*
*Do **any of** you speak English?*
*... **none of** them are very big.*

Practice

A Make sentences about Susie's shopping bag using *some*, *any* or *no*.

1 

2 
3 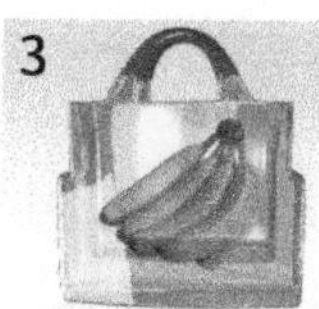
4 
5
6 SOAP

1 She has some chocolate.
2 She doesn't have any fish. / She has no fish.
3 ....
4 ....
5 ....
6 ....

B Underline the correct option.

1 I'm lucky, I have <u>*some*</u> / *any* good friends.
2 It's a small room and there aren't *some* / *any* windows.
3 Sundays are quiet; there is *no* / *none* traffic on the streets.
4 I'd love *some* / *any* chocolate cake, please.
5 Bring some water because there is *no* / *none* here.
6 I'm afraid there's *no* / *none* beach.
7 Sheila doesn't need *no* / *any* help.
8 We need help because *some* / *none* of us understand.
9 There aren't *some* / *any* questions.
10 *Some* / *None* tourists prefer to travel by train.

C In your notebook, rewrite these dialogues with *some*, *any* or *none* to make them more natural. Sometimes more than one answer is possible.

1 A: Can I have six or seven potatoes?
B: Sorry, we don't have them.
A: Can I have some potatoes?
B: Sorry, we don't have any.

2 A: Have you got a small amount of American dollars with you?
B: Yes, I've got a small amount.

3 A: Would you like a little bit of help?
B: I don't need help, thanks.

4 A: I need three or four biscuits.
B: I'm sorry, we don't have three or four biscuits. We don't even have one biscuit!

5 A: Do you understand one or more of the questions?
B: No, not one.

6 A: Yes, we've got three or four. Which do you want?
B: It doesn't matter.

D Complete the sentences using the words in the box and *some*, *any* and *no*.

Some people like Knoydart for these reasons:

beautiful walks	delicious seafood	noisy factories
friendly people	money	~~traffic~~

1 The roads are very quiet. There is ......no traffic...... .
2 .... live in the area.
3 There aren't ....
4 The hotel restaurants serve ....
5 There are .... through the country.
6 You don't need .... to enjoy the fresh air.

MY TURN!

In your notebook, write five good reasons to visit your town or village, using *some*, *any* and *no*.

Examples:
1 It has some interesting museums.
2 There aren't any expensive hotels.

MY TEST!

Circle the correct option.

1 You'll have to walk because the island doesn't have .... taxis. **a** some **b** no **c** any
2 I invited all my friends to come with me to Knoydart, but .... them wanted to come. **a** none of **b** no **c** any of
3 A: Does Knoydart have .... casinos? B: No, I don't think so. **a** any of **b** some of **c** any
4 Could I have .... more information about the hotel, please? **a** no **b** none **c** some
5 A: How many people live on Knoydart? B: I have .... idea. **a** none **b** no **c** any

My Test answers: 1c 2a 3c 4c 5b

46 *Something, everywhere, nobody, anyone*

Say nothing.

When you have **nothing** to say, say **nothing**. (Charles Caleb Colton)

He knows **nothing** and he thinks he knows **everything**. That clearly points to a political career. (George Bernard Shaw)

Anyone can catch your eye, but it takes **someone** special to catch your heart. (Anon)

Learning is a treasure that will follow its owner **everywhere**. (Chinese proverb)

Which of these quotes do you like best?

Something, everywhere, nobody, anyone

1 **Use the pronouns *anything* or *something* to talk about a thing or an idea.**

Use the pronouns *anybody, somebody, anyone* or *someone* to talk about a person. (The words ending in *-body* or *-one* are the same in meaning.)

Anyone can catch your eye.

Use the pronouns *anywhere* or *somewhere* to talk about a place.

2 ***Everywhere* (= all places), *everybody* or *everyone* (= all people), *everything* (= all things)**
***Nowhere* (= no place), *nobody* or *no one* (= no person), *nothing* (= no thing or not anything)**

*He knows **nothing** and he thinks he knows **everything**.*

3 **We usually use *something, somewhere, somebody* and *someone* in statements.**

*It takes **someone** special to catch your heart.*

We often use *anything, anywhere, anybody* and *anyone* in negative sentences and questions.

*I can't see **anything**.*
*Is **anybody** at home?*

4 **We can also use pronouns beginning with *any-* in statements to mean 'all' when it doesn't matter who, what or where.**

***Anyone** can catch your eye.* (= all people; it doesn't matter who they are)
*He can go **anywhere** he wants.* (= He can go to all places; it doesn't matter where.)

5 **Use *nothing, nowhere, nobody* and *no one* in statements and questions.**

*He knows **nothing**. Why is **no one** here? He has **nowhere** to live.*

TIP

We don't have two negative words in one sentence.
*I didn't hear **anything**.* OR *I heard **nothing**.*
NOT ~~*I didn't hear nothing*~~.

6 **We usually use *everything, everywhere, everybody* and *everyone* in statements.**

***Everybody** says it's true. I met **everyone**.*

TIP

everyone / everybody / everything **+ singular verb**
*Everybody **was** there.* NOT ~~*Everybody were there.*~~

Practice

A Match the sentence beginnings to the correct endings.

1 Anything that can go wrong, — d
2 Worrying
3 Try something
4 Nothing
5 If you have hope,
6 Nobody's
7 Everyone needs

a someone to talk to.
b lasts forever.
c perfect.
d will go wrong.
e won't help anyone.
f new today.
g you have everything.

B Underline the correct option.

1 Let's go *somewhere* / *everywhere* special.
2 She doesn't have *anything* / *nothing* nice to wear.
3 I think there's *something* / *anything* strange about him.
4 I have *nothing* / *anything* new to read.
5 Look in the fridge if you're hungry. You can have *anything* / *something* you want.
6 This music is boring – I want to listen to *something* / *everything* different.
7 I've met *someone* / *anyone* special.
8 *Everybody* / *Everything* loves a good story.

C Complete the sentences with an appropriate pronoun. Sometimes there is more than one right answer.

1 A: Have you seen the dog?
B: No, I've looked everywhere.
2 I've got .... in my eye.
3 You must come to the party – .... is going to be there.
4 There's .... at the door.
5 Has .... seen my watch?
6 My cousin is very shy – she never says .... !
7 I need to buy .... for dinner.
8 Can .... come to the party or do you need a ticket?
9 She lives .... in France.

D Write sentences which mean the opposite.

1 She doesn't have anywhere to live.
She has somewhere to live.
2 I could see no one.
....
3 I told the police officer everything.
....
4 The woman told me something interesting.
....
5 Everyone is happy.
....
6 Nobody knows.
....
7 There was nothing unusual about her.
....
8 He hasn't been anywhere.
....

MY TURN!

Complete each sentence with an appropriate pronoun.

1 No one knows the answer.
2 There's .... in the garden.
3 .... says it's true.
4 I can't see him ....
5 Do .... and .... will happen.
6 .... loves a happy ending.
7 .... is always right.

MY TEST!

Circle the correct option.

1 Please tell me .... about your family. a something b anywhere c everyone
2 A: What do you want for your birthday? B: .... I don't mind. I'll be happy with something small. a Everything b Anything c Something
3 I didn't know .... at the party, so I went home again. a nobody b anybody c no one
4 .... mistakes. a Everyone makes b Anybody make c Everybody make
5 A: I can't find my keys .... B: Where have you looked? A: Everywhere. a somewhere b anything c anywhere

My Test! answers: 1a 2b 3b 4a 5c

47 Much, many, a lot of, a little, a few

A lot of fun!

? Do tourists at Port Stephens usually see dolphins?

Answer: Yes. There are not many trips where you don't see a dolphin.

The Eco-Blog **Read what our eco-tourists say about travelling in Australia.**

A lot of fun!	by Kelly, 24th October

I've been on dolphin-watching trips before and often you only get **a little** time with the dolphins ... but this was different. Port Stephens on the coast of New South Wales is the perfect place to watch dolphins. I saw **lots** of dolphins jumping over the waves ... fantastic!

There are **not many** trips where you don't see a dolphin. But if you are unlucky and only see a dolphin for **a few** moments, the captain will give you a free ticket for another trip.

And the best thing is – it doesn't cost **much**. What are you waiting for? Buy your ticket today!

Much, many, a lot of, a little, a few

many, a lot of, lots of	some	not many, a few

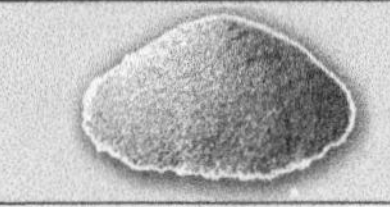		
much, a lot of, lots of	some	not much, a little

1 **Use *much* with singular uncountable nouns and *many* with plural countable nouns.**
*We do not have **much** time.*
*There are not **many** trips.*

2 **Use *a lot of* or *lots of* with both singular uncountable nouns and plural countable nouns.**
*It was **a lot of** / **lots of** fun.*
*I saw **a lot of** / **lots of** dolphins.*

3 **We use *a lot of* or *lots of* in statements and negative sentences and in questions.**
*There is **a lot of** marine life in the Port Stephens bay area.*
*Not **a lot of** tourists know this place.*
*Are there **a lot of** different types of dolphin?*

4 **We usually use *much* and *many* in negative sentences and questions.**
*We do not have **much** time.*
*Are there **many** dolphins in the Port Stephens bay area?*

5 **We don't usually use *much* in statements – we prefer *a lot of* or *lots of***
*It was **a lot of** fun!* NOT ~~*It was much fun!*~~

6 **We sometimes use *many* in formal statements.**
*Scientists have discovered that **many** female dolphins live in groups of six or eight animals.*

7 ***A lot of* or *lots of* are more common in informal statements.**
*I saw **lots of** dolphins jumping over the waves.*

8 **Use *a little* with singular uncountable nouns and *a few* with plural nouns.**
*You only get **a little** time with the dolphins.*
*You only see a dolphin for **a few** moments.*

You can leave out the noun after *much, many, a little, a few, a lot of* and *lots of*.
*It doesn't cost **much**.* (= It doesn't cost much money.)
*How much time do we have? Only **a little**.* (= Only a little time.)
*It doesn't cost **a lot**.* (= It doesn't cost a lot of money.)
*How much money do we have? **Lots**!*

Practice

A Complete the sentences with *much* or *many*.

1. There aren't ....many.......... days before the exam.
2. Not .... snow has fallen in the Alps this winter.
3. .... people are surprised when they first see the dolphins.
4. Do the boys have .... homework tonight?
5. Did .... children come to the party?
6. There won't be .... hotel rooms at this time of year.
7. Do you eat .... meat?
8. Did you get .... presents for your birthday?
9. Maria didn't give me .... good advice.
10. There are .... different plants, animals and insects in the rainforest.

B Complete each of these sentences in two different ways, using phrases from the box and appropriate forms of the verb.

a little a few	love knowledge arguments bad marks salt in your food sweets rain days off

1. A little rain is / A few days off are } a good thing.
2. .... / .... } not bad for you.
3. .... / .... } better than none.
4. .... / .... } nothing to worry about.

C Complete the blog using *a lot of, lots of, much, many, a little* or *a few*.

Kuranda Train and Skyrail, Australia
by Ido, 4th July

This is a great day trip. Take the train through the mountains and come back by Skyrail.
The train trip was beautiful – we went past [1] ....a lot of.......... waterfalls and through [2] .... tunnels! We wanted to see the traditional markets at Kuranda, but there weren't [3] .... good shops – just shops selling tourist souvenirs – so you won't need [4] .... money.
[5] .... hours in town should be enough for most people. You can visit the Butterfly Sanctuary – if you want to – but there are [6] .... butterflies flying around you for free!
You don't need [7] .... time to get to the Skyrail. Skyrail is a cable car that travels only [8] .... metres above the top of the rainforest. Unfortunately we only had [9] .... time. I wanted to stay all day!

MY TURN!

Answer the questions in your notebook using *a lot, not much, some, only a little, not many* or *only a few*.

1. How much time do you spend on your homework every evening? ....A lot!..........
2. How much time do you spend watching TV every week?
3. How many plants do you know the names of?
4. How many different butterflies do you know?
5. How much money do you have in your pocket?
6. How many hours' sleep did you have last night?
7. How much snow was there last winter?
8. How many times have you been on a plane?

MY TEST!

Circle the correct option.

1. We travelled around Australia with .... friends. There were about six of us. **a** a little **b** a few **c** much
2. We didn't have .... time in Port Stephens – only a few days. **a** many **b** a lot **c** much
3. We had a .... free time at the end of our trip, so we did some shopping. **a** few **b** lot **c** little
4. A: Did you see .... other animals? B: Yes, lots. **a** many **b** much **c** a lot
5. A: How much did it cost to fly to Australia? B: .... It was very expensive. **a** Much **b** A lot of **c** A lot

My Test! answers: 1b 2c 3c 4a 5c

48 Subject and object pronouns

I don't know them and they don't know me.

I'm Susan. Simon is my husband. **We** live in Green Street. **It** is a big street and our house is in the middle of **it**. John lives next to **me**. **He**'s a doctor and **I** like **him** a lot. His wife Jane is noisy. **She** sings in the shower very loudly. Sometimes **we** tell **her** to be quiet but **she** doesn't listen to **us**. My other neighbours are Mr and Mrs Strange. **They** are very quiet. **I** don't know **them** very well. **We** have two sons. **They** know a story about Mr and Mrs Strange. **We** don't believe **them** but **you** will read about **it** in Exercise E.

? True or False? There are four people in Susan's family.

Answer: True

Subject and object pronouns

1 We can replace nouns with pronouns.

I have two neighbours. ***They*** *are nice.* (*they* = two neighbours)
This is Jane. ***She****'s my wife.* (*She* = Jane)

2 There are different forms for subject pronouns and object pronouns, but *you* and *it* stay the same.

subject	verb	object
I	like	**him**
She	likes	**me**

I'm Susan.
She *sings in the shower.*
Sometimes ***we*** *tell* ***her****.*

3 Use object pronouns after prepositions (e.g. *to, in, at, around*).

John lives next to ***them****.*
Look at ***me****!*
The story is about ***her****.*

subject pronoun	object pronoun
I	me
you	you
he	him
she	her
it	it
we	us
they	them

TIP

In English, a full sentence needs a subject. The subject can be a noun or a pronoun.
I want an apple. NOT ~~*Want an apple.*~~
It*'s eight o'clock.* NOT ~~*Is eight o'clock.*~~

▶ **See Unit 51 for more information on *it* as a pronoun.**

Practice

A **Underline the subject pronouns and circle the object pronouns.**

1 I know him.
2 It is my birthday.
3 She likes them.
4 Where is he?
5 Can you see me?
6 Give it to us.
7 You don't understand her.
8 We're with you.

B **Complete the sentences with the correct pronouns.**

1 ......I...... am the winner!
2 .... likes chocolate.
3 .... can't sing very well.
4 .... go first, please.
5 .... smell very nice.
6 .... costs a lot of money.

C **Complete the sentences with the correct pronouns.**

1 She's our new neighbour. Do you know ......her...... ?
2 .... are going to visit John. Will you come with us?
3 Your bags are heavy. I'll carry ....
4 Listen, boys, can .... be quiet, please?
5 Mr Jones isn't ill. I saw .... this morning.
6 Where are my glasses? I can't find ....
7 Dolphins are very intelligent. .... have their own language.
8 Susan needs the book. Give .... to .... now, please.
9 I don't understand the instructions. Please explain .... to ....
10 Hello? It's ...., we're back.

D **Complete the text with the correct pronouns.**

Neighbours is an Australian soap opera. [1] ......It...... is now famous around the world. Kylie Minogue started her career in *Neighbours*. [2] .... married Jason Donovan in the show and [3] .... both became pop stars. When Kylie left *Neighbours*, thousands of people wrote to [4] .... [5] .... wanted Kylie to stay in the show. '[6] .... all love [7] ...., Kylie, please don't leave [8] .... !' wrote many sad *Neighbours* fans. Kylie left, but *Neighbours* continued. Today you can watch [9] .... in many countries including Uganda, Ukraine and Laos. Of course, the actors and characters change. [10] .... are not the same today, but fans still love [11] .... all.

E **Replace the nouns in the text with pronouns to make the story more natural.**

Mr and Mrs Strange are my neighbours. ~~Mr and Mrs Strange~~ They live in a very old house. The very old house has a big garden but most people don't know that the big garden is a magic garden! Mr and Mrs Strange have a daughter, Mary Strange. Last summer, my brother and I saw Mary Strange outside. Mary Strange had a golden key. Mary Strange took the golden key, went to the gate of the garden and opened the gate of the garden. Quietly, my brother and I followed Mary Strange inside. My brother and I saw Mr and Mrs Strange. Mr and Mrs Strange were sitting in a tree. Mary flew to Mr and Mrs Strange. A bird in the tree spoke to Mary and Mary answered the bird. My brother and I ran away.

MY TURN!

Do you like these things / people? Use pronouns in your answers and write them in your notebook.

1 English ......I like it......
2 Swimming ......I don't like it......
3 Red shoes
4 Jazz
5 Your doctor
6 Basketball
7 Jennifer Lopez
8 Brad Pitt
9 Your neighbours

MY TEST!

Circle the correct option.

1 He is my neighbour. I like .... likes me.
a him and he b them and they c he and him
2 Please visit .... soon.
a us b we c they
3 I spend a lot of time with ....
a it b them c they
4 That's me in the picture. .... an old picture.
a Is b He's c It's
5 Can I give .... a message?
a her b he c she

My Test! answers: 1a 2a 3b 4c 5a

Possessive *'s*

My great-grandfather's letters

My name is Joe. I live in Philadelphia in the United States. I work in my **father's bakery**.

My great-grandfather, Emilio, came here from Italy in 1902. **Emilio's brother** arrived two years later. At first, my great-grandmother, Rosa, did not want to leave her **parents' home** in Italy. But she loved getting my **great-grandfather's letters**, and finally she decided to come. She came in 1905 with their young children. The family was happy to be together again.

The family had little money. **Emilio's first jobs** were selling fruit and building roads. They worked very hard to save money, and in 1915 they bought their first little home. They were happy that their **children's future** was more certain.

Where is Joe from?

Answer: Joe is from the United States, but his great-grandparents came from Italy.

Possessive *'s*

1 **Add *'s* to a singular noun to mean 'belongs to'.**
my father's bakery
Emilio's brother

2 **After a plural noun which ends in *-s*, just add *'*.**
her parents' home

3 **Add *'s* to irregular plural nouns (which do not end in *-s*).**
their children's future

4 **We can use *'s* without a following noun, for example when we answer questions with *Whose?***
A: Whose bakery is it? B: It's my father's.

▶ **See Units 26 and 50 for *Whose?***

We often use *'s* without a noun to talk about shops, businesses or someone's house
*My aunt stayed at **Rosa's**.* (= Rosa's house)
*We had a great pizza at **Mario's**.* (= Mario's restaurant)

5 **When there are two nouns, we usually add *'s* to the second noun.**
It's my mother and father's bakery. (The bakery belongs to both my mother and father.)

***'s* can mean:**

1 possessive: *Emilio's letters*
2 *is*: *he's poor*
3 *has*: *he's worked* (*he has worked*)

6 **When a name ends in *'s* we still add *'s*.**
Lois's house.

Practice

A Look at Joe's family tree and complete the sentences.

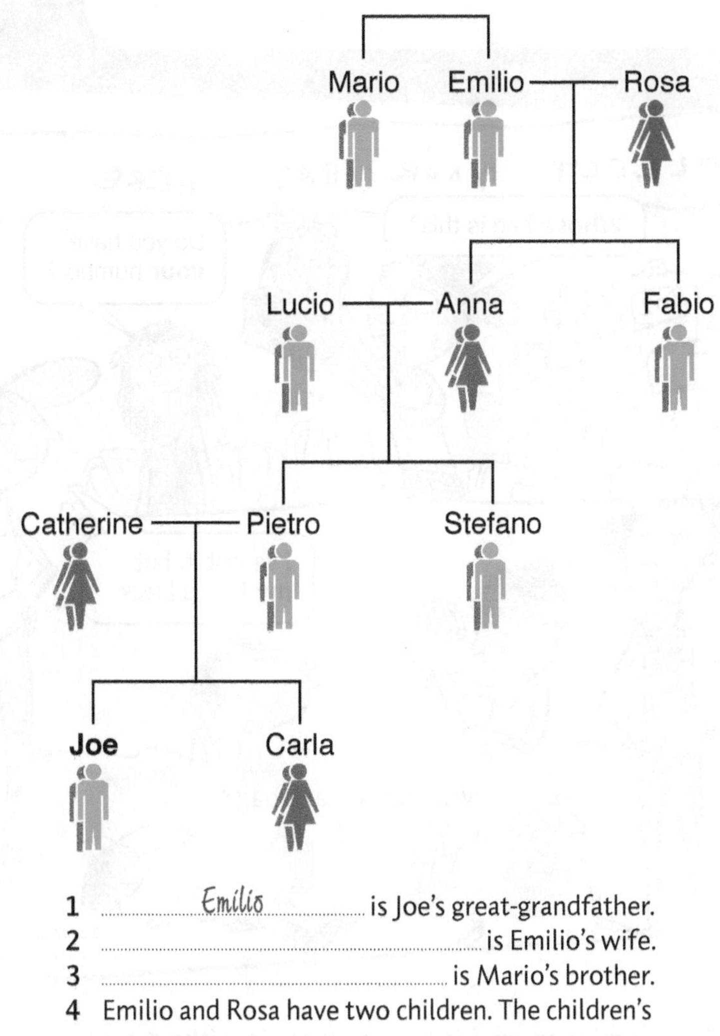

1 ......Emilio...... is Joe's great-grandfather.
2 .... is Emilio's wife.
3 .... is Mario's brother.
4 Emilio and Rosa have two children. The children's names are ....
5 .... are Lucio and Anna's sons.
6 .... is Emilio's great-grandson.
7 Fabio is ......Stefano and Pietro's uncle.......
8 Lucio ....
9 Catherine ....
10 Stefano ....
11 Carla ....
12 Joe and Carla ....

B Complete the sentences using the correct names.

1 This is ......Rosa's...... hat.
2 These are .... boots.
3 This is .... stick.
4 This is .... baby.
5 These are .... shoes.
6 This is .... house.

C Add ' or 's in the correct places.

1 The president's son is coming this afternoon .
2 Jack daughter is taking her exams this summer .
3 Could you get this man coat for him, please ?
4 Women football is becoming more popular .
5 There was a managers meeting last week .
6 Young people diets are not always very healthy .
7 What does your country flag look like ?
8 My parents apartment is in San Francisco .
9 A: Is this your card?
B: No, it's my husband .

Write sentences about your family in your notebook. Use the words in the box.

birthday hobby home job name room school favourite sport

Example: My grandfather's name is Emilio.

MY TEST!

Circle the correct option.

1 .... stayed in Italy. **a** Rosa parents **b** Rosa's parents **c** Rosa's parent's
2 .... children came to Philadelphia in 1905. **a** Emilio's and Rosa **b** Emilio and Rosa's **c** Emilio and Rosa
3 In the 1900s, many .... hats were very beautiful. **a** womans' **b** women's **c** womens'
4 .... lived in Philadelphia all his life. His name's Pietro. **a** Joe's father's **b** Joes fathers' **c** Joe's fathers
5 We always buy our bread at .... He has the best bakery in town. **a** Pietro's **b** Pietros **c** Pietros'

My Test answers: 1b 2b 3b 4a 5a

50 Whose?, my, mine

We ran a 10 km race in town today. After the race we went to get our bags ...
COLLECT YOUR BAGS HERE
Whose bag is this?

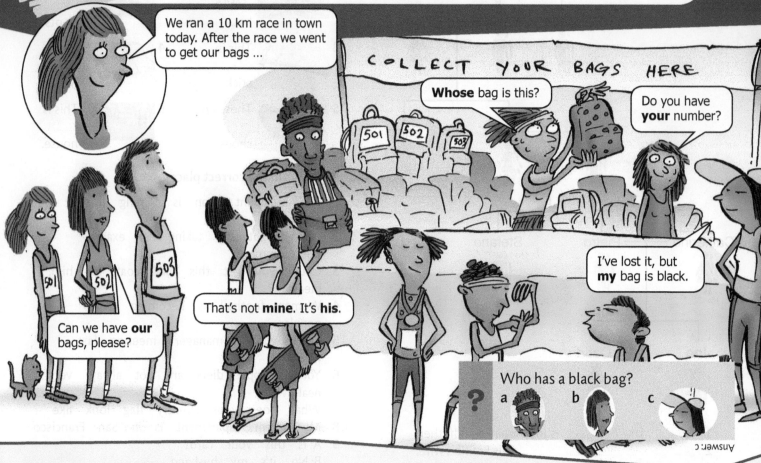

? Who has a black bag?

a b c

Answer: c

Whose?, my, mine

1 Use *Whose?* to ask who something belongs to.

*A: **Whose** bag is this? B: It's Julie's.*

▶ See Unit 26 for questions with *Whose?*

2 Use *my, your, his, her, our, their* with a noun.

__My bag__ is black.
Do you have __your number__?
The boy doesn't have __his bag__.
The woman has lost __her number__.
Can we have __our bags__, please?
That's __their little girl__.

We don't use *a, an* or *the* before *my, your, his, her, our* or *their*.

I went to the cinema with my new friend, Luke.
NOT ~~*... with a my new friend, Luke.*~~
His first day at school was good.
NOT ~~*The his first day ...*~~

3 Use *mine, yours, his, hers, ours, theirs* without a noun.

*That's not **mine**.*
*Do you have **yours**?*
*The boy doesn't have **his**.*
*The woman has lost **hers**.*
*Can we have **ours**?*
*That's **theirs**.*

I	**my** bag	It's **mine**.
You	**your** book	It's **yours**.
He	**his** skateboard	It's **his**.
She	**her** number	It's **hers**.
It	**its** name	–
We	**our** house	It's **ours**.
They	**their** car	It's **theirs**.

***It's* is different from *its*.**

It's a dog. (= it is)
What's its name? (= *What's the dog's name?*)

Practice

A Complete the letter with *my, your, his, her, our* or *their*.

Dear Jez,
This is a photo of [1] ......my...... family. We are just finishing the run. This is [2] .... dad. He was really pleased with [3] .... time. He ran 10 km in 55 minutes. This is [4] .... mum. She's wearing [5] .... race number. This is [6] .... dog. The dog's wearing [7] .... medals. Do you and [8] .... family do any sports together?
Love, Stacey x
PS In the photo you can also see [9] .... friends, Hari and Jay. They always do the race on [10] .... skateboards.

B <u>Underline</u> the correct option.

1 She lives at the end of <u>*our*</u> / *ours* street.
2 A: Is that Claudia's bike?
B: No, that's *her* / *hers* over there.
3 A: *My* / *Mine* new computer is really fast.
B: Lucky you! *My* / *Mine* is really slow!
4 My grandparents live in this village. That's *their* / *theirs* flat on the top floor.
5 A: Is Stella OK?
B: No, I think she has hurt *her* / *hers* arm.
6 *My* / *mine* eyes are blue and *your* / *yours* are brown.
7 I went to San Gimignano on holiday. *It's* / *Its* a very beautiful town.
8 The Black Pharaohs ruled Egypt for 75 years. Until recently, we did not know much about *their* / *theirs* history.
9 Welcome to the museum, everybody. Please leave *your* / *yours* bags at the desk.

C Complete the sentences using an appropriate possessive form.

1 Do these sunglasses belong to you?
No, they're not ......mine...... .
2 I've just seen Teresa. She was with .... husband.
3 A: How is Luke getting home?
B: .... parents are coming to collect him.
4 We would like to have the Olympic games in .... country.
5 A: Are your parents in?
B: No, they've gone to visit a friend of ....
6 I had a phone call from my brother yesterday. It was great to hear .... news.
7 The company is having a meeting for all .... members on Friday.
8 That's Mrs Stanley, my doctor. And that's .... big house.
9 A: Does that blue car belong to your friends?
B: No, ... is red.
10 A: We're staying in this hotel. .... room is on the ground floor.
B: So are we! But .... is on the top floor.
11 That's Michael's bag, but those boots aren't ....
12 A: Mum, me and Jack have had an idea ... .
B: I'm just going to finish my lunch and then you can tell me about that idea of ....

MY TURN!

Answer the questions truthfully in your notebook. If the answer is no, use an appropriate possessive form in the answer.

1 Do you have black jeans?
Yes, I do. / No, mine are blue. / No, my jeans are blue.
2 Do you have a pink mobile phone?
3 Does your teacher have a sports car?
4 Does your friend have a white bag?
5 Is your family home very large?
6 Do your parents have a fast computer?
7 Do you have a tidy bedroom?

MY TEST!

Circle the correct option.

1 .... bag is black and red. That's it under your table. a My the b The my c My
2 This little girl can't find .... running shoes. a she's b her c hers
3 A: Whose medals are these? B: They're .... I saw those boys winning them. a theirs b their c their's
4 My dog has lost .... bone. Is it here? a it's b its' c its
5 My sister and I love running with .... parents. a our b ours c our's

My Test! answers: 1c 2b 3a 4c 5a

51 There and it

It's a very unusual book.

There's a very unusual book in Cincinnati University library. **It's** only 0.99mm². **It's** very small but **it's** a real book: there are 30 pages and **there are** three colour pictures. We asked the librarian Mark Palkovic some questions about the book:

'**Is it** an interesting book?'

'Yes, **it is**. **It's** a story by the Russian author Chekhov.'

'**Is it** in Russian?'

'No, **it isn't**. **It's** a translation into English.'

'**Are there** any other copies?'

'Yes, **there are** 99 other copies. They're in different museums and libraries. Our copy is in very good condition. For example, **there aren't** any missing pages. **It's** beautiful.'

'Can I see it, please?'

'No, **it's** too small!'

True or False? The book has pictures but no words.

Answer: False

There and it

1 Use *there* + *be* to show that something is present or exists.

There is an unusual book in the library.

2 Use *there is* with singular subjects and *there are* with plural subjects. We often use *there* + *be* with *a*, *some* and *any*.

*There isn't a Post Office but **there are** three shops.*

*A: **Are there** any flowers? B: Yes, **there are** some here.*

▶ See Unit 45 for *some* and *any*.

3 Use *there is* with uncountable nouns and with a series of singular and uncountable nouns.

There is milk in your coffee.

There's an apple, some bread and a bottle of milk.

4 We can use *there* in different tenses.

***There was** a problem but **there won't be** tomorrow.*

5 In conversation, the short form *there's* is used. Don't use *there's* in questions or short answers.

*A: **Is there** a computer I can use? B: Yes, **there is**.*

	statement ✓	negative ✗
singular	There is ... (There's ...)	There is not ... (There isn't ... / There's not ...)
plural	There are ...	There are not ... (There aren't ...)

question ?	short answer ✓✗
Is there ...?	Yes, there is. / No, there isn't.
Are there ...?	Yes, there are. / No, there aren't.

6 Use *it* + *be* with a singular or uncountable noun (e.g. *Monday, information*) or adjective (e.g. *big, red*) to identify or describe something or someone.

It's a library, not a museum.

It is quiet in Cincinnati.

*Look Lisa, **it's** David!*

7 Use *it* + *be* to describe days, dates, times and weather.

It's Monday.

It's two o'clock.

It isn't cold.

8 Use *it* + *be* for nouns which have already been mentioned or which are already known to exist.

*A: Is **there** a cafe here? B: Yes, but **it's** not open.*

*A: What's that? B: **It's** a mouse!*

statement ✓	negative ✗
It is ... (It's ...)	It is not ... (It isn't ... / It's not ...)

question ?	short answer ✓✗
Is it ...?	Yes, it is. / No, it isn't.

TIP

Use *It's* to introduce yourself on the phone.

*Hi Jane. **It's** Simon here.*

▶ See Unit 2 for more information on *be*.

Practice

A Look at the picture for one minute, then cover it. If the things in the box were in the picture, write sentences in your notebook beginning *There's ... / There are some ....* If the things were not in the picture, write sentences beginning *There isn't ... / There aren't any ....*

books boxes clock computer ~~door~~ lamp people pictures telephone ~~windows~~

Examples: There aren't any windows. There's a door.

B <u>Underline</u> the correct option.

1 I'm happy. *There's / <u>It's</u>* Friday and I love Fridays.
2 *There isn't / It isn't* a lesson today.
3 *There is / It is* white bread if you don't like brown bread.
4 Is *there / it* five o'clock already?
5 I like Norwich. *There's / It's* a great city.
6 *There / It* is next to the bank.
7 Listen, *there is / it is* something I need to tell you.
8 Here's a letter. *There's / It's* for you.
9 *There isn't / It isn't* my book.
10 Oh no! Is *there / it* closed?
11 Is *there / it* any more news?

C Put the words in the correct order and add *there* or *it* and *was* or *were*.

1 you / to / a / next / pen
There was a pen next to you.
2 birthday / my / yesterday
....
3 you / to / see / lovely / again
....
4 of / a / people / lot
....
5 in / once / bears / England
....
6 time / bed / for / almost
....
7 bottle / the / in / water / some
....
8 long / three / kilometres
....

D Complete the text with the correct forms of *there + be* and *it + be*. (Some are negatives.)

The Three Sisters is a famous play by Anton Chekhov. [1] It isn't a small book but [2] .... very famous. [3] .... three sisters. They live in a boring town at the beginning of the 20th century. [4] .... nothing to do in this town. They want to live in Moscow because [5] .... the capital. [6] .... more opportunities in Moscow. However, [7] .... a long way to Moscow and [8] .... many trains. [9] .... easy to move from a small town to the capital. So, the sisters never go to Moscow. *The Three Sisters* is a classic play and [10] .... translations into many languages.

MY TURN!

In your notebook, write two sentences about each item in the left-hand column using words in the right-hand column. One sentence should begin *There's ...* and one sentence should begin *It's ....*

a bus a good programme a door some information a text message	on the website really interesting on television for you open at the bus stop in the wall from Susie very late! really funny!

Example: There's a door in the wall. It's open.

MY TEST!

Circle the correct option.

1 .... a lot of information on the website.
a There are b There's c It's
2 I like our library. .... very good and there are a lot of useful books. a Its b There's c It's
3 .... very cold in our library.
a There's b It's c Is
4 There .... any colour pictures in the book.
a isn't b hasn't c aren't
5 A: Is there a copy in the library? B: Yes, ...
a there is b there's c it is

My Test! answers: 1b 2c 3b 4c 5a

R9 Review: pronouns; possessives; quantifiers

A Replace the underlined words with pronouns to make this story more natural.

Hi. My name's Will. I live in a house with [1]~~Will's~~ *my* parents and brother, Tom. [2]~~Will's family's~~ *Our* house has a nice big garden where my brother and I like playing football.

One day, [3]Will kicked the ball over the garden wall and into [4]Will's family's neighbours' garden. The neighbours are called Mr and Mrs Stark and [5]the neighbours are not very nice people. [6]The neighbours don't like [7]Will's family and [8]Will's family don't like [9]the neighbours.

[10]Will and Tom asked [11]the neighbours for [12]Will and Tom's ball back, but Mrs Stark didn't give [13]the ball to us. Mrs Stark said '[14]The ball is in [15]Mr and Mrs Stark's garden so [16]the ball is [17]Mr and Mrs Stark's.'

Later that day, Mrs Stark came to [18]Will's family's house. [19]Mrs Stark had [20]Will and Tom's ball. 'Sorry. Here's the ball,' [21]Mrs Stark said to me. 'I need [22]Will's help. Today a bird took [23]Mrs Stark's gold watch and dropped [24]the watch in [25]Will's family's garden. Can [26]Will give [27]Mrs Stark the watch back, please?'

What do you think [28]Will said?

B Answer the questions with sentences beginning *there* or *it*.

1 How many people are in your class?
There are 26.

2 What is the time?
....

3 What colour is your country's flag?
....

4 What can you see outside the window?
....

5 Does your town have a lot of tourists?
....

6 Who is your best friend?
....

7 What wild animals live in your country?
....

8 What day was your birthday on last year?
....

9 What was on TV last night?
....

10 What was the weather like yesterday?
....

C Put apostrophes (') in the correct places in these sentences.

1 Robert's got some new trousers, but they're not very nice.
2 My brothers friend is very kind but hes not very clever.
3 Samanthas baby brother sleeps in her parents bedroom.
4 Its good that she isnt angry.
5 My friends computer doesnt work.
6 Ill do my work and you can do yours.
7 My sister likes my brothers friends but he doesnt like hers.
8 The childrens rooms are very dirty.
9 Marias horses names are Daisy and Rosy.
10 Terrys parents took his keys and he took theirs.

D Complete each sentence b so that it means the same as sentence a. Use two to four words including the word in brackets.

1 a Who does this phone belong to? (is)
b *Whose phone is* this?

2 a Barry and Gary have a house by the sea. We stayed there last summer. (in)
b We stayed .... house by the sea last summer.

3 a My dad owns these skis. (are)
b These skis ....

4 a You can use my dictionary. Have you lost yours? (lend)
b Have you lost your dictionary? I'll ....

5 a Al and Paula live near a lake. They're very lucky. (house)
b Al and Paula are very lucky. .... near a lake.

6 a She talks but he never listens. (to)
b He never .... when she talks.

7 a Can I have a new bike, please? (give)
b Can .... a new bike, please?

E Complete this report. Write one word from the box in each space.

a	any	anything	everybody	~~few~~	little	lot of	lots
many	many	many	much	much	nobody	of	

A [1] ......few...... days ago I interviewed 25 students about their cinema habits. Here are the results of my survey.

1 or 2× a month
5× a month
4× a month
3× a month

Number of visits to cinema every month

Question 1: How [2] .... times do you go to the cinema every month?

[3] .... in the class goes to the cinema sometimes.
[4] .... people go to the cinema once or twice a month.
[5] .... few people go three, four or five times.
[6] .... goes more than five times a month.

Question 2: How [7] .... cola do you usually drink at the cinema?

[8] .... of people buy cola at the cinema, and some [9] .... them say they drink a [10] .... cola (1 litre or more) while they are watching a film. Seventeen people say they drink a [11] .... cola (less than 1 litre). A few people never drink [12] .... cola.

Question 3: How [13] .... food do you usually buy at the cinema?

People in my class don't buy [14] .... snacks (sandwiches, hot dogs, etc.) at the cinema. Four people in the group never buy [15] .... at the cinema because it is very expensive.

F Underline the correct option.

Alison: Hello. [1] *That* / *This* / *Here* is Alison. Is [2] *that* / *you* / *there*, Sally?
Sally: Yes, it is. Hi, Alison. Where are you?
Alison: I'm camping [3] *anywhere* / *nowhere* / *somewhere* in the forest. I'm here with [4] *some* / *any* / *a little* of the girls from my class.
Sally: [5] *That* / *This* / *Those* sounds nice.
Alison: Yeah, it's great. It's so big – we can walk a long way in [6] *any* / *this* / *no* direction and we never see [7] *any* / *an* / *no* other people. But we've seen [8] *that* / *an* / *lots of* animals.
Sally: Really? Have you seen [9] *a* / *much* / *any* bears?
Alison: No, none. We've heard [10] *a few* / *few of* / *a few of*, but we haven't seen [11] *any of* / *any* / *none*. We have seen [12] *some* / *lots* / *a few of* rabbits. We've even seen [13] *any* / *a little* / *a few* snakes.
Sally: That's fantastic. What's [14] *the* / *a* / *–* weather like?
Alison: Well, we've had [15] *some* / *a* / *a few* nice weather, but we've also had [16] *a few* / *a few of* / *a lot of* rain. Last night we all got wet while we were coming home. [17] *A little of* / *Much of* / *A few of* the girls got sick.
Sally: That doesn't sound like [18] *many* / *much* / *a* fun. Are you going [19] *nowhere* / *anywhere* / *everywhere* today?
Alison: No, [20] *somewhere* / *nowhere* / *anywhere*. We're going to stay at the campsite and wait for the doctor.
Sally: Oh no.
Alison: Listen, I have to go. I'll see you soon.
Sally: OK, bye. Have [21] *any* / *a* / *–* fun!

52 Adjectives

It's a wonderful place.

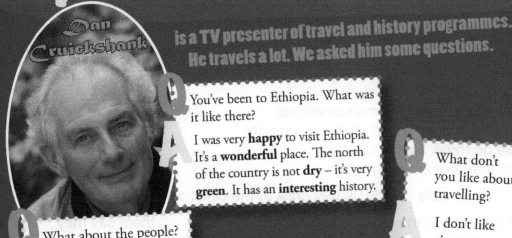

is a TV presenter of travel and history programmes. He travels a lot. We asked him some questions.

Q You've been to Ethiopia. What was it like there?

A I was very **happy** to visit Ethiopia. It's a **wonderful** place. The north of the country is not **dry** – it's very **green**. It has an **interesting** history.

Q What about the people? What are they like?

A The **Ethiopian** people are **beautiful** and **kind**.

Q What don't you like about travelling?

A I don't like airports – they're **boring**!

Q Do you have a **favourite** city?

A I have two favourite cities: Damascus and Calcutta. They are both **ancient** cities. Calcutta has some **great** palaces and it seems very **safe**.

Calcutta

? What places does Dan Cruickshank talk about?

Answer: Damascus, Calcutta and Ethiopia.

Adjectives

1 **An adjective describes a noun or a pronoun.**
*It's a **wonderful** country. They are **beautiful**.*

2 **Put the adjective before the noun.**
*It has an **interesting** history.*
NOT ~~*It has a history interesting.*~~

TIP

There are a few adjectives which we only use after the noun or pronoun. For example: *afraid, alive, alone, asleep, awake, glad.* We prefer to use *ill* and *well* (= healthy) after the noun, too.
*The baby is **awake**.* NOT ~~*... the awake baby ...*~~
*The man is **ill**.* NOT ~~*... the ill man ...*~~

3 **We use adjectives after the verbs *be, feel, look, seem, smell, sound, taste.***
*It is **safe**. They **seem beautiful** and **charming**.*

4 **A number of adjectives end in *-y*.**
ugly, funny, happy

***-ful* at the end of an adjective often has a meaning similar to 'full of'.**
careful, useful

***-less* often means 'without'.**
careless, useless

TIP

Adjectives don't change in the plural.
ancient cities NOT ~~*ancients cities*~~

5 **We can use words like *very, quite, a bit* and *a little* with adjectives. Use *quite, a bit* and *a little* after the noun or pronoun.**
*He's **quite** tall.* (= not tall, but not short)
NOT ~~*He's quite tall man.*~~
*The weather's **a bit** cold. The weather's **a little** cold.*
NOT ~~*It's a bit cold weather.*~~

***Very* can be used before or after the noun or pronoun.**
*She's a **very** kind person.* OR *She's **very** kind.*

We don't use words like *a bit* or *really* in front of all adjectives. For example, we say *He is married*, but NOT ~~*He is quite married*~~. We say *It is delicious*, but NOT ~~*It's very delicious*~~. Other examples are: *dead, enormous, exhausted, impossible, perfect.*

6 **Sometimes we use another noun instead of an adjective.**
shoe + shop = a shoe shop
dog + food = dog food

Practice

A Find at least ten pairs of adjectives and nouns that go together and write them in your notebook. (Some adjectives may go with more than one noun.)

ancient careless city cold day empty face glass great information man terrible time weather worker ugly useful young

Example: *young man*

B Put a noun from box A with a noun from box B to make words which match the definitions.

A	bed ~~book~~ CD credit post taxi tooth train
B	brush card driver man player room ~~shop~~ station

1 You buy books here. ......*a book shop*......
2 You can use this if you don't have any money.
....
3 You can use this to listen to music. ....
4 You clean your teeth with this. ....
5 You sleep here. ....
6 You go here to travel to a different place. ....
7 This person brings your letters. ....
8 This person takes people to other places. ....

C Make sentences by putting the words in order, then suggest who or what each sentence is about.

1 stories / writes / wonderful / he / think / I
I think he writes wonderful stories. (Paolo Coelho)
2 from / far / it / not / is / here
....
3 was / busy / very / it / place / a
....
4 well / very / doesn't / she / look
....
5 these / lovely / smell / flowers
....
6 friendly / very / not / she / does / seem
....
7 it / idea / not / is / good / a
....
8 actor / my / he / favourite / is
....
9 do / nice / taste / they / not
....
10 always / is / he / asleep!
....

D Complete the sentences using *a bit, a little, quite* or *very* where possible.

1 ......*My dad is quite*...... tall.
2 .... impossible.
3 .... nice.
4 .... enormous
5 .... tired
6 .... short.
7 .... small.
8 .... perfect.
9 .... happy.
10 .... cold.

MY TURN!

Answer the questions about your favourite city in your notebook. Use an adjective in each answer.

1 Do you have a favourite city?
2 When you first arrived in this city, how did you feel?
3 Think of one place every visitor must see. What is it? Tell us something interesting about it.
4 Imagine you are flying over the city in an aeroplane. What does the city look like?
5 What are the people like there?
6 What is the city like at night?
7 What do you miss about this city?

1 ......*My favourite city is Prague. It's a beautiful city.*......

MY TEST!

Circle the correct option.

1 Istanbul and Barcelona are both .... a beautifuls cities b beautiful cities c cities beautifuls
2 He has met many .... people. a afraid b awake c interesting
3 I am .... I often lose things. a quite careless man b quite careless c quite careful
4 The king's palace is very .... a old b enormous c perfect
5 I spend a lot of time in .... a airport's restaurants b airport restaurants c restaurant airports

My Test answers: 1b 2c 3b 4a 5b

53 Order of adjectives

… wonderful golden shoes …

The **International Olympic** Museum in Lausanne, Switzerland has many unique exhibits. Here are some examples:

The **original wooden** torch from Montreal (1976).

The **wonderful golden** shoes of the **brilliant 100 m** sprinter, Carl Lewis.

A **fascinating short** film clip of the first modern Olympics (1896).

An **ancient Greek** vase from Olympia (450 BC).

An **interesting small** stamp from London (1948).

Which country were the 1976 Olympics in?

Answer: Canada

Order of adjectives

1 **When there is more than one adjective before a noun, the adjectives usually go in a specific order.**

*an **interesting old** museum* NOT ~~*an old interesting museum*~~

*a **popular British** sport* NOT ~~*a British popular sport*~~

2 **Opinion adjectives (e.g. *nice, terrible, strange*, etc.) go before factual adjectives (e.g. *old, green, plastic*, etc.).**

the wonderful golden shoes

a brilliant educational experience

3 **The usual order of adjectives is:**

opinion	size	quality	age	shape	colour	origin	material
lovely	big	clever	old	round	red	Italian	paper
strange	long	happy	recent	square	black	African	stone

*an **ancient Greek** vase* (age + origin)

*a **small square** stamp* (size + shape)

*a **big strong wooden** box* (size + quality + material)

*my **lovely warm new green** jumper* (opinion + quality + age + colour)

4 **If there is an adjective phrase with numbers before a noun, we often use hyphens (-) to separate the words.**

*We stayed in a **five-star** hotel.*

*A horse is a **four-legged** animal.*

Practice

A Write these adjectives in the correct column.

amazing Asian ~~big~~ brown cheese dirty enormous famous glass golden handsome happy modern new quiet Roman short Swiss white

opinion	size	quality	age	colour	origin	material
....	big	....	....	....	....	....
....	....	....	....	....	....	....
....	....	....	....	....	....	....

B Describe the pictures using one word from each column.

amazing ~~enormous~~ heavy long tall tired	~~golden~~ Kenyan new slim silver 70-metre	basketball discus ~~golf~~ marathon Olympic 100-metre

1

2

3

4
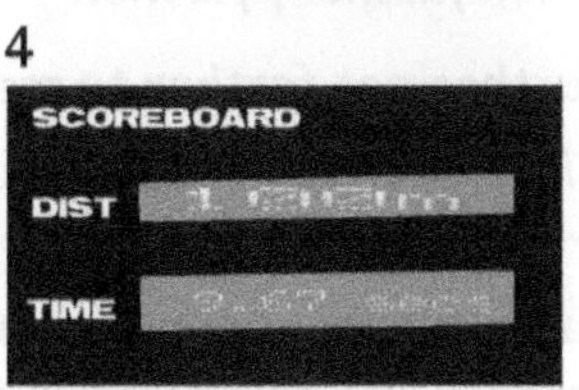

5

6
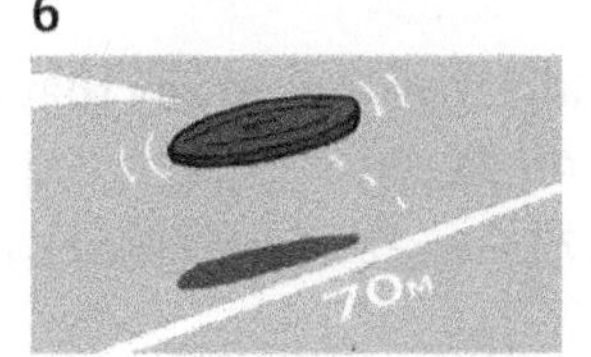

1 an *enormous golden golf* .... cup
2 a .... medal
3 a .... runner
4 a really .... record
5 a .... player
6 a really .... throw

C Complete each sentence with the correct adjective.

1 It's a red *English* teapot. (English / small)
2 I got a new .... poster for my birthday. (football / beautiful)
3 Paint a square .... house. (big / brown)
4 It's a .... Japanese boat. (real / fishing)
5 The police are looking for a .... blonde girl. (tall / French)
6 It was a .... round ball. (plastic / hard)
7 Do you really need silver .... shoes? (expensive / golf)
8 I bought a red .... car. (fast / family)

MY TURN!

In your notebook, write six phrases describing the nouns in the box using three adjectives. Don't use any adjective more than once.

armchair bear dress footballer friend sandwich shoes watch window

Example: *a big brown Russian bear*

MY TEST!

Circle the correct option.

1 Lausanne is a .... a beautiful Swiss-town b beautiful Swiss town c Swiss beautiful town
2 We saw .... medal at the museum.
a an ancient gold incredible b a gold ancient incredible c an incredible ancient gold
3 The winner of the race was a young .... girl. a amazing b small c Chinese
4 They are building .... stadium in the city.
a an enormous new Olympic b a new Olympic enormous c an Olympic new enormous
5 The ancient Romans loved .... a horses race b horse races c horses races

My Test! answers: 1b 2c 3c 4a 5b

Comparatives

It's nearer than you think.

Are you looking for a really different skiing holiday?

Try Sochi, Russia, location of the 2014 winter Olympics. Now it's **easier** than ever to travel to Sochi and it's **nearer** than you think. The new airport terminal is **nicer** and much **more convenient** than the old one. Things are a bit **more expensive** than in Switzerland but Russians say the snow is **whiter** and **faster**. After all that skiing you will go home **slimmer** and **fitter** than when you arrived! If you get tired of skiing, Sochi beach is close and the entertainment is even **better** there. Some tourists think the nightlife is **more interesting** than the skiing!

Try Sochi – it really is as good as we say!

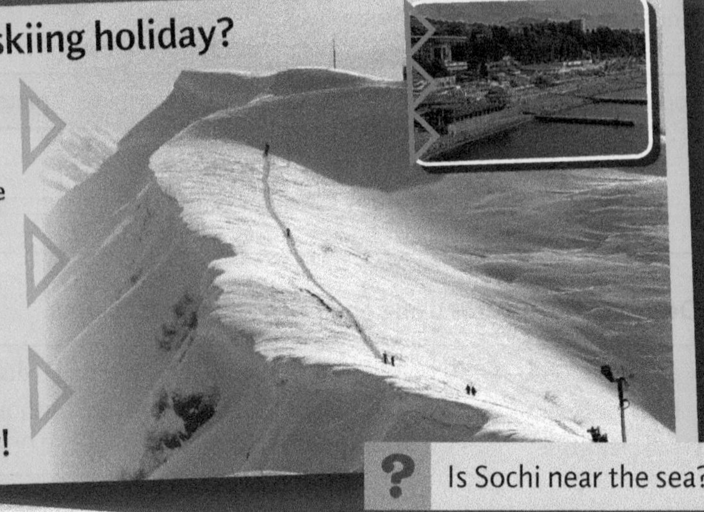

? Is Sochi near the sea?

Answer: Yes

Comparatives

1 **Use the comparative form of adjectives to compare people, things, actions and events.**
*The airport is **smaller** but **more convenient**.*
*The Sochi Olympics will be **better** than the Vancouver Olympics.*

2 **To make the comparative of one-syllable adjectives, add *-er* to the adjective.**
slow → slower, long → longer

3 **Some two-syllable adjectives form comparatives with *-er*, or *more* before the adjective.**
clever → cleverer, narrow → narrower, simple → simpler

4 **To make the comparative of long adjectives (at least two syllables) put *more* before the adjective.**
intelligent → more intelligent
hard-working → more hard-working

> **TIP**
> **Two-syllable adjectives ending in *-y* have *-er* endings.**
> *The journey was **easier** last year.*
> *I feel **happier** now.*

5 **A few comparative adjectives have irregular forms.**
good → better, bad → worse, far → further / farther

> **TIP**
> ***further* or *farther***
> **When we talk about distance, the meaning is the same.**
> *It is 10 km **further** / **farther**.*
> **Use *further*, not *farther*, to mean 'extra'.**
> *There is **further** information about Sochi on the website.*

6 **To compare different people, things, actions and events in the same sentence, use comparative adjective + *than*.**
*Winter is **colder than** summer.*

7 **Use *as* + adjective + *as* to say that people or things are equal.**
*I'm **as tall as** you.*

▶ See Unit 57 for more information on *as ... as*.

8 **The opposite of *more* is *less*. We usually use *less* before adjectives of two syllables and more.**
*Are people **less** happy today?*
*Travelling is **less** difficult now.*

We often use *not as ...* (*as*) instead of *less* in speaking and informal language.
*Travelling is **not as** difficult now.*

▶ See Unit 57 for *less* before adverbs (*less quickly*).

9 **Don't use *very* on its own before a comparative adjective. Use *much*, *far* or *a lot*. *A lot* is more informal. If you want to say that the difference compared is small, use *a little* or *a bit*. *A bit* is more informal.**
*Sochi is **much hotter** than Moscow.* NOT ~~*... very hotter ...*~~
*Our hotel is **a little more** expensive.*

Practice

A Complete the quiz questions using comparative forms of the adjectives in brackets. Then underline the answers.

1 Which are ......higher...... : the Carpathians or the Rocky Mountains? (high)
2 Which month is .... : February or March? (long)
3 Which is .... : driving or flying? (dangerous)
4 Which is .... : 'I want the bread.' or 'Can you give me the bread?' (polite)
5 Which is .... : gold or silver? (rare)
6 Which is .... : one mile or one kilometre? (far)
7 Which city is .... : Tokyo or Seoul? (expensive)
8 Which town is .... : Moscow or Madrid? (old)
9 Who was .... when he died: Mozart or Shakespeare? (young)
10 Which is .... : a kilogram of water or a kilogram of ice? (heavy)

Now check your answers at the bottom of the page.

B Use the information from Exercise A to complete these sentences using *less than* or *not as ... as*.

1 February ......is not as long as March...... .
2 Flying ....
3 Silver ....
4 One kilometre ....
5 Seoul ....
6 Moscow ....

C Complete the sentences about the two hotels, using the information in the table and the adjectives in the box.

	Seaview	Pushkin
1 Atmosphere	☺☺	☺☺☺
2 Management	☺☺☺	☺☺☺
3 Price per day	100 euros	70 euros
4 Size	67 rooms	67 rooms
5 Distance from the beach	400m	15 minute walk
6 Service	☺☺	☺☺☺
7 Food	☺☺☺	☺☺☺☺
8 Check-out time	11.00	12.00

bad big expensive far ~~good~~ good interesting late ~~nice~~

1 The atmosphere at Pushkin is ......nicer...... .
2 The management at Seaview is ......as good as...... the management at Pushkin.
3 Seaview is 30 euros ....
4 Pushkin is .... Seaview.
5 Pushkin is .... from the beach.
6 The service at Pushkin is .... than at Seaview.
7 The food at Seaview is .... than at Pushkin.
8 The check-out time at Pushkin is ....

MY TURN!

In your notebook, write sentences comparing the animals. Use *much, far, a lot, a little* or *a bit* and comparative adjectives.

Example: *The giraffe is much taller than the zebra.*

MY TEST!

Circle the correct option.

1 The beach in Sochi was .... the beach in my town.
a nicer than b nicer then c more nice than
2 The mountains in Sochi are a little .... than the mountains in my country.
a bigger b biger c more big
3 This hotel used to be very bad, but now it's ....
a very better b much better c much more good
4 Do you think the winter Olympics are .... as the summer Olympics?
a more interesting b as interesting c as much interesting
5 I'm much .... than I was a few years ago.
a less healthier b not as healthy c less healthy

My Test! answers: 1a 2a 3b 4b 5c

Exercise A answers:
2 March 3 driving 4 Can you give me the bread? 5 gold
6 one mile 7 Tokyo 8 Madrid 9 Mozart 10 Both are the same!

55 Superlatives

The lowest point on Earth

Amazing facts

The **lowest** point on Earth is the Mariana Trench. It is the **deepest** part of the Pacific Ocean at 11 km down.

Antarctica has the **most extreme** climate. The temperature can be –50º C and wind speeds 200 km / hour. The penguins there live in probably the world's **most difficult** conditions.

The **biggest** tree is the Giant Sequoia, which grows in California, USA. *General Sherman* is the world's **largest** living tree and the **most famous** Sequoia. (William Sherman was one of the **most important** generals in American history.)

The shortest river is the Roe River in Montana, USA. It is only 61 metres long but it is one of the **most popular** tourist attractions in Montana.

? Which is a good place for tourists? **a** The Mariana Trench **b** Antarctica **c** Montana

Answer: c

Superlatives

1 Use superlatives to compare people, things, actions and events.

*The **biggest** tree is the Giant Sequoia.*
*William Sherman was one of the **most important** generals.*
*It's the **best** thing I've ever seen.*

2 To make the superlative of one-syllable adjectives, add *-est*.

quick → quickest, low → lowest

3 To make the superlative of long adjectives (at least two syllables), put *most* before the adjective, e.g. *most popular, most famous*.

4 We can use *-est* with some two-syllable adjectives, and some adjectives ending in *-y*, e.g. *simplest, happiest*.

*Which is the **simplest**?*
*That was the **happiest** day of my life.*

5 Some superlatives have irregular forms.

good → best, bad → worst, far → furthest / farthest

6 The opposite of *most* is *least*.

*I bought it because it was the **least expensive**.*

7 We usually use *the* before superlatives.

***The oldest** rock in the world is in Australia.*

8 We can use superlatives without a noun.

*My essay is not the longest, but it's **the most interesting**.*

TIP

Use *in* + the name of a group or place (*class, team, Italy, world*, etc.) after a superlative.

*He is the **most important** player **in** the team.*
NOT *~~... of the team.~~*

Use *of* + plurals after a superlative.

*This is the **hardest** question **of** them all.*

Practice

A Match the pairs of opposite adjectives and write the superlative forms.

dangerous good hard-working interesting ~~long~~ old sad strong wet	bad boring dry happy lazy new ~~short~~ safe weak

1 longest ≠ shortest
2 .... ≠ ....
3 .... ≠ ....
4 .... ≠ ....
5 .... ≠ ....
6 .... ≠ ....
7 .... ≠ ....
8 .... ≠ ....
9 .... ≠ ....

B Complete the sentences with the superlatives of the words in brackets.

1 Gran is the fittest. (fit)
2 Dad is the most tired. (tired)
3 Mum is the tallest. (tall)

4 .... has .... ears. (long)
5 .... has .... eyes. (big)

6 .... (cheap)
7 .... (expensive)

8 .... has .... T-shirt. (unusual)

C Put the numbers 1–5 under each heading, then write sentences with superlatives or *least* + adjective in your notebook.

	heavy	nice	useful	interesting	fast	dangerous
elephant	1					
horse	4					
mouse	5					
dog	3					
sheep	2					

1 The elephant is the heaviest.

D Make sentences using words and phrases from the table and write them in your notebook.

~~The Roe~~	large	star
Mount Everest	~~short~~	continent
The Vatican City	common	mountain
The blue whale	bright	country
Antarctica	high	~~river~~
Hydrogen	deep	lake
Sirius	cold	gas
Baikal	small	animal

1 The Roe is the shortest river.

MY TURN!

Write superlative phrases advertising these things in your notebook.

1 A computer game: This is the most exciting game!
2 A car
3 A mobile phone
4 A dog
5 A flat
6 A café

MY TEST!

Circle the correct option.

1 Moscow is the world's .... city for foreigners. a expensivest b more expensive c most expensive
2 The .... Africa is Kilimanjaro.
a most tall mountain of
b tallest mountain in
c most tall mountain in
3 .... place in the world is El Azizia.
a The most hot b Hottest
c The hottest
4 The .... interesting place in the world is my town – nothing ever happens there.
a least b less c not very
5 The largest .... the American Great Lakes is Lake Superior. a in b from c of

My Test! answers: 1c 2b 3c 4a 5c

56 Adverbs of manner

Eat healthily.

Teenagers are busy people, but eating **fast** doesn't have to mean eating **badly**. Feel good, look good, have more energy and sleep **well**; these are four good reasons to eat **healthily**.

Carbohydrates are an important part of a healthy diet. Simple carbohydrates, or sugars, give us energy **quickly**, but only for a short time. But you can also find complex carbohydrates in food such as bananas, rice, pasta and bread. These give us energy **slowly**, and for longer.

Most people don't eat enough complex carbohydrates, but you can **easily** eat more. For example: 1. Eat more pasta. 2. Have more potatoes and less meat. 3. Make sure you eat bread or toast for breakfast.

? Which food is **not** a carbohydrate? **a** pasta **b** meat **c** rice **d** bananas

Answer: b

Adverbs of manner

1 **Use adverbs of manner to describe how something happens.**

He eats very ***healthily****. They give us energy* ***quickly****.*

2 **We usually form adverbs of manner by adding *-ly* to the adjective.**

bad → *badly, careful* → *carefully*

If the adjective ends in *-e*, take off the *-e*.

gentle → *gently*

If the adjective ends in *-y*, we usually change the *-y* to *i*.

angry → *angrily*   *healthy* → *healthily*
easy → *easily*   *heavy* → *heavily*
(un)happy → *(un)happily*   *noisy* → *noisily*
BUT *shy* → *shyly*

3 **Some adjectives end in *-ly*, e.g. *friendly, lonely, lovely, silly, ugly*. We don't add *-ly* to make the adverb. We say, for example:**

He spoke to them ***in a friendly way****.*

4 **Some adverbs are the same as the adjectives, e.g. *early, far, fast, hard, high, late, low*.**

a ***fast*** *car* (= adjective), *eating* ***fast*** (= adverb)

5 ***Well*** **is the adverb from *good*.**

Sleep ***well****.*

TIP
Well **can also be an adjective. It means 'healthy'.**
My teacher was not at school today. He is not ***well****.*

6 **Adverbs of manner often come at the end of a sentence.**

Simple carbohydrates provide energy ***quickly****.*

TIP
An adverb does not usually come between a verb and the object.
She plays tennis well. NOT ~~*She plays well tennis.*~~
Complex carbohydrates provide energy slowly.
NOT ~~*Complex carbohydrates provide slowly energy.*~~

▶ See page 183 for more spelling rules.

Practice

A Read each sentence a, then complete sentence b with a suitable adverb.

1. a They have a healthy diet.
   b They eat *healthily*.
2. a I had a bad diet when I was a student.
   b I ate .... when I was a student.
3. a I like eating fish because it is quick to cook.
   b I like eating fish because you can cook it ....
4. a My little sister is noisy when she eats.
   b My little sister eats ....
5. a It was easy to find the restaurant.
   b We found the restaurant ....
6. a My friend prepared the meal but he was very slow.
   b My friend prepared the meal ....
7. a When he put the food on the plates, he was very careful.
   b He put the food on the plates very ....

B Complete the sentences using adverbs made from the adjectives in the box.

careful early far fast good happy ~~hard~~
immediate late sudden

1. My class has studied very *hard* for our exam.
2. Where is the hotel? Do we have to go .... ?
3. My dog loves water, he will swim .... for hours.
4. I never go on motorways – I don't like driving ....
5. My aunt lives in Japan. She speaks Japanese .... now.
6. Please drive .... through the village.
7. It's only six o'clock. Why did you get up so .... ?
8. My friend invited me to stay and I said 'yes' ....
9. We were walking in the park when a man .... shouted at us.
10. He left home .... and had to run to work.

C Complete the sentences about the famous people using the words in the table. Choose a verb and make an adverb from an appropriate adjective.

could	dance hit paint play football play chess run sing	beautiful brilliant very good hard quick

1. Rudolf Nureyev *could dance beautifully*.
2. Leonardo da Vinci ....
3. Rocky Marciano ....
4. Carl Lewis ....
5. The Beatles ....
6. Pelé ....
7. Garry Kasparov ....

Make sentences about famous people today and write them in your notebook.

Example: *Cristiano Ronaldo can play football brilliantly.*

MY TURN!

In your notebook, write sentences about what the people are doing and how.

1 
2 
3 
4 
5 
6 

1 *She is running quickly / fast.*

MY TEST!

Circle the correct option.

1. She always eats .... a her food quick b her food quickly c quickly her food
2. Wash your hands .... before cooking. a carefuly b careful c carefully
3. She cooks really .... a good b goodly c well
4. They worked very .... in the kitchen. a hard b harder c hardly
5. He speaks .... when he's excited. a sillily b sillyly c in a silly way

My Test! answers: 1b 2c 3c 4a 5c

57 Comparative and superlative adverbs

Which will fall faster?

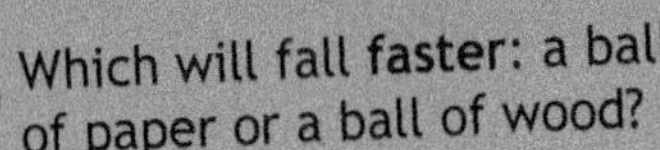

Q Which will fall **faster**: a ball of paper or a ball of wood?

A Many people think that light objects always fall **more slowly**. But – remember Galileo – if the balls are the same size they will hit the ground at the same time.

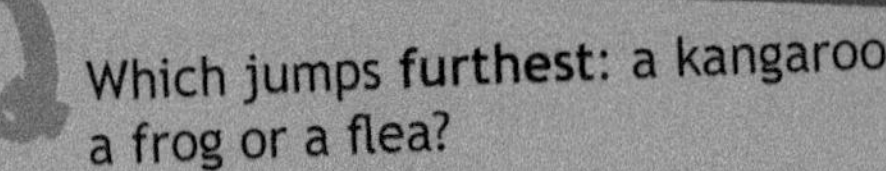

Q Which jumps **furthest**: a kangaroo, a frog or a flea?

A A kangaroo jumps **furthest** – about 9 metres. But the flea jumps **best**. It jumps 200 times its own body length.

Q In a storm we see the lightning before we hear the thunder. Why?

A Because light travels **more quickly** than sound.

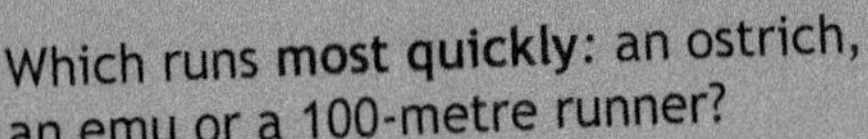

Q Which runs **most quickly**: an ostrich, an emu or a 100-metre runner?

A An ostrich runs **most quickly** at around 56 km an hour. An emu runs at about 48 km an hour and a 100-metre runner at about 32 km an hour.

Underline the correct option. A kangaroo can jump *9 metres / 32 metres / 200 metres*.

Answer: 9 metres

Comparative and superlative adverbs

1 **Add *more* or *less* to make the comparative form of most adverbs.**
*Light travels **more quickly** than sound.*
*Light objects do not fall **less quickly**.*

2 **Add *most* or *least* to make the superlative form of most adverbs.**
*Which runs **most quickly**?*
*Which runs **least quickly**?*

3 **Many short adverbs, such as *early, fast, hard, high, late, long* and *soon* have comparative forms with *-er* and superlative forms with *-est*.**
early → earlier → earliest, fast → faster → fastest
early → less early → least early, fast → less fast → least fast

4 **Some common adverbs have irregular comparative and superlative forms.**
well → better → best
badly → worse → worst
far → farther / further → farthest / furthest

5 **Use *as* + adverb + *as* when two or more people or things are equal.**
*I work **as hard as** you.*

▶ See Units 54 and 55 for comparative and superlative forms of adjectives.
▶ See Unit 56 for more information on forming adverbs.

Practice

A Complete the table.

	adverb	comparative	superlative
1	badly	worse	worst
2	early	....	....
3	....	more easily	....
4	far	....	....
5	....	better	....
6	....	....	most happily
7	....	more slowly	....
8	safely	....	....

B Underline the correct option.

1 Can you explain your ideas *more simply / most simply*?
2 The storm arrived *soon / sooner* than we expected.
3 There are many different types of plane, but rocket planes like the X-15 fly *higher / highest*.
4 Special cycle roads mean people can cycle *more safely / most safely*.
5 I don't know who plays the guitar *badly / worse* – you or me!
6 Why aren't you studying? You need to take your exams *more seriously / most seriously*.
7 Robots can do many jobs as *accurately / more accurately* as humans.
8 Of all the boys, he did the work *more carefully / most carefully*.

C Complete the sentences using the adjectives in brackets to make comparative adverbs. Circle True or False.

1 A man runs .... more slowly .... than a cheetah. (slow) True / False
2 A frog jumps .... than a kangaroo. (far) True / False
3 Dolphins swim .... than most fish. (quick) True / False
4 Light travels .... than sound. (fast) True / False
5 A balloon can fly .... than a plane. (high) True / False
6 Most plants grow .... in the sun. (good) True / False
7 A knife cuts .... when it's not sharp. (easy) True / False
8 Most people sleep .... in the winter. (deep) True / False

D Complete the sentences using the adjectives in brackets to make superlative adverbs.

Of all the people I know ...
1 .... My dad .... drives .... most slowly .... (slow)
2 .... draws .... (good)
3 .... works .... (hard)
4 .... writes .... (clear)
5 .... lives .... from here. (far)
6 .... sings .... (bad)
7 .... sleeps .... (long)
8 .... eats his / her lunch .... (quick)

MY TURN!

In your notebook, write at least six sentences comparing what Tim, Jim and Kim are doing or have done. Use *more, most, less, least, -er, -est* and adverbs made from the adjectives in the box.

fast	happy	high	hungry	quick	slow	tidy

TIM JIM KIM

Example: Tim is eating most quickly.

MY TEST!

Circle the correct option.

1 My cat is great: she plays much .... than my big, noisy dog.
a quieter b most quietly c more quietly
2 Elephants can live much .... than people.
a more longly b longer c more long
3 The bird that flies .... is the peregrine falcon.
a most fastly b most fast c fastest
4 Many birds fly a long way, but Arctic terns fly ....
a most far b farest c furthest
5 Sorry, can you please speak .... ? I can't understand you.
a more slowly b slowlier c more slow

My Test! answers: 1c 2b 3c 4c 5a

58 *-ed* and *-ing* adjectives

Is it exciting?

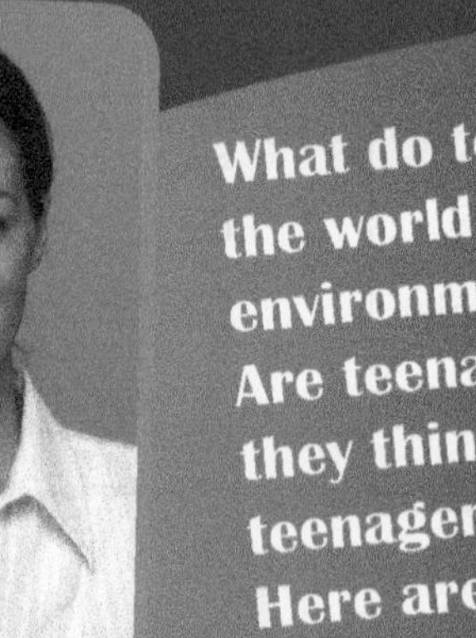

What do teenagers really think about the world today? News, technology, the environment, politics, social problems ... Are teenagers bored with all this or do they think it is interesting? 215 Russian teenagers completed a questionnaire. Here are their answers.

	Agree (%)	Disagree (%)	Not sure (%)
Climate change is **worrying**.	30	17	53
The price of food today is **shocking**.	90	0	10
No one is **interested** in my opinion.	69	12	19
Politics is **boring**.	84	7	9
I am very **worried** about crime.	15	30	55
TV advertisements are **annoying**.	65	20	15
It is **exciting** to live in the 21st century.	42	25	33

Do this questionnaire in your class. What do the students in your class think?

True or False? Most Russian teenagers like politics.

Answer: False

-ed and *-ing* adjectives

1 Many adjectives end in *-ing* or *-ed*.
*an **exciting** day*
*The United manager was **pleased** with the result of the game.*

2 Adjectives with *-ed* endings describe how we feel. They show our reaction to something or somebody.
*No one is **interested** in my opinion.*
*I felt less **worried** after listening to Bill.*

3 Adjectives with *-ing* endings describe what or who causes the feeling. They show the effect that something or somebody has on us.
*Politics is **boring**.*
*Sam is **amazing** – he speaks six languages.*

4 Some adjectives have both *-ed* and *-ing* endings but there is a difference in meaning.
*She is **tired**. Tennis is a **tiring** sport.*
*I am **shocked**. The news is **shocking**.*

5 Some examples of adjectives which end in *-ing* and *-ed* are:

amazing – amazed	*frightening – frightened*
annoying – annoyed	*interesting – interested*
boring – bored	*pleased – pleasing*
confusing – confused	*surprising – surprised*
depressing – depressed	*shocking – shocked*
disappointing – disappointed	*terrifying – terrified*
exciting – excited	*tiring – tired*
	worrying – worried

Practice

A Underline the correct option.

1 It was a long and very *tiring / tired* day for her.
2 I'm *disappointing / disappointed* that you can't come.
3 It's not a very *interesting / interested* idea.
4 Something really *exciting / excited* happened at the weekend.
5 Bears are *terrifying / terrified* when they get angry.
6 When you're nice and *relaxing / relaxed*, we can begin.
7 That's not *surprising / surprised* news.
8 Jack always looks very *worrying / worried* before a test.
9 Shopping is so *boring / bored*.
10 Is the boss *annoying / annoyed* because you were late?

B Add an *-ing* or *-ed* ending to the adjectives in the text.

Time travel is an [1]interest...ing... concept. It is not [2]surpris........ that people are so [3]interest........ in time travel because the idea is very romantic. In the 19th century, H. G. Wells wrote a very [4]excit........ book called *The Time Machine*. It's a great novel and you won't be [5]disappoint........ if you read it. The book also shows the dangers of time travel. The hero is [6]shock........ and [7]confus........ when he visits the past and future. At the end of the book he is lost in time and cannot come back to the present. This is a [8]frighten........finish to the book and readers who are [9]bor........ with living in the present must read it carefully. We cannot change the past or know the future so we must live in the present. The world around us is full of [10]amaz........ things. We don't need to visit the past or future to have an [11]interest........ life.

C Do you care about the world? Complete the questions with the correct adjectives, then tick ✓ your answers a, b or c.

1 You are walking down the street and see somebody drop a can on the ground. What do you think?
a) I'm not ...surprised... (surprising / surprised) ✓
b) That's ...shocking...! (shocking / shocked)
c) That's OK.

2 There is an election. What do you think?
a) Elections are very .... (boring / bored)
b) How .... ! (exciting / excited)
c) What's an election?

3 Do you think one day there will be too many people in the world to feed?
a) I'm not sure.
b) Yes and I'm very .... (worrying / worried)
c) I don't care. I'm not .... in the future. (interesting / interested)

4 Will robots do all the work in the future?
a) I hope so, I'm .... of work. (tiring / tired)
b) It's an .... thought but it won't happen soon. (amazing / amazed)
c) Perhaps.

5 Does technology make life better?
a) Yes, of course.
b) Yes, but too much change can be .... (frightening / frightened)
c) I play computer games six hours a day, which is very .... (relaxing / relaxed)

What do your results mean?

Mostly a: You don't care about the world and find many things boring.

Mostly b: You care about the world around you.

Mostly c: You don't know much about the world around you.

MY TURN!

Imagine you are in these situations. In your notebook, write what you feel using *-ing* and *-ed* adjectives.

1 You are riding an elephant.
It's exciting but I'm a bit scared!
2 You see a snake in your garden.
3 It snows in July.
4 Julia Roberts phones you.
5 You come first in the English test.
6 You hear a strange noise in the middle of the night.
7 A police officer stops you in the street.
8 You are waiting for your best friend. He / She is late.

MY TEST!

Circle the correct option.

1 I'm not .... about the future. I'm sure everything's going to be fine. a worried b pleasing c pleased
2 She's so .... when she talks about politics all the time. She thinks it's really interesting, but it isn't. a exciting b boring c bored
3 People today are .... of giving their real opinions. a depressing b annoyed c frightened
4 I think all those numbers are very .... – I don't understand them at all. a confusing b shocked c confused
5 The results from the questionnaire weren't .... a surprising b tiring c surprised

My Test! answers: 1a 2b 3c 4a 5a

59 *Too and enough*

This chair is too soft.

? The lines below are from a famous children's story. What is the story?

Once upon a time …

There's **too much** sugar in this porridge!
There's **not enough** sugar in this porridge!
This porridge is just right!

This chair is **too** soft.
This chair is **too** hard.
This chair is just right!

This bed doesn't have **enough** pillows.
This bed has **too** many pillows.
This bed is just right …
… She's still there!

Answer: Goldilocks and the Three Bears

Too and enough

1 **Use *too* before an adjective or an adverb.**

It's too big.
NOT *~~It's too much big.~~*

He's driving too fast!
NOT *~~He's driving too much fast!~~*

2 **Use *too much* before a singular (uncountable) noun. Use *too many* before a plural (countable) noun.**

*There's **too much** sugar.*
*This bed has **too many** pillows.*

3 **We can also use *too much* as an adverb.**

*She eats **too much**.*

4 **Use *enough* before a noun.**

*There isn't **enough** salt.*

5 **Use *enough* after an adjective or adverb.**

*It is good **enough**.*
*She doesn't study hard **enough**.*

6 **We can sometimes omit the noun after *enough*, *too much* or *too many*.**

*There isn't **enough**.*
A: How many pillows are there?
*B: **Too many**.*

TIP

Note the difference between *very* and *too*:

It's **very** loud!
It's **too** loud!

Practice

A Make sentences by putting the words in the correct order. Which stories are the sentences from?

1 too / lies / He / many / told
He told too many lies. Pinocchio

2 The / small / shoe / too / was
....

3 were / mattresses / enough / There / not

....

4 city / in / many / rats / were / There / too / the
....

5 too / was / ugly / He
....

6 He / too / much / slept
....

B Complete the sentences using *too, too much* or *too many*.

1 I don't like this weather – it's ...too... hot.
2 Why don't you sit down? You work .... hard!
3 A: Did you buy the shirt? B: No, it was .... expensive.
4 There are .... people here.
5 A: Can you come out tonight? B: No, I'm .... busy.
6 It costs ....
7 It's .... late now.
8 Don't ask .... questions!
9 I can't watch television – I have .... homework.

C Add *enough* in the correct places in these sentences.

1 There's not (enough) salt. Can you buy some more?
2 There are not women police officers.
3 He doesn't work fast.
4 I can't reach it – I'm not tall.
5 Do you have money?
6 There's never time for everything.
7 This camera is small to fit in your pocket.

D Complete the sentences using *too, too much, too many* or *enough* and the words in the box.

butter hard money people rain sweet ~~sweets~~ traffic

1 I don't feel very well.
I've eaten ...too many sweets... .
2 You need 100 g to make the cake. I only have 50 g.
I don't have ....
3 The young boy pushed his brother and he fell over.
He pushed him ....
4 It hasn't rained much this summer. The river is dry.
There hasn't been ....
5 There's sugar in my coffee. I don't like sugar in my coffee.
The coffee ....
6 The tickets are 10 euros. I have 11 euros.
I have ....
7 I like driving on empty roads. I don't like driving in the city.
In the city, there's ....
8 This class is very full.
There are ....

MY TURN!

Complete the questions with *How much* or *How many*. Then answer using *too much, too many, not enough* or *enough*.

1 ...How much... coffee do you drink? ...Not enough!...
2 .... money have you saved? ....
3 .... football is there on TV? ....
4 .... exams do you have every month? ....
5 .... text messages do you receive? ....
6 .... sleep do you get? ....
7 .... weekends are there in a year? ....
8 .... music do you listen to? ....

MY TEST!

Circle the correct option.

1 My dad prefers his porridge to be .... hot. a too b very c enough
2 He sat on his son's chair, but it wasn't .... and it broke. a strong enough b too much strong c enough strong
3 She ate her porridge ...., and now she feels sick. a too quick b quick enough c too quickly
4 I didn't have .... for breakfast, so I just had tea. a too many time b too much time c enough time
5 A: How much porridge do you eat? B: .... We have it every day and I hate it! a Much b Too much c Not enough

My Test answers: 1b 2a 3c 4c 5b

60 Adverbs of frequency

We always have dreams.

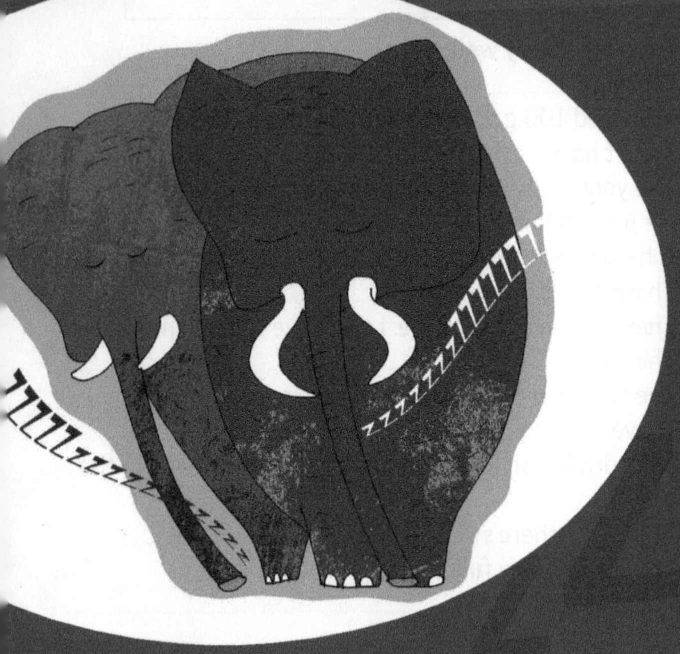

Most adults spend 30% of their lives in bed – but how much do you know about sleep? Here are six interesting facts.

- Elephants **often** sleep standing up.
- Animals **usually** sleep less than humans (maybe one reason why we **normally** live longer).
- Parents of a new baby **normally** lose a lot of sleep. New babies need a lot of sleep but they **hardly ever** sleep more than three hours at a time.
- Sleep is **sometimes** possible with your eyes open. Try it!
- Teenagers don't **usually** sleep enough. They need about ten hours but they **rarely** have this.
- When we are in deep sleep, we **always** have dreams, though we **rarely** remember them. Scientists have **never** understood the real reason for dreams and they are still a mystery.

Who sleeps more, a horse or a man?

Answer: a man

Adverbs of frequency

1 **Adverbs of frequency show how often we do things.**

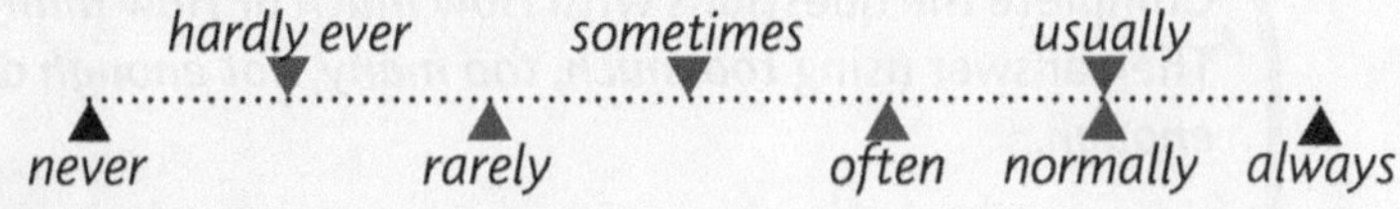

▶ **See Unit 62 for time phrases.**

2 **Adverbs of frequency usually go before the main verb of the sentence.**

*A new baby **normally** sleeps badly.*
*Teenagers don't **usually** sleep enough.*
*Do you **often** remember your dreams?*

3 **The adverb of frequency usually goes after the verb *be*.**

*Sleep is **sometimes** possible with your eyes open.*
*The class is **usually** in room 7.*

When *have* is a main verb, the adverb goes before *have*.

*New babies **normally** have strange sleeping habits.*

When *have* is an auxiliary, the adverb goes after *have*.

*I have **often** visited them.*

4 **In negative sentences, adverbs of frequency usually go after *not*. However, *sometimes* goes before *be*, auxiliaries and modals in negative sentences.**

*We don't **always** dream.*
*We **sometimes** don't dream.*

TIP

Never **and *hardly ever* are negative in meaning, so we don't use negative verbs in sentences containing them.**

*I **never** read in bed.* NOT ~~*... never don't read ...*~~

5 ***How often ...?* questions usually need an answer with an adverb of frequency.**

*A: **How often** do you sleep late?*
*B: I **rarely** get up late.*

▶ **See Unit 30 for *How often ...?* questions.**

Usually*, *normally*, *often* and *sometimes* can also go at the beginning or at the end of a sentence, especially when the adverb provides the most important information in the sentence.

***Usually** I get up late but yesterday was different.*

Practice

A Put the adverbs in the correct places in the sentences.

1 I ....usually.... have .... eggs for breakfast. (usually)
2 It .... snows .... here in winter. (rarely)
3 Computers .... don't .... save time. (always)
4 Dad .... is .... wrong. (hardly ever)
5 Do .... you .... take the bus to school? (often)
6 They .... go .... shopping together. (normally)
7 We .... have .... barbecues in the garden. (often)
8 The boss .... is .... on time so don't be late. (always)
9 My mum .... doesn't .... understand me. (sometimes)
10 Ivan .... has .... had a mobile phone. (never)

B How often does Sally do these things? Write sentences using *never, rarely, sometimes, often, usually* and *always*. (0% = 0 times; 100% = every time)

~~drive to work~~	50%
wear jeans in the office	15%
remember her boss's birthday	100%
be late	70%
work at the weekend	0%
have lunch in a café	85%

1 She sometimes drives to work.
2 ....
3 ....
4 ....
5 ....
6 ....

C Rewrite the sentences so that they have a similar meaning, using the adverbs in brackets.

1 Simon does the washing-up after every meal. (always)
Simon always does the washing-up.
2 Most of the time I wear jeans. (usually)
....
3 My sister is not late very much. (hardly ever)
....
4 Sandra phones me a lot. (often)
....
5 My boss has very little time to go on holiday. (rarely)
....
6 The book is useful about 50% of the time. (sometimes)
....
7 Guests must lock their rooms every time they go out. (always)
....
8 I have been to every European country except Portugal. (never)
....

MY TURN!

In your notebook, answer the questions with full sentences using adverbs of frequency.

1 How often do you remember your dreams?
I usually remember my dreams.
2 Do you always go to bed at the same time?
3 How often do you see animals in your dreams?
4 Has your dream ever come true?
5 Have you ever seen anyone you know in a dream?
6 How often do you wake up because of a bad dream?
7 Do you tell friends about your dreams?
8 Have you ever dreamed in English?

MY TEST!

Circle the correct option.

1 I .... on planes. a sleep never b don't sleep never c never sleep
2 Teenagers don't .... like going to bed. a usually b sometimes c never
3 My little sister .... awake all night. a rarely is b sometimes is c is often
4 Our baby .... slept more than four hours. a hardly ever hasn't b has hardly ever c hasn't hardly ever
5 .... bad dreams. a I have sometimes b Rarely I have c Sometimes I have

My Test! answers: 1c 2a 3c 4b 5c

R10 Review: adjectives and adverbs

A Complete the table with the correct forms.

	adjective	comparative adjective	superlative adjective	adverb	comparative adverb	superlative adverb
1	quick	quicker	the quickest	quickly	more quickly	most quickly
2	nice					
3	easy					
4	quiet					
5	fast					
6	sad					
7	good					
8	expensive					
9	bad					
10	far					
11	interesting					
12	friendly					

B Complete the email by writing one word in each space.

Delete Reply Reply All Forward Print

Hi Philip

I'm having a great time here in Warsaw. It's a [1] lot .... nicer than I expected. The weather's been really warm – about 28°C most days. Yesterday it was too hot to go outside, so we went to a shopping centre to stay cool.

Warsaw's [2] .... biggest city in Poland – nearly 2 million people live here. It's not as big [3] .... London, but it's much bigger [4] .... any other cities in Poland.

On Monday we went to the Palace of Culture. It's [5] .... tallest building in Poland. We went to the top, and we could see the whole city – it was fantastic. But little Danny didn't see much – he wasn't tall enough to see over the walls!

The Old Town is amazing – it looks really old, but in fact almost no buildings are [6] .... than about 60 years old. We wanted to eat in a restaurant in the Old Town, but it was [7] .... expensive than restaurants back home! Can you believe it? So we bought some sandwiches in the city centre – they were much [8] .... expensive than the food in the Old Town.

OK, so now it's your turn to write. You hardly ever write to me ☺.

Best wishes

Louise

C Complete each sentence b so that it means the same as sentence a. Use two to four words including the word in brackets.

1 a She has a beautiful singing voice. (sings)
  b She sings beautifully.
2 a Nobody in my town drives as badly as Harry. (driver)
  b Harry is .... in my town.
3 a Their house is nearer the sea than ours. (from)
  b Our house is .... than theirs.
4 a You are speaking too quietly. I can't hear you. (enough)
  b I can't hear you. You aren't speaking ....
5 a Her new sports shoes were very expensive. She bought them in America. (American, expensive, sports, new)
  b She has .... shoes.
6 a She is slower than me at learning English. (more)
  b She is learning English .... am.
7 a He did a silly dance. (way)
  b He danced ....
8 a This book isn't as interesting as her earlier one. (less)
  b This book .... her earlier one.
9 a Today is far colder than yesterday. (warm)
  b Today is a .... than yesterday.

D Write complete sentences, putting the adjectives and adverbs in the best places. You may need to change *a* to *an* (or *an* to *a*).

1 We have a meal in a restaurant on Sundays. (big, expensive, usually)
We usually have a big meal in an expensive restaurant on Sundays.

2 I study before an exam. (always, hard, important)

3 Please speak. The baby is. (asleep, more, quietly)

4 I get up when I'm on holiday. (early, hardly ever)

5 You wear your coat. (blue, never, old)

6 I don't answer my emails. (important, quickly, sometimes)

7 He's a man, but he's. (a bit, boring, nice, very)

8 My car is than my one. (a lot, better, new, old)

9 She laughs and she doesn't smile. (never, often)

10 You eat and you don't eat vegetables. (enough, fresh, quickly, too)

E Match the pairs.

1 He's very careful. — a He always makes mistakes.
2 He's very careless. — b He never makes mistakes.

3 It's a bit — a windy weather.
4 It's very — b windy.

5 I bought an old — a big painting.
6 I bought a lovely — b Chinese vase.

7 He is an eleven-year-old — a today. It's his birthday.
8 He is eleven years old — b boy.

9 Bob is as clever — a as Mike.
10 Bob is cleverer — b than Mike.

11 She's the tallest in — a my class.
12 She's the tallest of — b my friends.

13 Alan is boring. — a He has nothing to do.
14 Alan is bored. — b He always talks about football.

15 They don't — a often go dancing.
16 They — b never go dancing.

F Make this story more interesting by adding adjectives and adverbs. You may need to change *a* to *an* (or *an* to *a*). Use the words in the table and/or your own ideas.

adjectives	adverbs
angry beautiful big black broken colourful dirty fat golden good happy horrible hungry magic old open poor sad silly small strange stupid thin young	angrily carefully enough happily in a friendly way kindly quickly quietly slowly sometimes strangely suddenly very usually

Once upon a time, there was a [silly, young] boy called Jack. He lived [quietly] with his mother. They were. They didn't have money. They had clothes. They had just one cow.

One day Jack's mother told Jack to take the cow to the market in the city. Jack and the cow walked to the market. Jack heard somebody calling his name. He turned round and saw a man. The man was wearing clothes.

'Give me some gold and I'll give you some beans,' the man said.

Jack thought about it. 'I don't have any gold,' he said. 'I only have this cow.'

The man took the cow and Jack took the beans home to his mother.

When Jack got home, his mother was. 'You boy!' she said. 'You sold our cow for these beans! You are!' Jack's mother threw the beans through the window and into the garden.

61 Prepositions of place

I've left my keys at home.

Jess: Hi Chris! I'm **at** work, but I've left my keys **at** home. Could you bring them?
Chris: Of course. Where are they?
Jess: I think they're **in** my room. They're probably **in front of** you – **on** the table. I usually put them **next to** the photos.
Chris: No, they're not there.
Jess: Can you see the flowers **in** the corner?
Chris: Yes ...
Jess: Maybe they're **behind** them ... or **under** some books?
Chris: Just a minute ... there's somebody **at** the door ... Hello, Jess? The postman found your keys. You left them **in** the door!

? What has Jess lost? Who finds them?

Answers: Jess has lost her keys. The postman finds them.

Prepositions of place

1 **We use prepositions of place in front of a noun or a pronoun to say where something or someone is.**
on the table, under some books, in front of you, next to that, at home (prepositions in bold)

2 **Some prepositions of place are *in*, *at* and *on*.**

 ***in*** *the box*  ***at*** *the door*  ***on*** *the table*

Use *in* to say something is inside a larger space.
in *the box,* ***in*** *the city,* ***in*** *my study*

Use at with a place or a point.
at *the station,* ***at*** *work,* ***at*** *the door*

The shop is ***at*** *42 Culver Road.* (*at* = point)
The shop is ***in*** *Culver Road.* (*in* = inside a larger space)

3 **Note the following uses of the prepositions *at*, *in* and *on*:**

at	+ place: *A: Where's Jo? B: He's **at the doctor's**.* the top / the bottom (of): *Look at the exercise **at the top** of the page.* the end (of): *The post office is **at the end** of the street.*
in	+ city / country: *They live **in Paris**.* *a taxi / the car: Let's go to the station **in a taxi / in the car**.* *the north / the south / the east / the west: They live **in the west** of the country.* *the corner: Let's sit **in the corner**.* *the centre: There are a lot of shops **in the centre** of the town.*
on	*the top / bottom shelf: The present's **on the top shelf** of the cupboard.* *the bus / plane / train: The passengers are **on the train**.* *the ground / first / second / top floor: His apartment is **on the first floor**.* *the left / the right: It's the second door **on the left**.* *TV: There's a good programme **on TV** tonight.*

4 **We don't use *the* after the preposition in some expressions.**
at home, at school, at college, in bed

5 **Some more prepositions of place are: *under, above, below, opposite, in front of, behind, next to, between, outside, near, by* and *inside*.**

under *the books*

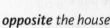

above *the clouds*
below *the clouds*

opposite *the house*

in front of *him*
behind *him*

next to *the photos*

between *the houses*
in / inside *the house*

near / by *the house*
outside *the house*

Practice

A Where's Edward? Match the prepositions from the box to each picture.

above	at	in	in front of	near	~~next to~~	on	opposite

1 
2 
3 
4 
5 
6 
7 
8 

1 *next to* the man
2 .... the bus stop
3 .... his sister
4 .... the old man
5 .... his brother
6 .... the window
7 .... the cupboard
8 .... TV

B What's the opposite of ...?

1 on the table .... *under the table*
2 in the north of the island ....
3 at the top of the page ....
4 below the line ....
5 in the shop ....
6 far from me ....
7 in front of the building ....
8 outside the city ....
9 at the beginning of the film ....

C Underline the correct option.

1 My cousin lives *at* / *in* Sydney now.
2 Be careful! There's some water *in* / *on* the floor.
3 There was a clock *at* / *in* the corner of the room.
4 Look out! There's a car *behind* / *between* you.
5 I'm going to a party *at* / *in* my uncle's tonight.
6 The castle is *between* / *in front of* the mountains and the sea.
7 Are you staying *at* / *by* home tonight?
8 We drove very slowly. There was a tractor *opposite* / *in front of* us.
9 They live *by* / *outside* the sea.
10 I've left my bag *at* / *in* the car.

MY TURN!

Answer these questions in your notebook using a preposition from the list on page 146.

1 Where do you keep your keys? *on the shelf*
2 Where do you keep your mobile phone?
3 You've lost something. Where do you look for it first?
4 Where did you meet your best friend?
5 Where does your best friend live?
6 Where were you born?
7 Where do your parents park their car?
8 Where are you now?

MY TEST!

Circle the correct option.

1 I think I left my bag .... the bedroom. Can you check? a on b at c in
2 I was .... Lucy's flat yesterday. Maybe I left my glasses there. a at b on c next
3 I think I've found your phone. It's .... the sofa, but I can't reach it and the sofa's too heavy to move. a outside b between c behind
4 I was .... bed this morning when I found my watch. It was under the pillow. a in b at c in the
5 Her house is at the end of this street. It's the last house .... the left. a at b by c on

My Test! answers: 1c 2a 3c 4a 5c

62 Prepositions of time: *at, in, on*

It happened at night.

The Hindenburg was a German airship. It exploded **on** 6 May 1937 and killed 36 people. The airship first flew **on** Monday, 4 March 1936 and it made many trips between Germany and America. **In** summer 1936 the airship was part of the opening of the Berlin Olympics. The trip **in** May 1937 was its first transatlantic trip of the year. The Hindenburg left Germany **at** night **on** 3 May and reached America **in** the afternoon **on** 6 May. The Hindenburg started to come down but **at** 7.25 there was a problem. A fire started and **in** less than a minute the airship exploded. No one knows why it happened.

? Match the dates to the events:

1 4 March 1936	**a** The Hindenburg goes to America.
2 Summer 1936	**b** The Hindenburg flies for the first time.
3 3 May 1937	**c** 36 people die.
4 6 May 1937	**d** At the Berlin Olympics.

Answers: 1b 2d 3a 4c

Prepositions of time: *at, in, on*

1 Use *at, in* and *on* before time expressions.
*The tragedy happened **in** 1937.*
*The story was in all the newspapers **on** 7 May.*

2 Use *at* for a point in time such as a clock time, meal time and short holidays.
***At** 7.25 there was a problem.*
*I'll see you **at** breakfast.*
*There are flights **at** New Year.*

3 Use *at* with '… *time*' and '… *moment*'.
*There is a meeting **at** lunchtime.*
*I always get up **at** the same time.*
*She's busy **at** the moment.*

4 Use *in* with parts of the day (*morning, afternoon, evening*).
*It reached America **in** the afternoon.*
*It's much cooler **in** the evening.*

5 Use *in* for longer time periods like months, seasons, years and centuries.
*It happened **in** the spring.*
*President Hindenburg died **in** 1934.*

TIP
A common expression is *in … 's time*.
*What will air transport be like **in** 100 years' **time**?*

6 *In* can also mean 'after' a future time interval.
*I'll speak to you **in** an hour.*

TIP
***in** the day, **on** Friday afternoon* BUT ***at** night, **at** the weekend*

7 Use *on* with days and dates.
*The Hindenburg Museum is closed **on** Mondays.*
*The Olympics began **on** 15 July.*
***On** weekdays, I get up at 7.*

8 We do not normally use *at, in* or *on* before *this / that / some / each / every / last / next*.
*The airship landed **the next** evening.* NOT ~~*… in the next evening.*~~
*We go home **every** New Year.* NOT ~~*… at every New Year.*~~
*It will finish **next** Friday.* NOT ~~*… on next Friday.*~~

9 We do not usually use *at, in* or *on* before the adverb phrases *later / today / tonight / tomorrow / the day after tomorrow / yesterday / the day before yesterday*.
*We're going to Berlin **tomorrow**.* NOT ~~*… on tomorrow.*~~
*He arrived **the day before yesterday**.* NOT ~~*… on the day before yesterday.*~~

Practice

A Write the time expressions from the box under the correct prepositions.

~~2:00~~ 1999 breakfast 22 June midnight Monday your birthday 13 September the afternoon the moment the rainy season the weekend Thursday two years' time winter

on	in	at
		2:00

B Match the pairs.

1 I was born on   a March.
2 It's my birthday in   b 10 March.

3 I'll see you in   a Wednesday.
4 I'll see you on   b three weeks.

5 Come at   a lunchtime.
6 Come on   b 15 August.

7 We left school in   a 2010.
8 We left school at   b 5:00.

9 The film starts in   a ten past three.
10 The film starts at   b half an hour.

C Write *on, in, at* or – (= no preposition).

1 I play golf ...on... Sundays.
2 Is the play ...—... next Tuesday?
3 She'll be fifteen .... 26 May.
4 My family goes to Greece .... every summer.
5 It's 11 o'clock .... night.
6 Phone me .... two days.
7 Are you free .... this weekend?
8 It was a mistake to go .... November.

D Complete the text with *on, in, at* or – (= no preposition).

Airship Tours (www.airshiptours.net) offers airship trips [1] ...on... weekdays and [2] .... the weekends. You can travel [3] .... any season, [4] .... the morning, afternoon or even [5] .... night. It's a wonderful trip. Remember, [6] .... this month we have a special flight across San Francisco. The trip starts [7] .... 9:00 so you will have plenty of time to enjoy the views. For romantic travellers, it's not too late to book a place for the trip [8] .... Valentine's Day. The perfect present for the person you love! This trip leaves early so we hope to see you all [9] .... breakfast [10] .... next February.

MY TURN!

What are your plans? Complete these sentences with time expressions.

1 I'm going to watch TV at ...7 o'clock tonight... .
2 I want to go to the cinema at ....
3 I will leave school in ....
4 I'd like to see my friends on ....
5 I will probably go to bed tonight at ....
6 My parents hope we will go on holiday in .... time.
7 I think I'll buy some new shoes in ....
8 I'll have a really good time on ....

MY TEST!

Circle the correct option.

1 The fire started at ....   a the day before yesterday   b the morning   c midnight
2 I read a book about the Hindenburg on ....   a yesterday   b July   c Tuesday
3 He first flew the airship in ....   a the 1930s   b his birthday   c last month
4 A: When will you arrive in America? B: .... three weeks.   a On   b In   c At
5 Two airships flew across the Atlantic .... same time.   a the   b in the   c at the

My Test! answers: 1c 2c 3a 4b 5c

63 Prepositions of movement

Get off the boat and swim to the island.

Go **to** the island. Get **off** the boat. Walk **along** the beach and **into** the forest. Go **through** the forest, **out of** the gate and take the road **between** the mountains. Walk **up** the road and **over** the mountains. You will walk **past** two small houses. You will come **to** a big tree. Go **round** the tree and look carefully. There is a small door in the tree. Open the door, and go **through** the door **into** the tree. Look **under** a big stone. There is the treasure. Take it. Now go back **to** the beach, get **on** the boat and go home – quickly!

? Underline the correct option: On the island you will **not** see *a forest / mountains / houses / pirates*.

Answer: pirates

Prepositions of movement

1 *Into, through,* etc. are prepositions of movement. They show where somebody or something is going.

*Walk **into** the forest*
*Go **through** the door.*

More prepositions of movement:

across	*Walk **across** the bridge.*
along	*She's driving **along** the road.*
between	*The mouse ran **between** two chairs.*
by	*You will pass **by** some shops.*
down	*Jill fell **down** the hill.*
from	*Has Max come back **from** London?*
in	*Jump **in** the water!*
off	*Get **off** the horse carefully.*
on	*Spider-Man climbed **on** the wall.*
onto	*We got **onto** the ship.*
out of	*I walked **out of** the disco.*
over	*They ran **over** a big hill.*
past	*You will go **past** Jim's house.*
round (= *around*)	*The plane flew **round** the town twice.*
towards	*The dog came **towards** me.*
to	*Throw the ball **to** Simon.*
under	*Go **under** the apple trees.*
up	*Walk **up** Oxford Street for 10 minutes.*

2 Some of these prepositions can also show position, not movement.

*Walk **under** the bridge.*
*She's **under** the bridge.*

► **See Unit 61 for prepositions of place.**

3 Don't use *to* after *arrive*. Use *arrive* before *at* (places) or *in* (very big places, e.g. cities, countries).

*When you arrive **at** the hotel, ...* NOT ~~*... to the hotel ...*~~
*I arrived **in** Paris.* NOT ~~*... to Paris.*~~

Use *to* after verbs of movement like *go, walk, come, fly* and *travel*.

*Don't go **to** the island.*

Don't use *to* after *visit*.

I visited my brother. NOT ~~*I visited to my brother.*~~

Don't use *to* before *home*.

Run home! NOT ~~*Run to home!*~~

Don't use *go* + *to* + an *-ing* word.

4 Use *by* to show how you travel.

*Go **by** train.*
*It is faster **by** plane.*

5 Use *get on / onto* and *off* with trains, buses, planes, bikes, boats and animals.

*Get **on** your bike.*
*Get **off** the boat.*

6 Use *get in / into* and *out of* with cars (and small boats and small planes).

*I got **into** my Mercedes.*
*Get **out of** my taxi!*

Practice

A Rewrite these sentences using different prepositions to make them mean the opposite.

1 I'm flying to Nice.
I'm flying from Nice.

2 Get in the car.
....

3 Walk over it.
....

4 Jack went up the hill.
....

5 We got off the train.
....

6 She is coming from Palermo.
....

7 I walked from the park.
....

8 We got onto the plane.
....

9 Walk slowly away from the lion.
....

B Where is the mouse going? Answer using the prepositions on page 150.

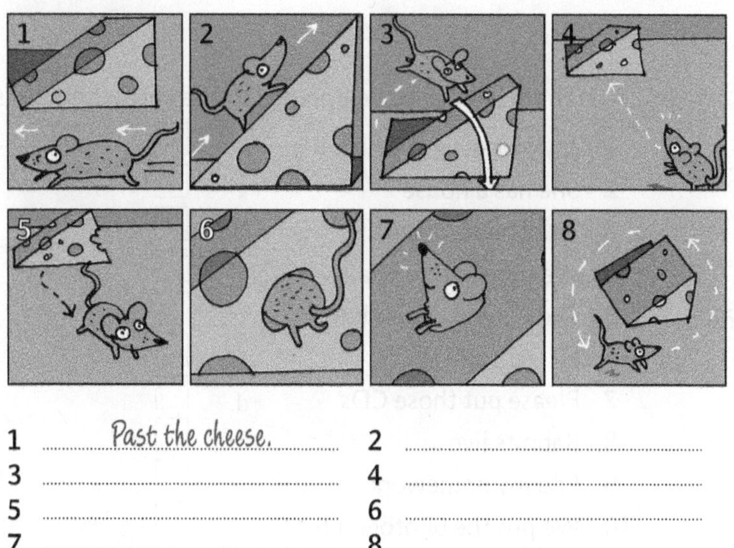

1 Past the cheese. 2 ....
3 .... 4 ....
5 .... 6 ....
7 .... 8 ....

C Circle the correct option.

Max,
Here are the directions to get [1] .... my house. If you come [2] .... train you will arrive [3] .... Central Station. Go [4] .... the station and walk [5] .... the road. You are then on North Street. Go [6] .... this street. You will walk [7] .... a supermarket and a bookshop. My house is number 61. Go [8] .... the garden – the back door will be open. If you get lost, you can always go back [9] .... the station and get [10] .... a taxi.
See you soon, Amelia.

	a	b	c	d
1	a in	b on	ⓒ to	d at
2	a by	b in	c on	d with
3	a in	b on	c to	d at
4	a from	b out of	c into	d between
5	a on	b back	c through	d across
6	a over	b to	c along	d across
7	a over	b past	c up	d at
8	a between	b on	c at	d through
9	a off	b by	c to	d at
10	a in	b on	c at	d to

MY TURN!

Mark X on the map to show where your treasure is. Then draw the route to the treasure using ....➔. In your notebook, write instructions for finding the treasure.

MY TEST!

Circle the correct option.

1 The pirate ship went .... the ocean, from the Caribbean to Africa. a off b across c towards
2 The pirates walked .... us. a through b past c along
3 We came to the island .... ship, but we had to swim home. a on b in c by
4 I was hiding the treasure on the beach when two pirates came .... the forest behind me. a under b off c out of
5 When I arrived .... the treasure tree, the treasure had gone. a at b to c in

My Test! answers: 1b 2b 3c 4c 5a

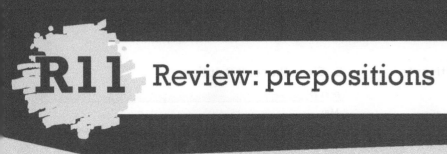

R11 Review: prepositions

A Complete each sentence b so that it means the same as sentence a. Use two to four words, including the word in brackets.

1 a It's 10 o'clock now – we're going to leave at 11 o'clock. (hour)
  b We're going to leave ....in an hour.........., at 11 o'clock.
2 a There's a red house on one side of our house and another red house on the other side. (two)
  b Our house is .... red houses.
3 a Walter stood behind us while we were waiting to buy tickets. (front)
  b We stood .... Walter while we were waiting to buy tickets.
4 a The best time to phone is 3 pm. (at)
  b You should phone .... the afternoon.
5 a We met her two days ago. (yesterday)
  b We met her ....
6 a They left the shop and went home. (out)
  b They came .... the shop and went home.
7 a I went to see my grandmother in New York 12 months ago. (visited)
  b My grandmother lives in New York. I .... year.
8 a Sorry – I can't help you right now. (moment)
  b Sorry – I can't help you ....

B Complete the sentences with *in*, *on* or *at*.

1 There's someone ....at.......... the door.
2 He got .... his bike and went home.
3 They got up .... lunchtime.
4 She's asleep .... bed.
5 The cup is .... the shelf.
6 What happens .... the end of the story?
7 I'll see you .... Sunday.
8 She was born .... 1998.
9 I go to ballet classes .... Fridays.
10 He's still .... work.
11 We'll be there .... about an hour.
12 There's a spider .... the wall.
13 It was cold .... the evening.
14 Our house is the third .... the left.
15 She arrived .... the hotel very late.
16 They jumped .... the water.
17 What are you doing .... the weekend?
18 Put the box .... the corner.

C Match the sentence beginnings to the correct endings.

1 My parents got married [g]
2 She has a house [ ]
3 A tall man was sitting [ ]
4 We travelled to Spain [ ]
5 The Queen is standing [ ]
6 I'll see you [ ]
7 Please put those CDs [ ]
8 Rabbits live [ ]
9 I do my homework [ ]
10 We put the photograph [ ]

a on the wall above the television.
b by plane.
c next to the President.
d into their boxes.
e in five minutes.
f by the sea.
g in 1992.
h at night.
i in front of us in the cinema.
j under the ground.

D Complete the story using the prepositions in the boxes.

Scarface sat [1] ....on.... the bed in his small room [2] .... the prison. [3] .... midnight he got [4] .... the bed, took the knife [5] .... his pocket and started cutting the metal bar in the window.

at in off ~~on~~ out of

Ten minutes later, the bar was cut and he climbed [6] .... the hole in the window.
He then climbed carefully [7] .... the wall.

down through

When he was [8] .... the ground, he ran [9] .... the corner and [10] .... the prison kitchen. It was very dark. He waited [11] .... the door and listened carefully.

behind into round on

There was another wall [12] .... the door of the kitchen.
When he was sure no one was there, he ran [13] .... the kitchen [14] .... the wall. When he arrived [15] .... the wall, he stopped again and listened. He heard a noise – a guard was coming [16] .... him.

at opposite out of towards towards

There was a car [17] .... the wall, so he lay down [18] .... it and waited. He heard the guard walk [19] .... him and [20] .... the kitchen. He went back [21] .... the wall and started to climb [22] .... it.

into near past to under up

[23] .... the top of the wall he could see a car [24] .... him on the other side. It was his wife's car – she was waiting to take him home. He started walking [25] .... the top of the wall ... when suddenly he fell [26] .... the wall. He landed [27] .... the ground [28] .... two guards.

along at below between off on

E Make sentences by putting the words in the correct order. The first and last words are already in the right places.

1 We / the / 3 / arrived / the / at / o'clock / in / at / airport / morning.
We ....arrived at the airport at 3 o'clock in the.... morning.

2 I'll / half / in / meet / in / you / of / the / an / front / hour / cinema.
I'll .... cinema.

3 He / box / out / the / took / into / of / the / and / put / the / it / pizza / oven.
He .... oven.

4 I'm / after / day / to / the / her / in / going / visit / hospital / tomorrow.
I'm .... tomorrow.

5 They / on / eighth / an / live / apartment / in / the / floor.
They .... floor.

6 I / best / my / next / friend / sit / at / always / to / school.
I .... school.

7 We / on / to / usually / by / went / by / work / train / but / Tuesday / go / we / taxi.
We .... taxi.

8 The / over / the / along / the / road / dog / jumped / ran / and / wall.
The .... wall.

64 Passive: present and past simple

A lot of rubbish is produced.

Look at this beach.

It **was cleaned** yesterday (it **is cleaned** every morning by hotel workers) but it is dirty again now. The beach **is covered** with rubbish. Why?

Some cans **were left** by people having a picnic.

The bags **weren't taken** to the bin.

A bottle **was broken**.

Those sweets **were brought** by some children but **they weren't eaten**.

This is a small part of a big problem. Every year 1.3 billion tons of rubbish **are produced** in Europe. **Are you shocked** by this?

 Underline the correct option: The best place for rubbish is *in the bin / on the beach / in the sea.*

Answer: In the bin

Passive: present and past simple

1 **We usually use the passive when we want to focus on the process or result rather than who or what does or did it.**

*The beach **is cleaned** every day.*
I am not surprised.

2 **Make the passive with *be* and the past participle (*cleaned, seen, driven,* etc.).**

*Bottles **are** sometimes **used** again.*
*It **is made** of glass.*

▶ See Unit 2 for forms of *be*.

3 **The negative and questions are formed like this:**

*Most rubbish **isn't recycled**.*
*The food **wasn't eaten**.*
***Are you shocked** by this?*
***Were the hotels built** in the 1980s?*

4 **In the past, use *was* or *were*. In the future, use *will be*.**

*In the 1970s, less rubbish **was produced**.*
*Tomorrow the beach **will be cleaned** again.*

5 **If you want to say who or what causes the action, add *by* + noun.**

*A lot of money **is made** by the recycling business.*
***Were** the dinosaurs **killed** by a meteorite?*

TIP

be born is only used in the passive.
*I **was born** in 1998.*

Practice

A Match the sentence beginnings to the correct endings. If you don't know the answers, look on the Internet.

1 Tea was invented — h
2 The euro is used
3 Hydrogen (H_2) was discovered
4 The women's football world cup is held
5 The Fiat car company was started
6 *Dracula* was written
7 Most coffee beans are grown
8 President Lincoln was killed
9 The original hamburgers were cooked
10 In 2002 water was found

a by Henry Cavendish.
b on Mars.
c in the nineteenth century.
d by over 300 million people.
e in a theatre.
f every four years.
g in New York.
h in China.
i by Giovanni Agnelli.
j in Africa.

B Complete the sentences with passive forms (present and past simple) of the verbs in brackets.

1 The Olympics *are watched* by billions of people today. (watch)
2 Nowadays the work .... by computer. (do)
3 Now, prizes .... every week. (give)
4 The course .... two years ago. (start)
5 In Europe, most food .... in supermarkets. (buy)
6 .... Latin still .... in schools? (learn)
7 Gold .... in California in the 19th century. (discover)
8 Cars .... all over the world nowadays. (produce)
9 .... you .... any information about it? (send)
10 Radio .... by Marconi. (invent)

C Complete each sentence b so that it means the same as sentence a. Use no more than three words.

1 a John took Cindy to the cinema.
b Cindy *was taken* to the cinema.
2 a The cat ate the cheese.
b The cheese .... the cat.
3 a The shop was opened by the Queen.
b .... the shop.
4 a Somebody called the police.
b The police ....
5 a Was it written by him?
b .... it?
6 a This computer does not accept my password.
b My password ....

D Gerald is talking about his job as a dustman. Complete the text with passive forms of the verbs in the box.

~~ask~~ break empty give leave put sell shock take wake

I [1] *was asked* to tell you about my job, so I'll begin. I [2] .... up by my wife at 5 o'clock and I am at work at 5.45. We go round and take rubbish from people's bins. In my area, 6,000 rubbish bins a day [3] .... Often I [4] .... by what people don't need! Yesterday a new TV [5] .... next to a bin! That [6] .... very quickly, I can tell you! It [7] .... for 700 euros the same day. The job can be dangerous. Once a big bin [8] .... on the van. It fell off and my friend's leg [9] .... She didn't work for a month but she [10] .... some money to help her.

MY TURN!

What is done in these places? In your notebook, write at least two sentences for each place using the passive and the words in brackets.

1 Your neighbourhood. (people, rubbish, streets)
Rubbish is collected. Streets are cleaned.
2 A supermarket. (customers, food, money)
3 A school. (children, friends, lessons).
4 A cinema. (films, popcorn, tickets)
5 An office. (computers, emails, work)
6 A hotel. (beds, food, rooms)
7 A train station. (coffee, tickets, trains)
8 The Internet. (information, websites, emails)

MY TEST!

Circle the correct option.

1 The rubbish .... to the bin. a is take b is took c is taken
2 The workers are paid .... hotels to pick up the rubbish. a by b through c from
3 A lot of this rubbish .... fish or birds. a eat b is eaten by c is ate by
4 These birds .... when they ate these plastic bags. a was kill b were killed c was killed
5 How often ....? a is the beach cleaned b is cleaned the beach c the beach is cleaned

My Test! answers: 1c 2a 3b 4b 5a

65 Zero and first conditionals

If you study chemistry, you'll never stop learning.

Thinking About Your Future – Why Study Chemistry?

Chemistry **is** a good subject to study **if** you **are thinking** about your future. **You'll be able to** choose from a lot of different jobs **if** you **have** a qualification in chemistry. Maybe you want to find some new medicine, or solutions to pollution …

Karin Beyer, 23
marine chemist

Peter Willcox, 37
food scientist

If you **study** chemistry, you **will understand** how many everyday things work. For example, **if** you **cut** an onion, it **makes** you cry. But did you know this is a chemical reaction? There is sulphur in onions which turns to sulphuric acid in your eyes. **If** you **cut** the onion under water, the sulphur **reacts** with the water and not your eyes.

If you **study** chemistry, you**'ll** never **stop** learning.

? Find one reason why it is a good idea to study chemistry.

Answer: You'll be able to get a lot of different jobs. You will understand how many everyday things work. You'll never stop learning.

Zero and first conditionals

1 **Use the zero conditional to talk about things that are generally true.**
If you cut an onion, it makes you cry.

2 **In zero conditional sentences, use *if* + present tense ... present tense.**
*If you **cut** the onion under water, the sulphur **reacts** with the water.*

3 **Use the first conditional to talk about something that we think is possible in the future, and its result.**
If I see Jack tomorrow, I'll talk to him about the problem.

4 **The basic pattern for first conditional sentences is: *if* + present tense ... *will* + infinitive without *to*.**
*If you **study** chemistry, you**'ll** never **stop** learning.*

TIP

Both parts of a first conditional sentence talk about the future, even though a present tense is used after *if*. We do not usually use *will* after *if*.

*If you **study** chemistry next year, you **will learn** how lots of things work.* NOT ~~*If you will study chemistry next year, ...*~~

5 **Use *might* or *could* in the main part of the sentence to indicate that something is possible and not certain.**
*If you have a qualification in chemistry, you **might** get a good job.*
*You **could** work with antibiotics if you are interested in this.*

▶ See Units 20, 21 and 24 for more information on *could* and *might*.

6 **When *if* comes at the beginning of the sentence, we need a comma in the middle.**
If you cut an onion, it makes you cry.
Chemistry is a good subject to study if you are thinking about your future.

7 **We can use *unless* to mean *if ... not*.**
I run every morning if it isn't cold.
OR *I run every morning **unless** it's cold.*
That plant will die if you don't water it.
OR *That plant will die **unless** you water it.*

Practice

A Complete the sentences with the correct forms of the verbs in the box.

eat ~~keep~~ kill make melt not mix

1 Ice cream melts unless you ......keep...... it in the fridge.
2 If you put sulphur in water, it .... sulphuric acid.
3 Ice .... quickly if you put salt on it.
4 Chillies burn your mouth if you .... them.
5 If you put chlorine in water, it .... bacteria.
6 If you put water and oil together, they ....

B Match the two parts of each sentence and make them into one whole sentence using *if*. Decide whether to put *if* at the beginning or in the middle.

1 I see Alice
2 you'll get cold
3 we study hard
4 the men do not leave
5 What will you do
6 I don't work very well
7 I might go to school tomorrow
8 I give you some money

a the army will attack
b the shop is closed?
c I feel better
d we will do well in our exams
e you don't put your coat on
f the TV is on
g will you pay for the tickets?
h I'll tell her to ring you

1 If I see Alice, I'll tell her to ring you.
2 ....
3 ....
4 ....
5 ....
6 ....
7 ....
8 ....

C Complete the sentences using the correct forms of the verbs in brackets.

1 If you ......push...... this button, water ......comes...... out. (push / come)
2 If the weather .... bad this year, food prices .... (be / go up)
3 I phone my mum every evening. If I .... her, she .... worried. (not phone / get)
4 If I .... to the airport, I .... there on time. (drive / get)
5 You can .... to bed if you .... tired. (go / feel)
6 If he .... he .... in the team. (not practise / not be)
7 Why don't you leave now? If you .... there early, you .... more relaxed. (get / be)
8 You .... very tired tomorrow unless you .... working now. (be / stop)

MY TURN!

You are planning to go to the beach for the day with your cousin. Copy and complete the sentences in your notebook.

1 If I arrive late, ...he'll be angry...... .
2 If the sun's shining, ...
3 We'll stay at home ....
4 If my cousin's ill, ...
5 We'll walk ....
6 If we're tired, ...

MY TEST!

Circle the correct option.

1 If you put lemon juice on a .... go black. a banana it doesn't b banana, it doesn't c banana, it don't
2 Water boils faster if you .... salt in it. a doesn't put b won't put c don't put
3 If I pass my exams, I .... chemistry at university. a might study b might be study c might to study
4 The chemicals in cola will be bad for your teeth unless .... them carefully. a you don't clean b you won't clean c you clean
5 Be careful! If .... those sweets in your cola, the bottle might explode. a you put b you might put c you'll put

My Test! answers: 1b 2c 3a 4c 5a

66 Second conditional

I'd throw a cake at him if he didn't stop.

Tim wants a job in a restaurant.
The chef interviews him.

Chef: Now Tim, some more difficult questions. Don't worry, these are not everyday situations. **What would you do if there was a fire in the kitchen?**

Tim: **I would run away if I saw a fire.**

Chef: I see. **If a waiter shouted at you, would you do anything?**

Tim: Yes, **I'd throw a cake at him if he didn't stop.**

Chef: Hmm. **If the shops were closed and you needed some eggs, where would you get some?**

Tim: **If I wanted some eggs, I'd look for a chicken.**

? Well, have you decided? If you were the chef, would Tim get the job?

Answer: No

Second conditional

1 **Use the second conditional for events and situations which are unlikely, imaginary or impossible in the present and future.**

If I didn't like anything on the menu, I would go home. (Unlikely: there is usually something you like.)
I would run away if I saw a fire. (Imaginary: Tim is imagining a fire that might happen in the future.)
If I were the chef, I wouldn't give Tim the job. (Impossible: you are not the chef.)

2 **In second conditional sentences, use *if* + past tense ... *would* + infinitive without *to*. We can use the short forms *'d* for *would* and *wouldn't* for *would not*.**

*If the customer **complained**, I'd tell the manager.*
*If Tim **worked** here, he **wouldn't** do a good job.*

3 **The short form answer is *Yes, I / you* / etc. *would* or *No, I / you* / etc. *would not / wouldn't*.**

A: If you were the chef, would Tim get the job?
*B: **No, he wouldn't.***
A: Would you run outside if there was a fire in the kitchen?
*B: **Yes, I would.***

4 **When the *if* comes at the beginning of the sentence, we need a comma in the middle.**

If the food was bad, there wouldn't be many customers.
There wouldn't be many customers if the food was bad.

5 **Use *might* or *could* in the main clause to indicate that something is possible and not certain.**

*If you ate Tim's cooking, you **might** get sick.*
*You **could** complain if you didn't like the food.*
*I **could** be a chef if I wanted.*

▶ **See Units 20, 21 and 24 for more information on *could* and *might*.**

6 **We often use *if* + *were* instead of *was* after the pronouns *I, she, he, it* and singular nouns. This is more common in formal language and American English.**

If it were cheaper, I'd go to restaurants more often.

7 **We often use *If I were you ... I would* (*not*) ... for advice and suggestions.**

***If I were you, I'd find** another job.*
I wouldn't eat** here **if I were you.

Practice

A Complete the second conditional sentences using the correct forms of the verbs in brackets.

1 If I ......lost...... my phone, I ......would buy...... a new one. (lose / buy)
2 If you .... the race, you .... famous. (win / be)
3 If I .... really bad, I .... a doctor. (feel / see)
4 My sister .... to me if I .... it. (not speak / break)
5 We .... to Mars if too many people .... on this planet. (move / live)
6 If you .... more time, ... you .... another language? (have / learn)
7 If I .... my name, I .... it. (not like / change)
8 .... you .... away if you .... a wolf? (run / see)

B Circle the correct option.

Interviewer: You're a famous British chef but if you [1]... a chef, what would you do?
Chef: I would play football if I [2]... because I love it. But, I love cooking too. I [3]... all day if my wife let me.
Interviewer: Where [4]... to open a restaurant next?
Chef: If I [5]... a restaurant in Paris, that would be fantastic. It would be great if I [6]... shop in the markets there. If that restaurant was successful, I [7]... more in France.
Interviewer: People think British food is not very good. Why?
Chef: I really don't know. If I [8]... why, I would tell you. If you [9]... my cooking, you would never say English food is bad. If I [10]... you, I'd buy my new book.

1 a were (b) weren't c would be d wouldn't be
2 a could b can c will d would
3 a cooked b would cook c didn't cook d wouldn't cook
4 a do you like b did you like c are you liking d would you like
5 a had b did have c would have d might have
6 a would b might c could d did
7 a opened b might open c might opened d might to open
8 a know b knew c would know d would knew
9 a might taste b wouldn't taste c didn't taste d tasted
10 a am b be c were d would

C Match the pairs, then make them into second conditional sentences using *could* and *might* (*not*) and write them in your notebook.

1 watch too much TV
2 see a strange light in the sky
3 have no friends
4 learn 700 new words today
5 find a book of magic
6 travel back in time
7 write a pop song
8 spend three hours in the bathroom every morning

a become a pop star
b make my family very angry
c my eyes get tired
d not want to read it
e visit Cleopatra
f think it was a spaceship
g join a sports club
h not remember them all

1 If I watched too much TV, my eyes might get tired.

MY TURN!

In your notebook, copy and complete at least four of these sentences with *If* ..., using a comma if necessary.

1 If I found some money on the street, I'd give it to a police officer.
2 .... I'd fly to Peru.
3 .... I might jump out of the window.
4 The world would be a happier place ....
5 .... she wouldn't be very pleased.
6 I would be really worried ....
7 .... I'd invite all my friends to a big party.
8 .... I couldn't get home.

MY TEST!

Circle the correct option.

1 If I found an insect in my salad, I wouldn't .... it. a eat b ate c eating
2 I'd be a chef if I .... better at cooking. a would be b were c am
3 A: This soup tastes terrible. B: If I .... speak to the waiter. a were you, I'd b would be you, I'd c would be you I'd
4 If the food in this restaurant were better, I .... eat here more often. a may b will c might
5 A: If a waiter threw a cake at you, would you eat it? B: No, ... a I don't b he didn't c I wouldn't

My Test answers: 1a 2b 3a 4c 5c

R12 Review: the passive; conditionals

A Match the sentence beginnings to the correct endings.

1 Stonehenge was built
2 Mickey Mouse was created
3 Some people think the dinosaurs were killed
4 Champagne is made
5 Honey is made
6 Chinese is spoken
7 Paper is made
8 Bananas are grown
9 Mice are eaten

a by a meteor from space.
b from trees.
c by over 1 billion people.
d by snakes.
e by Walt Disney.
f in France.
g about 4,500 years ago.
h in Central America.
i by bees.

B Change the active sentences into passive sentences. You don't always need to include *by*.

1 Somebody stole my phone last night.
My phone was stolen last night.
2 They sell mobile phones in that shop.
Mobile phones ....
3 My sister gave me this sweater.
I ....
4 My aunt cuts my hair.
My ....
5 A famous opera singer taught me to sing.
I ....
6 Mr Hill teaches us to swim.
We ....
7 Uncle Brian will cook tomorrow's dinner.
Tomorrow's ....
8 I told you to stay in your room.
You ....

C Complete these newspaper stories using the correct form of the verbs in brackets. Some verbs should be active and some should be passive.

More bikes stolen from city centre

Last weekend four bicycles [1] were stolen (steal) in the city centre. This brings the total of bikes stolen this month to fourteen. Police [2] .... (think) there is a gang of bike thieves. 'The thieves always [3] .... (use) the same methods. Every time, the chains [4] .... (cut) using metal cutters and the bikes [5] .... (put) into a big white truck. We know it's a white van because it [6] .... (film) last night by cameras.'

New element number 112 has a name

Yesterday, one of the newest and heaviest elements [7] .... (give) a name, Copernicium. The element [8] .... (discover) in 1996, but it [9] .... (add) to the periodic table only last month, because other scientists [10] .... (need) to check that there really is such an element. The name 'Copernicium' [11] .... (choose) by Professor Hofmann, the man who [12] .... (discover) the element.

£1 million damage caused by Wednesday's wild weather

The strong winds last Wednesday night [13] .... (cause) over £1 million worth of damage in the city. More than 40 shop windows [14] .... (break). Several trees [15] .... (blow down). Eleven cars [16] .... (damage) when tree branches [17] .... (fall) on them. Six houses [18] .... (lose) their roofs. Fortunately, nobody [19] .... (hurt).

D **Complete the conditional sentences using the words in brackets. Add commas if necessary.**

1 If you (not understand), I (help) you.
If *you don't understand, I'll help* you.
2 If Mick (be) taller, he (be) a great basketball player.
If ……………………………………
…………………………………… player.
3 This computer (not work) unless you (turn) it on.
This ……………………………………
…………………………………… on.
4 If I (know) the answer, I (tell) you.
If ……………………………………
…………………………………… you.
5 If I (be) you, I (not wear) that hat.
If ……………………………………
…………………………………… hat.
6 You can't come in unless you (have) a ticket.
You ……………………………………
…………………………………… ticket.
7 Where (go) if you could fly?
Where ……………………………………
…………………………………… fly?
8 I might win the competition if I (be) lucky.
I ……………………………………
…………………………………… lucky.

E **Complete the sentences using the correct verb forms.**

1 If I met a Hollywood star, ……………………
I'd take a photo.
2 If I go to the cinema this week, ……………………
…………………………………… .
3 I'd buy a new MP3 player ……………………
…………………………………… .
4 I'll take an umbrella if ……………………
…………………………………… .
5 If my grandparents phoned me, ……………………
…………………………………… .
6 If I got a car for my birthday, ……………………
…………………………………… .
7 I'd phone the police if ……………………
…………………………………… .
8 If I were invited onto a TV show, ……………………
…………………………………… .

F **Complete the conversation using the correct forms of the verbs in brackets. Sometimes there is more than one right answer.**

A: So what shall we get for Maggie's birthday?
B: I don't know. What does she want?
A: Well, if I [1] *knew* (know) that, I [2] …………… (not / ask) you, would I?
B: OK ... but what does she like?
C: Well, she loves tennis, of course. We could buy her a new racket.
A: Are you joking? They're really expensive. If we [3] …………… (have) more money, it might be a good idea.
C: Yes, but if we [4] …………… (buy) her a cheap one on the Internet, it might not be too bad ...
B: Hmm ... I think she's already got a racket.
C: But if she [5] …………… (have) two, she [6] …………… (be able to) play with her sister.
B: No ... we shouldn't buy her a racket. We don't know anything about rackets. What if we [7] …………… (buy) her the wrong one ...?
A: ... like a children's racket ...
C: ... or a squash racket.
B: Yeah. It [8] …………… (be) terrible.
A: So what do you think? How about tennis balls?
C: Maybe ... but it's a bit boring. How [9] …………… (you / feel) if somebody [10] …………… (give) you a tennis ball for your birthday?
A: Well, if I [11] …………… (be) a tennis player, I [12] …………… (be) happy, I think.
B: Hang on ... I've just remembered something. You can buy night-time tennis balls. They're made of some special plastic. If you [13] …………… (hit) them, they [14] …………… (light up).
C: Er ... why [15] …………… (she / want) a night-time tennis ball?
B: Well, if she [16] …………… (want) to play tennis outside at night, for example, and she [17] …………… (lose) the ball, she [18] …………… (be able to) find it again.
A: It sounds really useful. I think we should get it.
B: OK, so unless anyone [19] …………… (have) any better ideas, I [20] …………… (try) to buy one on the Internet. If I [21] …………… (not can) find one, or if they [22] …………… (be) really expensive, I [23] …………… (phone) you and we [24] …………… (have to) think of something else.

67 Reported speech

She said she would never have a party again.

Sophie Brown's 18th birthday party was really bad. A radio station **told listeners that there was going to be a party** the next day, so many teenagers **thought the party was open to** everyone. The teenagers caused 30,000 euros of damage to the Browns' expensive house. One teenager **said he didn't know Sophie but he liked parties.** Sophie **said that she felt terrible and that she would never have another party** again. Her father **told reporters that he was thinking of getting the radio station to pay for the damage.** Sophie's mother **said she couldn't understand why** the teenagers wanted to damage their lovely house. We tried to talk to Sophie again today but her father **says she is not talking** to reporters any more.

How old was Sophie?

Answer: 18

Reported speech

1 **We can talk about what people said or thought by using reported speech.**
*Sophie **said that she wanted a party.***

2 **If the verb of saying or thinking is in the present, there is no change of tense for the words reported.**
*Her father **says that she is ill.***

3 **When the verb of saying or thinking is in the past, the verb in the reported speech usually moves into the past.**
*Sophie **told her mum she was sorry.***

direct speech	reported speech
present simple ⟶	past simple
'It seems strange.'	He thought that it **seemed** strange.
present continuous ⟶	past continuous
'I am staying for a few days.'	She said that she **was staying** for a few days.
can ⟶	*could*
'We can swim very well.'	They said that they **could** swim very well.
will ⟶	*would*
'It will be great!'	She thought that it **would** be great.

TIP

***Used to* and *would* do not change in reported speech.**
*I **used to** be Sophie's friend.* →
*She said she **used to** be Sophie's friend.*

4 **The verb in the reported speech does not need to change if the information is still true or relevant now.**
*Sophie **told me that she is 18.***

5 ***That* often links the verb of saying or thinking to the reported speech. *That* can be left out, especially in speaking and informal language.**
*She said **that** she wanted a big party. /*
She said she wanted a big party.

6 **Pronouns and time and place expressions may change in reported speech.**
we → they
now → then
next week → the week after
this morning → that morning
tomorrow → the next day
here → there

John: 'I love parties.' →
*John said **he** loved parties.*
*'There will be a party **tomorrow**.'* →
*A radio station told listeners that there would be a party **the next day**.*

▶ **See Unit 68 for more information on *say* and *tell*.**

Practice

A Change these sentences from reported speech into direct speech.

1 Jim said he was tired.
Jim: *'I'm tired.'*
2 Cathy said she wanted to go to Sophie's party.
Cathy: ....
3 Jim said he didn't know Sophie.
Jim: ....
4 Cathy told Jim that Sophie was having a party the next day.
Cathy: ....
5 Cathy also said that everyone was invited to the party.
Cathy: ....
6 Jim said that he was surprised that everyone was going.
Jim: ....
7 Cathy said that it would be great if they went together.
Cathy: ....
8 Jim told Cathy that he would think about it.
Jim: ....

B Report what the people are saying or thinking. Begin each sentence with *He / She / They said / thought*.

1 It's my ball!
2 I need a towel.
3 I have a lot of work to do.
4 The map isn't clear.
5 FINISH
We're winning!
6 I'm not answering your question!

1 *He said it was his ball.*
2 ....
3 ....
4 ....
5 ....
6 ....

C Complete each sentence b so that it means the same as sentence a in reported speech. Use no more than three words.

1 a John: 'I come from a small town in New Zealand.'
b John said *that he came* from a small town in New Zealand.
2 a Felicity: 'I need it this morning.'
b Felicity said she .... morning.
3 a John: 'We have a lot to do.'
b John told her .... a lot to do.
4 a Alice: 'I am busy now.'
b Alice said that she ....
5 a Olive: 'Gary, I'll go next week.'
b Olive told Gary that she would .... after.
6 a Mike: 'I'll phone tomorrow.'
b Mike said he would phone ....

MY TURN!

It was the morning after Sophie's party. Mr and Mrs Brown came home and found the house in a mess. What did they think and say? Write six sentences in reported speech in your notebook.

Example: *Mr Brown thought he was having a bad dream.*

MY TEST!

Circle the correct option.

1 'I like big parties': Sophie says she .... big parties. a likes b would like c liked
2 'Sophie will be 18 tomorrow': The radio station said that Sophie .... 18 the next day. a was b would be c will be
3 'You can't have a party next year': Mr Brown told Sophie that she .... have a party the next year.
a won't b can't c couldn't
4 'Sophie's helping to clean our house': Mrs Brown said that Sophie .... to clean their house.
a is helping b helped c was helping
5 'I'll come to your party tomorrow': Sophie's friend said she'd go to her party ....
a tomorrow b this day c the next day

My Test! answers: 1a 2b 3c 4c 5c

68 *Say* and *tell*

She told me to meet her.

? What do you think happens next?

Say and *tell*

1 ***Say* and *tell* have similar meanings.**
*What did he **say**?*
*What did she **tell** you?*

2 **Use *say* when it is not necessary to specify who is being spoken to.**
*What did she **say**?*
*She **said** (that) she would be here.*

3 **Use *tell* or *say* when you want to mention the person who is being spoken to.**
***Tell her** your name.* NOT ~~*Tell to her your name.*~~
*She **said to me** that she was happy.*
NOT ~~*She said me ...*~~, ~~*She told to me ...*~~

4 **We usually use *say* (not *tell*) to introduce direct speech.**
*'You must be home by midnight,' she **said**.*

5 **We can also use *tell* + object + *to*-infinitive to report instructions or commands.**
'Phone me!' ➜ *She **told me to phone**.*

The negative form is *tell* + object + *not* + *to*-infinitive.
'Don't phone!' ➜ *She told me not to phone.*
NOT ~~*She told me don't phone.*~~

6 **There are also a number of expressions using *tell* + noun. For example:**

tell a joke	*tell a secret*	*tell the time*
tell a lie	*tell a story*	*tell the truth*

*My mum likes **telling stories**. He **told me a good joke**.*

7 **Common expressions with *say* are:**

say goodbye	*say something / anything*
say hello	*say sorry*
say nothing	*say yes / no*

*I hate **saying goodbye**.*
*Please **say yes**.*

Practice

A Complete these sentences using an appropriate form of *say* or *tell*.

1 She looks really unhappy. What did you ......say...... to her?
2 He didn't .... that he would be late.
3 I'm not sure if he was .... me the truth.
4 He .... her to wait.
5 They .... goodbye at the station.
6 She's going to .... us everything tomorrow.
7 She didn't .... anyone she was going to the park.
8 She .... she doesn't like cheese.

B Make sentences by putting the words in the correct order.

1 please / phone / number / tell / Can / me / your / you?
Can you tell me your phone number please?
2 police officer / did / tell / you / What / the / do / to?
....
3 were / happy / not / said / customers / The / they
....
4 Have / problems / anyone / you / about / your / told?
....
5 She / she / get / up / would / said / early
....
6 later / will / you / about / I / the / tell / match
....
7 Passengers / platform 3 / told / go / were / to / to
....
8 very / well / said / not / My / dad / was / feeling / he
....
9 go / in / told / not / She / everyone / to
....
10 told / come / them / We / not / could / we
....

C Rewrite the sentences in reported speech using the pattern *tell* + object + (*not*) *to*-infinitive and the words in brackets.

1 'Come back in four weeks.' (The dentist / him)
The dentist told him to come back in four weeks.
2 'Call back later!' (He / me)
....
3 'Don't leave without us.' (We / the others)
....
4 'Wait outside.' (I will / her)
....
5 'Don't park in front of the house!' (Tell / the driver)
....
6 'Don't be late!' (I / Simon)
....
7 'Don't say anything!' (The girl / her friend)
....
8 'Don't worry!' (He / always / me)
....

MY TURN!

What do you think was happening? Write sentences using phrases with *say* and *tell* in your notebook.

1 The girl didn't believe the boy.
She thought he was telling a lie.
2 Everyone in the class was laughing.
3 The boy went red in the face.
4 The children were listening very carefully to the man.
5 The girl was speaking very quietly to her friend.
6 It was difficult for the boy to speak to his mother. But afterwards he felt better.

MY TEST!

Circle the correct option.

1 Jo .... me she was waiting for Beth. a told b told to c said
2 'There's a great film on at the cinema,' I .... a told b said her c said
3 I told Jo .... for Beth, but to come to the cinema with me. a to wait not b to don't wait c not to wait
4 When Beth arrived, she didn't even say .... for being late. a a lie b sorry c a joke
5 A: Hi. Are you angry with me? I thought it was still five o'clock. B: Can't you .... time? a say the b tell the c tell a

My Test! answers: 1a 2c 3c 4b 5b

69 Defining relative clauses

A ball game that is played in many countries

Jai-alai ...

... is a team ball game **that is played in many countries**. A team has eight players **who take turns to throw the ball against a wall**. The players throw the ball from a *cesta* (a basket **a player ties to his arm)**. The game is played in a *fronton* (a court **that has three walls)**.

The sport has been popular with famous people in the USA. Paul Newman was one famous person **who played the sport**.

It is an exciting ball game **which many people think is the fastest in the world.**

True or False? Jai-alai is played in the USA.

Answer: True

Defining relative clauses

1 **A relative clause gives us more information about a noun.**

A team has eight players who ***take turns to throw the ball against the wall.*** (gives more information about the players)

A fronton is a court ***that has three walls.*** (gives more information about the court)

2 **Many relative clauses begin with the relative pronouns *who*, *which* or *that*.**

Use *who* to refer to a person.

Paul Newman was one famous person ***who*** *played the sport.*

Use *which* to refer to a thing, an animal or an idea.

It is an exciting sport ***which*** *many people think is the fastest ball game in the world.*

Use *that* instead of *who* or *which* in informal English.

Jai-alai is a team ball game ***that*** *is played in many countries.*

3 **When the relative pronoun is the object of the relative clause we do not need to repeat the object pronoun.**

Handball is a game. People have played ***it*** *for centuries.*

Handball is a game ***which*** *people have played for centuries.* NOT ~~*Handball is a game which people have played it for centuries.*~~

4 **We can leave out the relative pronoun when it is the object of the relative clause.**

Handball is a game ***which people have played*** *for centuries.* OR *Handball is a game* ***people have played*** *for centuries.*

Practice

A **Underline the relative clauses in this text about the game of squash.**

Squash is a racket sport which boys in a London school invented in the 19th century. It is played by two players in a court that has four walls. Players hit the ball around the walls of the court. The ball travels very quickly.

Squash is a healthy sport but it is not good for people who are not very strong! It has become an internationally popular sport which many people think should be in the Olympics. But there is a problem with this. People who come to watch the matches do not always enjoy them. They find it difficult to see the ball!

B **Complete the sentences with the relative pronoun *who* or *which*.**

1 That's the woman ......who...... I saw.
2 The school .... she goes to is outside town.
3 People .... arrive late have to go to Reception.
4 The train .... he's catching leaves in half an hour.
5 The man .... lives there is an actor.
6 I've just seen the woman .... stole your bag!
7 Is that the book .... your teacher told you about?
8 *Who Wants to be a Millionaire?* is a TV show .... is very popular.

C **Join each pair of sentences to make one sentence. Use relative clauses with *who, which, that* (or nothing).**

1 A spade is a thing. You use it to dig the garden.
A spade is a thing which / that you use to dig the garden.
A spade is a thing you use to dig the garden.

2 *Matkot* is a beach game. It is played all over the world.

3 An ecologist is a scientist. An ecologist studies the environment.

4 Is that the girl? The girl you saw at the party?

5 A penguin is a bird. It can't fly.

6 I don't know the doctor. He is coming to see you.

7 The actress was in *Superman*. She is on TV tonight.

8 We're going to the hotel. It's near the beach.

MY TURN!

Write definitions for the people and things in your notebook.

1 A sunflower ......is a flower which grows very tall.
2 Neighbours
3 A musician
4 A chef
5 A telescope
6 An astronaut
7 Friends
8 A dinosaur
9 A ring
10 A knife

MY TEST!

Circle the correct option.

1 There are often eight players .... in a jai-alai game. a what play b that plays c who play
2 The most important things .... are very strong arms and good eyes. a that you need them b you need c which you need them
3 The first player .... seven points is the winner. a what gets b gets c who gets
4 The balls .... are made of rubber. a that they use b they use them c which they use them
5 A very high ball .... down near the back wall is called a *chula*. a it comes b which comes c which it comes

My Test! answers: 1c 2b 3c 4a 5b

R13 Review: reported speech; *say / tell*; relative clauses

A Change the direct speech to reported speech in the past.

1 'I have to go now, Steve. The baby's crying.'
Vicky told Steve she had to go then because the baby was crying.

2 'You can't go out tomorrow, Frank. Your aunt is coming to stay with us.'
Frank's mum told ....
....

3 'Come to my house later, Zoe. I'll show you my photos.'
Sue told .... She said ....
....

4 'I can't play the guitar but I'm quite good at singing.'
John said ....
....

5 'We used to have a dog but now we have a cat.'
Tina said ....
....

6 'Please put your coats here, children. You can collect them later.'
The teacher told the .... and that
....

7 'I'd like to speak English as well as you, Paula.'
Greg told ....
....

8 'If you don't stop talking, I'll phone your mother.'
Their grandmother said that ....
....

B Read this police officer's report and change the reported speech (underlined) to direct speech.

POLICE REPORT

I was walking through the park yesterday afternoon when I saw a young man. He was speaking very loudly on a mobile phone. I told him [1] to stop talking. The man said that [2] he couldn't because he was talking to his friend. He told me that [3] his friend was angry with him. He said [4] he would be very very angry if he turned the phone off.

I told him that [5] I would be very very very angry if he didn't turn the phone off. He told his friend that [6] he couldn't talk right then because a policeman wanted to talk to him. He turned the phone off. I told him [7] I was looking for a criminal. I said that [8] I wanted to look in his bag. He told me [9] I couldn't because it was full of stolen money from the bank. I laughed because I thought [10] he was joking. But then he ran away ...

1 'Please stop talking.'
2 ....
....
3 ....
4 ....
....
5 ....
....
6 ....
....
7 ....
8 ....
9 ....
....
10 ....

C Match the pairs.

1 He thinks a she is very nice.
2 He thought b she was very nice.

3 She told a a truth
4 She told the b lie

5 He said a her that he loved her.
6 He told b to her that he loved her

7 She said a 'I'm sorry.'
8 She told him b she was sorry.

9 He said a a story.
10 He told b nothing.

D Complete each sentence b so that it means the same as sentence a. Use two to four words, including the word in brackets.

1 a 'Don't be late,' Charles said to Pamela. (not)
b Charles told Pamela not to be late.
2 a The children listened to Bill's story. (told)
b Bill .... story.
3 a 'I'm sorry I broke your pen, Rob,' said Adam. (said)
b .... for breaking Rob's pen.
4 a Barry told Sylvia that he didn't like her. (I)
b Barry said, '...................., Sylvia.'
5 a He said he'd study the next day. (I'll)
b He said '....................'
6 a I'll say something to you, but you mustn't tell anybody. (you)
b I'll .... secret.
7 a 'I used to live here,' he said. (that)
b He said .... live there.
8 a She lied to me about her age. (told)
b When I asked her about her age, she
....

E Combine the pairs of sentences into one sentence, using *which* or *who*.

1 The shop closes at 7.00. We want to visit it.
The shop which we want to visit closes at 7.00.
2 The photo is terrible! You took the photo of me.
....
3 The student is from China. I'm teaching her.
....
4 Where did I put that book? I was reading it.
....
5 I met someone. He went to primary school with you.
....
6 Was the doctor nice? You saw her.
....
7 The bus doesn't stop here. It goes to the town centre.
....
8 The people live next door. They have eight cats.
....
9 Was the present expensive? You gave the present to me.
....
10 People are usually healthy. They run every day.
....

F Match the sentence beginnings to the correct endings, then write them below. Add the relative pronouns *who* or *which* only if they are necessary.

1 A tie is something a many people enjoy.
2 A shopaholic is a person b has six legs.
3 An insect is an animal c flies a plane.
4 A pet is an animal d writes poems.
5 Mercury is a planet e you wear with a shirt.
6 Oxygen is a gas f we need to live.
7 A pilot is someone g you look after at home.
8 A poet is someone h loves shopping!
9 Yoga is a type of exercise i is very close to the sun.

1 e 2 ..... 3 ..... 4 ..... 5 .....
6 ..... 7 ..... 8 ..... 9 .....

1 A tie is something you wear with a shirt.
2 ....
3 ....
4 ....
5 ....
6 ....
7 ....
8 ....
9 ....

70 Linking words: *and, but, or, so, because*

What is 6,700 km long and made of stone?

The Great Wall of China is 6,700 km long **and** it goes from the east to the west of China. The Wall was started more than 2,500 years ago, **but** the biggest part was built in the Ming dynasty (1368–1644).

The Mings needed the Wall **because** enemies were coming from the north. Millions of people – free people **and** slaves – built the Wall **or** guarded it. They worked day **and** night. They guarded the Wall during the day **and** built it at night. They didn't build in the morning **or** afternoon **because** it was often very hot **and** uncomfortable in the day.

The Wall is very old, **so** some of it is broken, **but** there are still many beautiful sections.

? Underline the correct option: The Mings were *builders / emperors / slaves.*

Answer: emperors

Linking words: *and, but, or, so, because*

1 Use *and, but, or, so* and *because* to link two or more words, sentences, or parts of sentences.

*day **and** night*
*the morning **or** afternoon*
*It was hot, **so** people worked at night.*

2 Use *and* to add information.

*I left my hotel **and** walked to the Wall.*
*a warm **and** beautiful night*

TIP

In a long list, separate the items with commas (,), but remember to put *and* before the last item.

*Chinese, Japanese, Thai **and** Korean*

3 Use *but* to contrast information.

*I love China **but** I don't like the food much.*
*nice **but** expensive*

4 Use *or* to show alternatives.

*Do you want to see the old town **or** go to the beach?*
*Don't shout **or** scream.*

5 Use *so* to show the result of something.

*The Wall is very old, **so** some of it is broken.*
*They worked all night, **so** they were tired in the morning.*

6 Use *because* to show the reason for something. *Because* usually goes in the middle of the sentence.

*The Chinese needed the Wall **because** they had enemies.*

If you put *because* at the beginning of the sentence, you need to use a comma.

***Because** you speak Chinese, you can buy the tickets.*

Practice

A Match the pairs.

1	I sat down	a	so I was tired.
2	I ran five km,	b	because I was tired.
3	I want to go out	a	and it's raining again.
4	It's Monday	b	but it's raining again.
5	Did you finish the test	a	and did you pass?
6	Did you fail the test	b	or did you pass?
7	Sarah looks older	a	but she is in the same class as me.
8	I know Sarah	b	because she is in the same class as me.
9	We can go for a meal	a	but we can have a coffee.
10	I don't have much time	b	or we can have a coffee.

B Complete the sentences using *and, so, but, or, because*.

1 It's very late, ...so...... go to bed.
2 Please come .... visit us in the summer.
3 Do you want to stay here .... do you need to get home?
4 It's a big house .... my bedroom is small.
5 We're ready, ... let's go.
6 John finished university .... got a job.
7 Lucy was happy .... she got a present.
8 We can watch it at the cinema .... buy the DVD. You choose.

C Join each pair of sentences using linking words and write them in your notebook.

1 Sally went to bed. She felt tired.
Sally went to bed because she felt tired.
2 Felix is friendly. His sister is really nice.
3 My dictionary is very small. The word isn't in it.
4 The party was OK. I felt a bit bored.
5 Have you been to Italy before? Is this your first time here?
6 I opened the bag. I saw the money.
7 Trevor can't sleep. He drank a lot of coffee.
8 We heard a strange noise. I phoned the police.

D Join some of the sentences in this story using linking words.

This is an interesting story~~. You~~ *so you* will like it. Shen-Nung was an Emperor. He lived in China. One day he went into the garden. He sat under a tree. It was a beautiful day. It was too hot. It was too dry. Shen-Nung was thirsty. He asked for a drink. Shen-Nung could drink something cold. He could have a cup of hot water. The Emperor chose hot water. It was his usual afternoon drink. He waited. The servant brought the hot water. Shen-Nung closed his eyes. He felt tired. He felt sleepy. Some leaves fell from the tree. They went into his cup of water. Shen-Nung woke up. He took his cup. He drank the tea. He didn't notice the leaves. The new drink was unusual. The new drink was very tasty. He made another cup of hot water with leaves. Shen-Nung is now famous. He invented tea.

MY TURN!

Copy these sentences into your notebook and complete them using *and, or, so, but* and *because*.

1 At the weekends I *go shopping or see my friends*.
2 This morning I got up ....
3 I like the place where I live ....
4 .... is difficult for me ....
5 When I leave school I might .... or ....
6 .... made me angry ....
7 I want .... or .... for my birthday.
8 English is important for me ....
9 Pollution is a problem ....
10 Two things I need for happiness are ....

MY TEST!

Circle the correct option.

1 Some people say you can easily see the Great Wall from the moon, ... it's not true. a or b but c so
2 You can't see the Wall from the moon .... it's only 9 metres wide. a and b so c because
3 Some people use the Wall's stones for building, ... parts of the Wall are broken. a and b but c so
4 I want to go to China to visit Beijing .... visit the Great Wall. a because b and c so
5 Nobody wanted to destroy the Wall .... build a road. a or b but c so

My Test! answers: 1b 2c 3c 4b 5a

71 Time and sequence adverbs: *first, then, afterwards*

After lunch we visit the Peguche waterfall.

Ecuadorian Andes Tour

The two-day tour of the Ecuadorian Andes starts from a five-star hotel in Quito. **First**, we'll take you on a beautiful drive, **then** for lunch at a local restaurant on the San Pablo lake. **Next**, we'll take you to the volcanic lake of Cuicocha. At night we will stay at a 17th-century hotel.

The next morning you are free to visit the market in Otavalo. **Afterwards**, we'll visit the Peguche waterfall, and **finally**, we'll have a lovely drive back to the five-star hotel in Quito.

Put the events in the correct order:

a Visit the market.
b See the waterfall.
c Drive back to the hotel.
d Have lunch at the restaurant.

Answer: d, a, b, c

Time and sequence adverbs: *first, then, afterwards*

1 **Use these words to describe the order of events:**
first, next / then, afterwards, finally

2 **Other phrases similar to *afterwards* include *after that* and *after + noun.***
The next morning, you are free to visit the market in Otavalo.
Afterwards / After that / After lunch, we visit the Peguche waterfall.

TIP

We don't usually use *after* as an adverb.
After the class we are going to the museum.
NOT ~~*After we are going to the museum.*~~

3 **When we describe a process, we can also use ordinal numbers to describe each stage, e.g. *first, second, third, fourth, fifth, sixth*. We can use *finally* for the last part of the process. We usually use commas after these words.**
***First**, turn the machine on. **Second**, take a cup. **Third**, choose water or juice. **Finally**, press the green button.*

Practice

A Complete this postcard using the words in the box.

afterwards	finally
first	next	~~then~~

I'm having a great time in Sicily! We arrived at the airport this morning and [1] ...then... we had a tour of Palermo. In Palermo, [2] ...., we visited the cathedral, [3] .... the Church of Martorana and [4] .... we travelled to Monreale. We are staying in a hotel tonight. Tomorrow morning we are visiting the theatre in Taormina. [5] .... we are going to the Palazzo Corvaja. Our last visit is to the top of Mount Etna in a coach. See you soon!

B Describe the process of taking money out of a cash machine. Use time and sequence adverbs and the words in the box.

bank card	pin code	amount of money	wallet

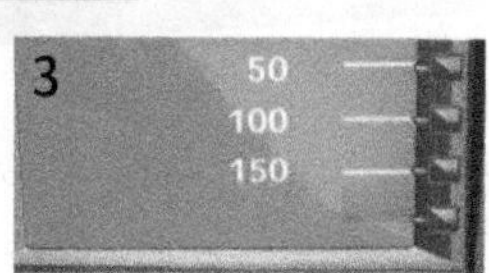

1 First, put your bank card in the machine.
2 ....
3 ....
4 ....
5 ....
6 ....

C Complete the sentences using *first, second, then, after that* or *finally*. Sometimes more than one answer is possible.

1 Do your homework. ...Then... you can go out.
2 ...., listen to all the instructions. Then write your answers.
3 We're not ready to leave yet. ...., we need to check the bikes. ...., we need to repair the tent and .... we need to buy some food.
4 Put the sugar in a bowl and .... add the eggs.
5 We had breakfast early. .... we went to the beach.
6 It was a good class. .... we learnt about rivers. .... we saw a film and .... we talked about river pollution.
7 The best advice I can give you about money is to save first and .... spend.

MY TURN!

Think of a food or drink you know how to make, e.g. a cake, a cup of coffee. Write sentences describing how to make it in your notebook. Use time and sequence adverbs in your description.

Example: First, cut two slices of bread.

MY TEST!

Circle the correct option.

1 When you arrive at the airport, first, collect your bags. ...., go through Passport Control. Third, go to the Arrivals hall and look for a man with 'Super Peru Tours' on a sign. **a** Two **b** Second **c** After
2 .... breakfast in Cuzco, we'll drive you to Pisac. **a** Afterwards **b** After that **c** After
3 After ...., we'll take you to your hotel in Yucay. **a** then **b** that **c** this
4 The next morning we'll take the early train to Machu Picchu for a tour. We'll have a two-hour tour, and .... you will have some free time. **a** then **b** second **c** after
5 ...., we'll return to the hotel in Cuzco. That's the end of the holiday. **a** Finally **b** After **c** Second

My Test! answers: 1b 2c 3b 4a 5a

72 Both, either, neither

They both live in a fantasy world.

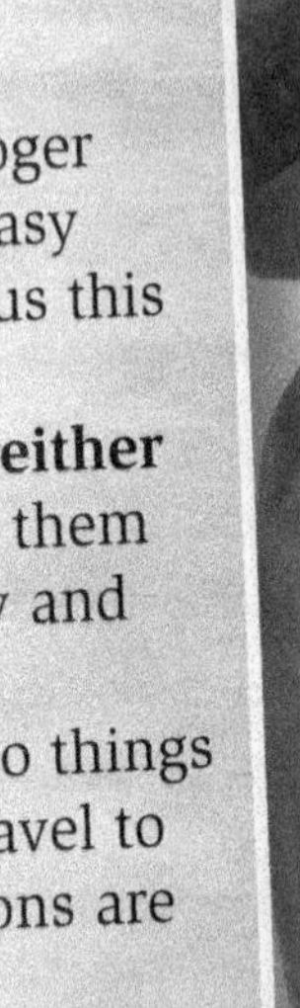

The Golden Compass is a story of **both** magic **and** adventure.

Lyra and Roger are friends. **Both** children enjoy playing **and** having fun but **neither** Lyra **nor** Roger is an ordinary child. **Both of** them live in a fantasy world. **Neither** child understands how dangerous this world is.

The strangeness of their world doesn't worry **either of** the children. But then other children around them start to disappear. **Neither of** them knows why and **both** are frightened.

One day even Roger disappears. There are two things Lyra can do. She can **either** stay at home **or** travel to the terrible North to find her friend. **Both** options are dangerous. What will Lyra do?

? Underline the correct option: Lyra is Roger's *daughter / friend / wife.*

Answer: friend

Both, either, neither

1 *Both* = A and B. *Neither* = not A and not B. *Either* = A or B.
Both compasses show north.
Neither is working.
Don't use *either*.

2 Use *both* either before or after nouns, but only after pronouns.
*Lyra and Roger **both** feel afraid.*
OR ***Both** Lyra and Roger feel afraid.*
*We **both** like fantasy books.*

3 Use *both of* before plural personal pronouns: *both of us / you / them*.
***Both of us** read it.*
*They will find **both of them**.*

4 Use *either* and *neither* before singular nouns.
***Either** day at the weekend is fine.*
***Neither** child understands.*

5 Use *either of* and *neither of* before plural nouns and pronouns.
*Do **either of** you understand?*
***Neither of** them knows why.*

6 We can use *both ... and, either ... or, neither ... nor* to join nouns, other kinds of words, phrases and even sentences.
*... a story of **both** magic **and** adventure.*
*The children **neither** know **nor** care.*
*... **either** take the train **or** the bus.*

7 We can use *both, either* and *neither* on their own as pronouns.
A: Do you want a sandwich or a pizza?
*B: **Both**! I'm hungry!*
*C: **Either**! One of them – it doesn't matter which.*
*D: **Neither**! I don't like sandwiches or pizzas! I want a hot dog.*

Practice

A Underline the correct word.

1. There are two nice cakes. *Both / Neither* are delicious.
2. *Either / Both* Russia and Korea are next to China.
3. A: Do you want an apple or a banana?
   B: *Both / Neither*. I'm not hungry.
4. We saw *both / both of* them at the station.
5. I'm not busy on Monday and Tuesday. *Either / Neither* day is good to meet.
6. We didn't pass the exam, so *either of / neither of* us is happy.
7. I have a sister. We *both / neither* like football.
8. My computer is slow. It's *either / neither* broken or it's very old.

B In your notebook, compare Lyra and Roger using *Both / Neither of them* ... and *Both / Neither Lyra and / nor Roger* ... .

	Lyra	Roger
1 Where do you come from?	Oxford	Oxford
2 Do you like Oxford?	No	No
3 Can you use a compass?	No	No
4 Do you feel afraid?	Yes	Yes
5 Have you been to the North?	No	No
6 Would you like a map?	Yes	Yes
7 Do you know where the children are?	No	No

1 *Both of them come from Oxford. / Both Lyra and Roger come from Oxford.*

C These symbols are used in computer logic. Make sentences using *both ... and, either ... or* and *neither ... nor*.

[AND symbol] = *both ... and* [OR symbol] = *either ... or* [NOR symbol] = *neither ... nor*

1 A computer is [OR] on / off.
A computer is either on or off.

2 Programming is [AND] a science / an art.
....

3 Computer logic is [NOR] difficult / boring.
....

4 The symbols are [AND] clear / useful.
....

5 The software is [OR] free / very cheap.
....

6 You need [AND] a monitor / keyboard.
....

D Complete the dialogue using *both (of), neither (of)* or *either (of)*.

Andrew: Hi, Clare. Have you see seen those two DVDs I bought? I can't find [1] *either of* them.

Clare: They are [2] .... on the coffee table. You should take them back to the shop. [3] .... them will play.

Andrew: Really? I watched [4] .... on Tuesday and they were OK.

Clare: Well, they don't work now. Take them back to the shop. You can [5] .... exchange them or get your money back. I didn't like [6] ...., anyway.

Andrew: I thought [7] .... films were good. [8] .... you like those kinds of films or you don't.

MY TURN!

In your notebook, write sentences about you and your best friend using *both (of)* and *neither (of)*. (Think about your favourite things; what you do every day; your family and friends; what you can / can't do and have / don't have.)

Example: *We were both born in 2000.*

MY TEST!

Circle the correct option.

1 I love *The Golden Compass*. I enjoyed .... the film and the book. **a** neither **b** both of **c** both

2 Lyra travels between her world and ours, but she doesn't feel comfortable in ....
a neither of **b** either **c** either of

3 Neither Lyra's mother .... her father understands her.
a or **b** nor **c** neither

4 Both Lyra and Roger leave Oxford, but will .... ever come home again?
a either them **b** they either
c either of them

5 A: Who wrote the book? Was it JK Rowling or Lemony Snicket? B: .... It was Philip Pullman.
a Nor **b** Neither **c** Either

My Test! answers: 1c 2b 3b 4c 5b

73 Word order
Outside the port today

Evening Times, 25 July
News in Brief

Police are looking for the driver of a car which hit a tree **by the side of the M79** motorway. The car was found **earlier today**.

Last night Fogmouth port was closed because of strong winds. There were long lines of trucks **outside the port today**. 'I have been here for ten hours,' one driver told us **angrily**.

The Fire Service was called to a fire in **Rexbrook town centre** yesterday. The fire started in some rubbish **in Kelly Road at about 9.10 pm**.

? Answer the questions.
1 When was the car found?
2 When was Fogmouth port closed?
3 Where did the fire start?

Answers: 1 earlier today 2 last night 3 in some rubbish in Kelly Road in Rexbrook town centre

Word order

1 Common expressions of time:

in the winter	*today*	*early*
in the afternoon	*tomorrow morning*	*again*
on Sunday	*next week*	*now*
on Mondays	*last month*	*then*
at the moment	*yesterday*	*recently*
at 9 o'clock	*daily*	*these days*
at lunchtime	*every year*	*at this time*
for ten years		

2 Common expressions of place:

here	*in the town centre*
there	*at the bank*
upstairs	*at the end of the street*
in Italy	*near the church*
in Milan	*outside the fire station*
in Ford Street	

3 We usually put expressions of time and place and adverbs of manner at the end of a sentence. Sometimes we put them at the beginning.

*The Fire Service was called to a fire **in Rexbrook town centre.***
*The police came **immediately.***
***Last night** Fogmouth port was closed because of strong winds.*

If there is more than one of these at the end of a sentence, the order is usually: manner, place, time.

*There were long queues of trucks **outside Fogmouth port today.*** (place + time)
*She brushed her teeth **carefully at bedtime.*** (manner + time)
*He ran **quickly to school in the morning.*** (manner + place + time)

▶ **See Unit 56 for more adverbs of manner.**

TIP

An adverb does not usually come between a verb and the object.
They closed the port yesterday.
NOT ~~*They closed yesterday the port.*~~

▶ **See Unit 1 for more information on word order.**

Practice

A **Underline the expressions of time and place in these short news stories and mark them either t (time) or p (place).**

1 Police are looking for three men who stole money from a restaurant in [p] Market Place. The robbery happened at Tony's Diner at 8 pm [t] on Monday.

2 There are plans for new buildings at the Barton Hospital. Work will start on the old people's buildings in the summer.

3 Rory Wright could play for Barton Football Club again. The club hopes the 23-year-old player will return next month.

4 The headteacher of Stoke Fields Primary School has retired at the age of 65. Ian Fletcher has worked at the city centre school for 18 years. Mr Fletcher owns a house in Florida. He plans to move there.

B **Complete the dialogues by putting the words in the correct order. Sometimes more than one answer is possible.**

1 A: What time do we leave in the morning?
B: We need to leave early. (we / early / leave / to / need)

2 A: Have you been to the holiday apartment recently?
B: Yes, ... (last / week / there / was / I)

3 A: Do you know this town?
B: Oh yes, ... (years / lived / have / for / here / I)

4 A: When do you go to the gym?
B: .... (Tuesdays / I / on / go / there)

5 A: Do you know where the town hall is?
B: .... (now / am / I / there / going)

6 A: Have you read the information?
B: No, but ....
(I / it / at / look/ tonight / carefully / will)

7 A: Have you seen my bag?
B: .... (was / upstairs / it / morning / this)

8 A: Where are we meeting?
B: ....
(are / outside / at / we / school / the / meeting / 9.15)

C **Add more information to the news stories by putting the expressions in the right places.**

1 ~~last week~~ on Sunday evening outside the port

Three young men were rescued from a boat near Fogmouth port last week. The boat hit large rocks. No one was hurt.

2 at home from St Francis Zoo recently yesterday

A bear escaped. Police told people to stay. A number of animals have escaped from the zoo, including a rare white tiger.

MY TURN!

Copy and complete the sentences in your notebook using appropriate expressions of time and / or place.

1 The baby was born at the hospital last night.
2 Buses go ....
3 I was ....
4 Shall we have the party ....?
5 I'm going to meet her ....
6 Could you give him the present ....?
7 I love going ....

MY TEST!

Circle the correct option.

1 Police stopped a woman driving ....
a dangerously in the city last night b in the city dangerously last night c in the city last night dangerously

2 .... the new airport. a Tomorrow the president is going to open
b The president tomorrow is going to open c The president is going to tomorrow open

3 Most teenagers don't do ....
a outside enough sport these days b these days enough sport outside c enough sport outside these days

4 Lynn Green played .... a chess well last Tuesday b chess last Tuesday well c well chess last Tuesday

5 13-year-old Harry White has made over £1 million buying and selling on the Internet. 'I spend ....,' he said.
a at the moment all my free time there b all my free time there at the moment c there all my free time at the moment

My Test! answers: 1a 2a 3c 4a 5b

R14 Review: linking words and word order

A Complete the sentences using the expressions in brackets. Remember the usual order is: manner, place, time.

1 She climbed ......slowly upstairs...... .
(slowly / upstairs)
2 I have an appointment ....
(in the park / at 11.00)
3 Can you meet me .... ?
(at the hospital / next Monday)
4 I always eat ....
(at lunchtime / quickly)
5 You don't see young people
....
(in this café / these days)
6 People must drive ....
(carefully / on Saturdays / in the town centre)
7 He's staying ....
(in Barcelona / on holiday)
8 I saw him ....
(here / last week)
9 Can you swim ....
(now / well)
10 I'm not studying ....
(at the moment / at school / hard)

B Underline the correct options.

1 It's hard work *or* / *but* I enjoy it.
2 I walk everywhere. I don't have a car *and* / *or* a bike.
3 I stayed at home on Saturday *so* / *because* I thought Andy would visit.
4 I thought Andy would visit, *so* / *because* I stayed at home on Saturday.
5 Amy got up too late, *so* / *because* she missed the bus.
6 Amy missed the bus *so* / *because* she had got up too late.
7 I'd like to buy this shirt for Charlie, *and* / *but* do you think it will be big enough?
8 I went back to the village *and* / *or* saw all the places I used to play in.
9 My sister and I *both* / *either* like rock climbing.
10 I haven't been there *either* / *neither*.

C Make sentences by putting the words in the correct order.

1 arrived / both / late / us / of
Both ...of us arrived late....
....
2 neither / nor / see / hear / I / him / could
I ....
....
3 stay / I / go / I / do / or / do?
Do ....
....
4 after / spoke / he / game / the / the / players / to
After ....
....
5 wasn't / the / either / joke / clever / funny / or
The ....
....
6 were / because / late / angry / they / was / I
Because ....
....
7 playing / team / was / neither / well
Neither ....
....
8 colds / my mum / my dad / have / and / both
My ....
....

D **Make one sentence from each pair using the linking words: *and, because, but, or, so.***

1 They sat down. She asked their names.
They sat down and she asked their names.
2 My computer is very slow now. I'm getting a new one.

3 Would you like a sandwich? Have you had something to eat?

4 I need some new shoes. These are really old.

5 I've joined the club. I'll get tickets half-price.

6 He loves music. He can't sing very well.

7 Laura agreed to help them. They had been kind to her in the past.

8 Just knock on the door! Go in!

9 I'll give you the book at school tomorrow. I'll bring it to your house later.

10 I'm going to the party. I have to leave early.

E **Put the sentences in the correct order and complete them with the time and sequence adverbs from the box.**

after five or ten minutes	finally	~~first~~	second	then

The perfect lunch.
........, cut into pieces and enjoy!
........, put the bread and cheese back in the oven at 180° C.
First, ~~warm some bread in the oven.~~
........, put some cheese on top.
........, take the toast out of the oven and put some tomato on top.

1 First, warm some bread in the oven.
2 ....
3 ....
4 ....
5 ....

F **Complete the text using the words and expressions from the box.**

and	at midnight	at the school	because
both	but	but	finally	~~in 1989~~
in New England	so		

The film *Dead Poets Society* was made [1] in 1989. It is still a very popular teen movie [2] .... its message is that a man should think for himself.

The film takes place [3] .... in the 1950s. The main characters in the film are new schoolboys Neil and Todd [4] .... a new English teacher, Mr Keating. The two boys [5] .... have difficult fathers who want them to do well [6] .... They soon become friends. The school and the parents are very traditional, [7] .... Mr Keating is a young free-thinking teacher. Mr Keating helps the boys to be different. They form a poetry club which meets to read poems [8] .... The headteacher becomes worried about Mr Keating's classes, [9] .... he tells the new teacher to leave.

[10] .... Mr Keating has to agree, [11] .... he has changed the boys' lives forever.

Verb tenses

	statement	negative	questions
Present simple			
I/you/we/they	work	**do not** work (I **don't** work)	**Do** I work?
he/she/it	works	**does not** work (he **doesn't** work)	**Does** he work?
Present continuous			
I	**am** working (**I'm** working)	**am not** working (**I'm not** working)	**Am** I working?
you/we/they	**are** working (**you're** working)	**are not** working (**you're not** / you **aren't** working)	**Are** you working?
he/she/it	**is** working (**it's** working)	**is not** working (**it's not** /it **isn't** working)	**Is** it working?
Past simple			
I/you/he/she/it/we/they	worked	**did not** work (you **didn't** work)	**Did** you work?
Present perfect			
I/you/we/they	**have** worked (**they've** worked)	**have not** worked (they **haven't** worked)	**Have** they worked?
he/she/it	**has** worked (**she's** worked)	**has not** worked (she **hasn't** worked)	**Has** she worked?

Irregular verbs

infinitive	past simple	past participle
be	was/were	been
beat	beat	beaten
become	became	become
begin	began	begun
bite	bit	bitten
blow	blew	blown
break	broke	broken
bring	brought	brought
build	caught	caught
buy	bought	bought
catch	caught	caught
choose	chose	chosen
come	came	come
cost	cost	cost
cut	cut	cut
do	did	done
draw	drew	drawn
drink	drank	drunk
drive	drove	driven
eat	ate	eaten
fall	fell	fallen
feel	felt	felt
fight	fought	fought
find	found	found
fly	flew	flown
forget	forgot	forgotten
get	got	got
give	gave	given
go	went	gone
grow	grew	grown
hang	hung	hung
have	had	had
hear	heard	heard
hide	hid	hidden
hit	hit	hit
hold	held	held
hurt	hurt	hurt
keep	kept	kept
know	knew	known
leave	left	left
lend	lent	lent

infinitive	past simple	past participle
let	let	let
lie	lay	lain
light	lit	lit
lose	lost	lost
make	made	made
mean	meant	meant
meet	met	met
pay	paid	paid
put	put	put
read	read	read
ride	rode	ridden
ring	rang	rung
rise	rose	risen
run	ran	run
say	said	said
see	saw	seen
sell	sold	sold
send	sent	sent
shine	shone	shone
shoot	shot	shot
show	showed	shown
shut	shut	shut
sing	sang	sung
sit	sat	sat
sleep	slept	slept
speak	spoke	spoken
spend	spent	spent
stand	stood	stood
steal	stole	stolen
swim	swam	swum
take	took	taken
teach	taught	taught
tear	tore	torn
tell	told	told
think	thought	thought
throw	threw	thrown
understand	understood	understood
wake	woke	woken
wear	wore	worn
win	won	won
write	wrote	written

Spelling verbs

Present simple verbs *he/she/it*

most verbs	+ -*s*	*work – works*
verbs ending -*s*, -*ss*, -*sh*, -*ch*, -*x*, -*z*	+ -*es*	*watch – watches*
verbs ending -*o*	+ -*es*	*go – goes*
verbs ending consonant + *y*	*y* ➜ *i* + -*es*	*study – studies*
verbs ending vowel + *y*	+ -*s*	*play – plays*

! *Have* and *be* are irregular.
I, you, we, they ***have*** *he, she, it* ***has***
I am *you, we, they* ***are*** *he, she, it* ***is***

-ing form

most verbs	+ -*ing*	*work – working*
verbs ending -*e*	remove *e* + -*ing*	*come – coming*
! except *be* is irregular		*be – being*
verbs ending -*ee*	+ -*ing*	*see – seeing*
verbs ending vowel + *b, g, m, n, p, t*	double consonant + -*ing*	*get – getting*
! except if final syllable is *not* stressed		*visit – visiting*
verbs ending -*l*	double *l* + -*ing*	*travel – travelling*
! North American English has one *l*		*traveling*
verbs ending in -*ie*	*ie* ➜ *y* + -*ing*	*lie – lying*

Past simple

most verbs	+ -*ed*	*work – worked*
verbs ending -*e*	+ -*d*	*like – liked*
verbs ending consonant +*y*	*y* ➜ *i* + -*ed*	*try – tried*
verbs ending in vowel + *y*	+ -*ed*	*play – played*
! except *pay, lay, say*	*y* ➜ *i* + -*d*	*paid, laid, said*
verb ends vowel + consonant	double consonant + -*ed*	*chat – chatted*
! except if final syllable is *not* stressed		*visit – visited*
verb ends -*l*	double *l* + -*ed*	*travel – travelled*
! North American English has one *l*		*traveled*

Spelling, adjectives, adverbs and nouns

Adjectives and adverbs

Comparative and superlative adjectives and adverbs

most words	+ *-er/-est*	*fast – faster – fastest*
words ending *-e*	+ *-r/-st*	*nice – nicer – nicest*
words ending consonant + *y*	*y* ➜ *i* + *-er/-est*	*early – earlier – earliest*
words ending vowel + consonant	double consonant + *-er/-est*	*big – bigger – biggest*

Adverbs ending in *-ly*

most adjectives	+ *-ly*	*bad – badly*
adjectives ending *-le*	*e* ➜ *y*	*simple – simply*
adjectives ending consonant + *y*	*y* ➜ *i* + *-ly*	*busy – busily*

Nouns

Regular noun plurals (countable nouns only)

most nouns	+ *-s*	*car – cars*
noun ends *-s, -ss, -sh, -ch, -x, -z*	+ *-es* [adds a syllable]	*watch – watches*
noun ends vowel + *-o*	+ *-s*	*radio – radios*
noun ends consonant + *o*	+ *-es*	*tomato – tomatoes*
noun ends consonant + *y*	*y* ➜ *i* + *-es*	*diary – diaries*
noun ends vowel + *y*	+ *-s*	*day – days*
noun ends *-f/fe* ! except roof – roofs	*f/fe* ➜ *ves*	*knife – knives*

Irregular noun plurals

man	*men*
woman	*women*
child	*children*
person	*people*
tooth	*teeth*
foot	*feet*

Glossary

bee a yellow and black insect that makes honey 1
amazed very surprised 58
amazing very surprising 58
ancient from a long time ago 10
army a large group of soldiers that fight wars 10
assertive behaving or speaking in a strong, confident way 37
assistant someone whose job is to help a person who has a more important job 13
atmosphere the feeling which exists in a place or situation 54
attraction somewhere you can visit that is interesting or enjoyable 55
axe a tool with a sharp piece of metal at one end, used for cutting trees or wood 26
bacteria very small living things that can cause disease 65
bakery a shop where you can buy bread, cakes, etc. 49
bat a small animal like a mouse with wings that flies at night 20
battle a fight between two armies in a war 10
bite to cut something using teeth 32
blood pressure the force with which blood flows around your body 35
bone one of the hard, white pieces inside the body of a person or animal 26
Briton someone who comes from Great Britain 10
butterfly an insect with large, coloured wings 47
cabbage a large, round vegetable with a lot of green or white leaves 31
calm If the weather or the sea is calm, it is quiet and peaceful. 30
captain the person in control of a ship or aeroplane 47
castle a large, strong building that was built in the past to protect the people inside from being attacked 8
cave a large hole in the ground or in the side of a mountain 12
chain a line of metal rings connected together R 12
charge up put electricity into 36
chlorine a gas with a strong smell, used to make water safe to drink and swim in (symbol Cl) 65
chopsticks thin sticks used for eating food in East Asia 13
cocoa bean the seed of the cacao tree. Chocolate is made from this. 40
colony a country or area controlled by a more powerful country 10
comic a magazine with stories told in pictures 6
compass a piece of equipment which shows you which direction you are going in 24
complain to say that something is wrong or that you are angry about something 38
contract a legal agreement between two people or organisations 18
convenient near or easy to get to 54
country the areas that are away from towns and cities 45
criminal someone who has done a crime 9
depressed very sad, often for a long time 58
depressing making you feel sad and without any hope for the future 58
desert a large, hot, dry area of land with very few plants 39
determined wanting so much to do something that you keep trying very hard 22
diet the type of food that someone usually eats 35
diplomat someone who is good at dealing with people in a sensitive way 37
dyslexic Someone who is dyslexic has difficulty with reading and writing. 15
elevator (AmE) a machine that carries people up and down in tall buildings (BrE **lift**) 7
empire a group of countries that is ruled by one person or government 33
enemy a person or country that you are arguing or fighting with 8
expedition an organised journey, especially a long one for a particular purpose 24
explode If a bomb explodes, it bursts (= breaks suddenly from inside) with noise and force. 62
fail to not be successful 9
faithful always liking and supporting someone or something 34
fan someone who likes a person or thing very much 31
fascinating very interesting 53
feather one of the soft, light things that cover a bird's skin 28
fishing boat a boat used to catch fish 44
flight a journey in an aircraft 62
float to stay on the surface of a liquid and not go under 35
forever for all time in the future 46
fox a wild animal like a dog with brown fur and a long thick tail 1
fur the thick hair that covers bodies of some animals like cats and rabbits 4
gravity the force that makes objects fall to the ground 26
guard to protect someone or something so that no one attacks or steals them. 70
guidebook a book that gives visitors information about a particular place 23
habitat the natural environment of an animal or plant 25
helmet a hard hat that protects your head 11
hero a very brave man that a lot of people admire 8
honey a sweet, sticky food that is made by bees 28
horizon the line in the distance where the sky and the land or sea seem to meet 39
hydrogen a gas that combines with oxygen to form water 55
image the way that other people think someone or something is 33
in danger when it is possible that something bad will happen 4
intend to want and plan to do something 38
invent to design or make something new 9
jealous upset and angry because someone you like likes another person 34
jogging the activity of running at a slow regular speed, especially as a form of exercise 32

jungle an area of land in a hot country where trees and plants grow close together 39
keyboard a set of keys on a computer, which you press to make it work 72
kiss to put your lips against another person's lips or skin because you love or like them 23
lake a large area of water which has land all around it 55
leaf (leaves) a flat, green part of a plant that grows from a stem or branch 1
lend to give something to someone for a period of time 37
lightning sudden bright light in the sky during a storm 57
lonely sad because you are not with other people 3
mechanic someone who repairs vehicles and machines 4
medicine something that you drink or eat when you are ill, to stop you being ill 16
monitor a screen that shows information or pictures, usually connected to a computer 72
monster an imaginary creature that is large, ugly, and frightening 10
mosquito a small flying insect that drinks your blood, sometimes causing a disease 25
mustard a spicy yellow or brown sauce often eaten in small amounts with meat 13
nest a home built by birds or insects for their eggs 29
oven a piece of kitchen equipment which is used for cooking food R 14
panic to suddenly feel very afraid so that you stop thinking clearly and do silly things 7
pet an animal that someone keeps in their home 11
pineapple a large fruit with leaves sticking out of the top which is sweet and yellow inside 35
pirate someone who attacks ships and steals from them 63
programming when someone writes computer programs 72
protest when people show that they disagree with something by standing somewhere, shouting, carrying signs, etc 9
qualification what you get when you pass an exam or a course 65
raw not cooked 13
react If a chemical substance reacts with another substance, it changes. 65
recycle to use paper, glass, plastic, etc. again and not throw it away 64
rent to pay money to live in a building that someone else owns 14
resident someone who lives in a particular place 14
rhyme If a word rhymes with another word, the end part of the words sound the same. 22
rhythm a regular, repeating pattern of sound 39
rugby a sport played by two teams with an oval ball and H-shaped goals 6
scream when someone makes a high, loud cry because they are afraid or upset 11
shake to make quick, short movements from side to side or up and down 11
shy not confident, especially about meeting new people 24
slave someone who is owned by someone else and has to work for them 70
slim Someone who is slim is thin in an attractive way. 54
soap opera a series of television or radio programmes that continues over a long period and is about the lives of a group of characters 48
sofa a large, comfortable seat for more than one person 5
software programs that you use to make a computer do different things 72
species a group of plants or animals which are the same in some way 25
spider a creature with eight long legs which catches insects in a web 1
sprinter someone who runs short distances in competitions 53
stripy with a pattern of stripes 1
suitcase a rectangular case with a handle that you use for carrying clothes when you are travelling 5
sulphur a yellow chemical element that has an unpleasant smell (symbol S) 28
survivor someone who continues to live after almost dying because of an accident, illness, etc. 20
temple a building where people in some religions go to pray 16
tent a structure for sleeping in, made of cloth fixed to metal poles 22
terrified very frightened 58
terrifying very frightening 58
thunder the loud noise in the sky that you hear during a storm 57
tragedy something very sad which happens, usually involving death 62
treasure something valuable; gold, silver and jewellery 46
tunnel a long passage under the ground or through a mountain 30
uniform a special set of clothes that are worn by people who do a particular job or by children at school 22
vegetarian someone who does not eat meat or fish 14
vet a doctor for animals 4
volcanic volcanic rocks come from a volcano (a mountain that sends gas and hot rocks out of a hole in the top) 40
wasp a flying insect with a thin, black and yellow body 29
waterfall a stream of water that falls from a high place, often to a pool below 71
wave to put your hand up and move it from side to side in order to attract someone's attention or to say goodbye 36
weep to cry, usually because you are sad 22
whale a very large animal that looks like a large fish and lives in the sea 55
wind a natural, fast movement of air 39
wipe your feet clean dirt from your shoes on a mat before entering a room or house 22
witch a woman who has magical powers 16
wonderful very good 53
worm a small creature with a long, thin, soft body and no legs 25

Grammar index

a / an 102, 104
a few 114
a little 114
a lot of / lots of 114
able to 52
adjectives 126, 128, 130, 132, 138
adverbs 134, 136, 142, 172
after 172
afterwards 172
and 170
any 110
anybody 112
anyone 112
anything 112
anywhere 112
articles 102, 104
be 8
because 170
both 174
but 170
can, can't 52, 54, 56
comparatives 130, 136
conditionals 156, 158
could 52, 54, 60, 156, 158
countable nouns 98
either 174
enough 140
ever 34
everybody 112
everyone 112
everything 112
everywhere 112
first 172
first conditional 156
going to 48
have (got) 82
have to 56
if 156, 158
infinitive 92
imperative 18
-ing form 14, 92
it is 122
like 70, 92
linking words 170, 172
many 114, 140
may 54, 60
might 60, 156, 158
much 114, 140
must 56
neither 76, 174
never 34
no 110
none 110
or 170
ought to 58
passive 154
past continuous 28
past simple 22, 24, 26, 38
phrasal verbs 88
plural nouns 100
possessive apostrophe ('s) 118
possessive adjectives 120
prepositional verbs 86
prepositions 86, 88, 146, 148, 150
present continuous 14, 16, 46
present perfect 32, 34, 36, 38
present simple 10, 12, 16
pronouns 116, 120
quantifiers 114
question tags 78
questions 64, 66, 68, 72, 74
relative clauses 166
reported speech 162
say 164
second conditional 158
shall 44
should 58
so 76, 170
some 110
somebody 112
someone 112
something 112
somewhere 112
state verbs 94
superlatives 132, 136
tell 164
that 108
the 102, 104
then 172
there is/are 122
these 108
this 108
those 108
to infinitive 92
too 140
uncountable nouns 98
unless 156
used to 40
was/were 22
will 44, 156
word order 6, 176
would 158
would like 92
zero conditional 156

Thanks and Acknowledgements

The authors would like to thank Penny Ur for her patience, knowledge and extremely helpful advice. We would also like to thank the editorial team for their encouragement and hard work, especially Alison Sharpe, Lynn Dunlop, Lynn Townsend, Matthew Duffy, Rhona Snelling, Janet Weller, Robert Vernon and Frances Disken. Fiona would like to thank Steve and Ollie for their support.

The authors and publishers would like to thank the following individuals who commented on the materials during the development stage:
Mauretta Bernardini, Davide Cafiero, Gloria Ciarpaglini, Patrizia Daniele, Chiara Ferdori, Sabina Fortunati, Marina Gardin, Julia Raskina, Giancarla Spagnolo, Olga Vinogradova, Angioletta Viviani, Cristiana Ziraldo.

The authors and publishers acknowledge the following sources of copyright material and are grateful for the permissions granted. While every effort has been made, it has not always been possible to identify the sources of all the material used, or to trace all copyright holders. If any omissions are brought to our notice, we will be happy to include the appropriate acknowledgements on reprinting.

p. 56: Coral Rumble for the text 'The First Bit' © Coral Rumble. Reproduced with permission; p 56: Wendy Cope for the text 'An Attempt at Unrhymed Verse' taken from *The Orchid Book of Funny Poems*. Reprinted by permission of United Agents on behalf of Wendy Cope; p56: Gerda Mayer for the translated German folk song. Reproduced with permission; p. 126: The Independent for the adapted text 'My Life in Travel: Dan Cruickshank' by Sophie Lam, *The Independent* 03.05.08. Copyright © Independent Newspapers.

The publishers are grateful to the following for permission to reproduce copyright photographs and materials:

Key: l = left, c = centre, r = right, t = top, b = bottom

Alamy /©Edward Bock/UpperCut Images for p. 14, /©Kevin Schafer/Peter Arnold, Inc for p. 18(l), /©PCL for p. 23, /©akg-images for p. 52(l), /©Hugh Threlfall for p. 52(r), /©image100 for p. 64(tl), /©Alfred Schauhuber/imagebroker for p. 65(tl), /©Redmond Durrell for p. 72(cr), /©Robin Wong/First Light for p. 78, /©Alan Howden - Japan Stock Photography for p. 88(r), /©music Alan King for p. 104(t), /©Ashley Cooper for p. 115, /©Neil McAllister for p. 126(r), /©Gerry Yardy for p. 128(bl), /©Cindy Miller Hopkins/Danita Delimont for p. 130(l), /©Doug Priebe for p. 132, /©Lister, Louise/Bon Appetit for p. 134, /©RTimages for p. 138, /©Interfoto for p. 148, /©louise murray for p. 155, /©Clover/amana images inc. for p. 162, /©Melba Photo Agency for p. 166, /©nagelestock.com for p. 170, /©Justin Black for p. 172, /©blickwinkel/Hauke for p. 173, /©Chris Laurens for p. 176; © The Trustees of the British Museum /©Iron Age, mid-1st century AD, found in Lindow Moss, Cheshire, England (1984) for p. 66; Corbis /©Toshiyuki Aizawa/Reuters for p. 88(l); Sarah Errington /© for p. 108(t), /© for p. 108(bl); Getty Images /©Gerard Burkhart for p. 24, /©Tony Avelar/AFP for p. 38(l), /©Ted Thai/Time Life Pictures for p. 38(r), /©Indigo for p. 39, /©Mansell/Time Life Pictures for p. 40(br), /©Popperfoto for p. 52(t), /©Frank Greenaway/Dorling Kindersley for p. 72(cl), /©Frank Greenaway/Dorling Kindersley for p. 72(bl), /©Pornchai Kittiwongsakul/ AFP for p. 82, /©ColorBlind Images/Iconica for p. 84, /©Frans Lemmens/The Image Bank for p. 114(t), /©David Levenson for p. 126(l), /©Hulton Archive for p. 128(bc), /©Robert George Young/Photographer's Choice for p. 128(tr), /©Joanna McCarthy/The Image Bank for p. 138; Penguin Books Ltd, H.G.Wells, *The Time Machine for* p.139; Robert Harding World Imagery /©Andrew McConnell for p. 108(br); iStockphoto.com /©Craig Dingle for p. 12(r), /©Juanmonino for p. 65(cr), /©Oleg Kozlov for p. 130(r); The Kobal Collection /©X-Men: The Last Stand/20th Century Fox/Michael Muller Michael for p. 70, /©The Golden Compass/New Line Cinema/Laurie Sparham for p. 174; Photolibrary.com /©Michael Krabs/ imagebroker.net for p. 12(l), /©Martin Harvey/Peter Arnold Images for p. 13, /©Charles Bowman/age fotostock for p. 17, /©FoodCollection for p. 34, /©Tam C Nguyen/Phototake Science for p. 64(cr), /©Frank Siteman/age fotostock for p. 72(t), /©Radius Images for p. 104(b); Rex Features /©Warner Br/Everett for p. 22(t), /© for p. 36(l), /©Jonathan Hordle for p. 36(r), /©News Ltd/Newspix for p. 117; Science Photo Library /©Earth Satellite Corporation for p. 6.

Review units written by Jeremy Day.
Picture research by Suzanne Williams/Pictureresearch.co.uk
Illustrations by David Shephard, Javier Joaquin, Julian Mosedale, Leo Brown, Mark Draisey, Mark Duffin, Rory Walker, Sean Sims and Tom Croft.

Notes